AF691256

From Civil Partnership to Same-Sex Marriage

The Civil Partnership Act 2004 and the Marriage (Same Sex Couples) Act 2013 are important legal, social and historic landmarks, rich in symbolic, material and cultural meanings. While fiercely opposed by many, within mainstream narratives they are often represented as a victory in a legal reform process that commenced with the decriminalisation of homosexuality. Yet, at the same time, for others they represent a problematic and ambivalent political engagement with the institution of marriage. Consequently, understood or labelled as 'revolutionary', 'progressive' and 'conservative', these legal reforms provide a space for thinking about issues that arguably affect everyone, regardless of sexual orientation or relationship status.

This edited collection brings together scholars and commentators from a range of backgrounds, generations and disciplines to reflect on the first ten years of civil partnerships and the introduction of same-sex marriage. Rather than rehearsing the arguments 'for' and 'against' relationship recognition, the essays ask original questions, draw on a variety of methods and collectively provide a detailed and reflective 'snap-shot' of a critical moment, a 'history of the present', as well as providing a foundation for innovative ways of thinking about and engaging with the possibilities and experiences arising from the new reality of relationship recognition for gays and lesbians.

Nicola Barker is Senior Lecturer in Law at the University of Kent.

Daniel Monk is Reader in Law, Birkbeck, University of London.

From Civil Partnership to Same-Sex Marriage

Interdisciplinary reflections

Edited by
Nicola Barker and Daniel Monk

Routledge
Taylor & Francis Group
a GlassHouse book

First published 2015
by Routledge
2 Park Square, Milton Park, Abingdon, Oxon, OX14 4RN

and by Routledge
711 Third Avenue, New York, NY 10017

a GlassHouse Book

Routledge is an imprint of the Taylor & Francis Group, an informa business

© 2015 Selection and editorial matter, Nicola Barker and Daniel Monk; individual chapters, the contributors

The rights of Nicola Barker and Daniel Monk to be identified as authors of this work have been asserted by them in accordance with sections 77 and 78 of the Copyright, Designs and Patents Act 1988.

All rights reserved. No part of this book may be reprinted or reproduced or utilised in any form or by any electronic, mechanical, or other means, now known or hereafter invented, including photocopying and recording, or in any information storage or retrieval system, without permission in writing from the publishers.

Trademark notice: Product or corporate names may be trademarks or registered trademarks, and are used only for identification and explanation without intent to infringe.

British Library Cataloguing in Publication Data
A catalogue record for this book is available from the British Library

Library of Congress Cataloging in Publication Data
From civil partnership to same-sex marriage : interdisciplinary reflections / edited by Nicola Barker and Daniel Monk.
pages cm
"a GlassHouse Book"
1. Same-sex marriage–Law and legislation–Great Britain. 2. Same-sex marriage–Great Britain. I. Barker, Nicola (Nicola J.), editor. II. Monk, Daniel, editor.
KD771.F76 2015
346.4101'68–dc23
2014036795

ISBN: 978-1-138-79753-6 (hbk)
ISBN: 978-1-315-75706-3 (ebk)

Typeset in Times New Roman
by Taylor & Francis Books

MIX
Paper from responsible sources
FSC® C013604

Printed and bound by CPI Group (UK) Ltd, Croydon, CR0 4YY

Contents

Acknowledgments

Most of the chapters in this collection were presented at a two-day workshop in January 2014. We would like to thank the Kent Centre for Law Gender and Sexuality, Birkbeck Gender and Sexuality and the Birkbeck School of Law for generously sponsoring the event. In an age of austerity we are both immensely fortunate – and proud – to be associated with, and members of, institutions which help to sustain a commitment to engaged critical interdisciplinary legal scholarship. The workshop was also made possible by the unstinting administrative support provided by Reina van der Wiel and the assistance at the event of Mayur Suresh; a big thank you to them both.

We are delighted that this collection is published by Routledge and thank Colin Perrin for his commitment to the project, and Laura Muir, Ashlie Jackman and Neil Dowden for their help in bringing the collection to fruition.

We also want to thank Routledge for supporting our front cover preference; Pierre Saurisse for bringing the artwork to our attention; the artists' studio manager Margo Lauras for her swift co-operation; and, of course, the artists Elmgreen and Dragset for providing their permission. Entitled 'Gay Marriage', the artwork is open to multiple playful and provocative readings. In doing so, it encapsulates perfectly what we hope the collection achieves; encouraging questions, reflections and debates about the pleasures and perils of civil partnership and same-sex marriage.

Nicola Barker and Daniel Monk
January 2015

List of contributors

Rosemary Auchmuty is Professor of Law at the University of Reading.

Nicola Barker is Senior Lecturer in Law at the University of Kent.

Kath Browne is Reader in Geography at the School of Environment and Technology, University of Brighton.

Christine Cocker is Senior Lecturer in Social Work at the University of East Anglia.

Chris Dietz is a research student and graduate teaching assistant at the University of Leeds.

Rev. Canon Giles Goddard is Vicar of St John's Church, Waterloo, Chair of Inclusive Church and a member of the General Synod.

Brian Heaphy is Professor of Sociology at the University of Manchester.

Daniel Monk is Reader in Law, Birkbeck, University of London.

Catherine Nash is Associate Professor at the Department of Geography, Brock University, Canada.

Kenneth Norrie is Professor of Law at Strathclyde University.

Flora Renz is a PhD student and teaching assistant at the University of Kent.

Yvette Taylor is Professor in Social and Policy Studies at the Weeks Centre for Social and Policy Research, London South Bank University.

Julie Wallbank is Senior Lecturer in Law at the University of Leeds.

Jeffrey Weeks is Emeritus Professor of Sociology at the London South Bank University.

Chapter 1

From civil partnership to same-sex marriage

A decade in British legal history

Nicola Barker and Daniel Monk

Introduction

The Civil Partnership Act 2004 (CPA) and the Marriage (Same Sex Couples) Act 2013 (MSSCA) are important legal, social and historic landmarks. For beyond their practical implications, same-sex relationship recognition, throughout the western world, has become a key site of political contestation, rich in symbolic, material and cultural meanings. While fiercely opposed by many, within mainstream narratives they are often represented as a victory in a legal reform process that commenced with the decriminalisation of homosexuality. Yet, at the same time, for others they represent a problematic and ambivalent political engagement with the institution of marriage. Consequently, understood or labelled as 'revolutionary', 'progressive' and 'conservative', these legal reforms provide a space for thinking about issues that arguably affect everyone, regardless of sexual orientation or relationship status.

This edited collection brings together scholars and commentators from a range of backgrounds, generations and disciplines to reflect on the first ten years of civil partnerships and the introduction of same-sex marriage. The contributors have different views about these reforms – some are in favour, others more ambivalent. But rather than simply rehearsing the arguments 'for' and 'against' relationship recognition, these essays, while informed by earlier debates, collectively ask a different set of original questions and provide a detailed and reflective 'snap-shot' of a critical moment, a 'history of the present'. At the same time, as globally same sex relationship recognition is no longer a proposal to debate but increasingly an aspect of lived experience (both for those who enter them but also for those who for various reasons remain outside them), we hope the essays will provide a foundation for both encouraging and suggesting ways of thinking about and engaging with this new reality.

In this opening chapter we provide an overview of the last decade of legal history relating to same-sex relationship recognition. We refer to this as

British rather than UK because while the CPA includes Scotland and Northern Ireland, in the former separate legislation introduced same-sex marriage (see Norrie in this collection) and, to date, the MSSCA does not include the latter. This introduction concludes with an outline of the subsequent chapters.

The legal background

Before civil partnerships were created through the CPA, same-sex relationships had been recognised only for some limited purposes through incremental changes in certain laws. For example, they were recognised in the Immigration Rules if, amongst other things, a couple could demonstrate that they were in a cohabiting relationship 'akin to marriage'.[1] Similarly, case law had come to recognise bereaved same-sex partners who had lived in rented property in their partner's name, as belonging to the category of 'family' for the purposes of tenancy succession.[2] Same-sex partners had, since 2002, also been able to jointly adopt prior to the CPA (see Cocker in this collection). This was particularly striking because while the other European jurisdictions that had created registered partnership provisions had done so with several exclusions relating to parenting, including prohibitions on joint adoption by same-sex couples, the UK had allowed joint adoption without any comprehensive recognition of the relationship between the same-sex parents who were adopting the child.

The CPA, introduced by the New Labour government in 2004, was not the first attempt to create civil partnerships. In the 2001–2 parliamentary session two Private Members' Bills introduced same-sex relationship recognition provisions.[3] Both Bills would have extended recognition not only to same-sex couples, but also to different-sex couples who chose not to marry. As a result, a key objection made to each of these Bills was their potential for undermining marriage through the inclusion of different-sex couples.[4] Pre-empting a debate that would recur in the context of the government's Civil Partnership Bill 2004, Baroness Buscombe also expressed disappointment at the exclusion of close relatives from the Bill:

> Why should close relatives – for example, two cohabiting sisters who may have pledged to care for each other – not register and thereby enjoy the same rights and responsibilities as others? Surely that exclusion is discriminatory in principle, particularly against the elderly. Is the noble Lord interested only in protecting the rights of couples in a sexual relationship?[5]

Though neither progressed beyond second reading, these two Private Members' Bills prompted the government to review the issues (Odysseus Trust

2002) and the government introduced its own Civil Partnership Bill in 2004, following a consultation process.[6] The government's Bill, which became the CPA, excluded heterosexual relationships and mirrored marriage much more closely than the previous Bills.[7]

The Civil Partnership Act 2004

The CPA, according to the government, provided 'a measured and proportionate response' to the exclusion of same-sex couples from marriage.[8] The government emphasised that its intention was to provide 'parity of treatment'[9] between registered same-sex couples and spouses in terms of legal protections and the focus of arguments in support of the Bill during the parliamentary debates was very much on access to financial provisions and formal equality arguments (see also Stonewall 2003, 2004a, 2004b, 2004c). There was surprisingly little overt homophobic reaction to the Civil Partnership Bill (though see further Browne and Nash in this collection). Instead, those opposed argued that as the Bill was an equality measure and not a 'gay marriage' measure, as the government had insisted, there ought to be no objection to extending this equality to deserving family members who remained 'unequal' through their exclusion from the Bill.[10] A series of amendments were attached to the Bill in both the House of Commons and House of Lords that would have allowed siblings and other close family members to register as civil partners in order to avoid inheritance tax. These were not only tax-avoidance measures but also wrecking amendments because the marriage-like provision would have become unworkable if it were extended to family. How would three or more siblings choose which two of them were to register? What if one of the siblings forms a romantic relationship and wants to marry or civilly partner their lover? How would they demonstrate irretrievable breakdown of their relationship? The amendments were designed to undermine the recognition of same-sex relationships as marriage-like relationships but they were all defeated during the parliamentary process (see further Barker 2014, and in this volume).

Key provisions of the Civil Partnership Act 2004

The CPA takes marriage as its template and replicates most of its legal rights and responsibilities so, from the beginning, there were few significant legal differences between civil partnerships and (heterosexual) marriage, and some of those that existed when the Act was first passed have now been removed. Originally, registration of civil partnerships could not take place in religious premises (s6(1)(b)) but this has now been permitted since 2011 with the implementation of the Equality Act 2010, s202. There is no provision for a civil partner to be assumed to be the legal parent of a child born to her partner during the relationship, unlike a husband who would be presumed to be the father of a child born to his wife, but the Human Fertilisation and Embryology Act 2008 changed this in relation to children born through assisted reproduction (s42). The differences that remain are those of language, sex and pensions.

In addition to the label 'civil partnership' rather than 'marriage', differences in language extend to the terminology of 'dissolution' rather than 'divorce' and there is no offence of 'bigamy'; rather, s80 amends the Perjury Act 1911, s3(1) to include making a false statement with regard to a civil partnership. These statutory language differences have often been ignored in practice, with civil partnership registrations referred to as weddings, dissolutions as divorces, and the first criminal conviction for making a false statement widely reported as being a bigamy conviction (see, for example, Barnett 2007; Walker 2007; and Auchmuty and Heaphy in this collection). Civil partnerships are contracted when the couple signs the register (s2) so there is also an absence of language where marriage vows would be spoken, though there is no prohibition on creating vows for civil partnership ceremonies and in practice many ceremonies do contain vows.

There is no consummation requirement and adultery is not a specific ground for dissolution of a civil partnership. This is not because civil partnerships were intended to be asexual or non-monogamous but rather it was explained by reference to the difficulties of attempting to apply a definition of consummation and adultery that is explicitly heterosexual to same-sex relationships (Baroness Scotland, HL *Hansard*, 10 May 2004, col GC19 and see Collier 1995: 152). For example, to divorce based on adultery there must be, amongst other things, 'consensual sexual intercourse between a married person and a person of the opposite sex during the subsistence of the marriage' (*Dennis v Dennis* [1955] P 153, at 160, per Singleton LJ). It is interesting that there was an assumption that someone in a civil partnership would never act in a way that meets the definition of adultery (i.e. have sex with someone of the opposite sex), thereby making invisible both bisexuals and the fluid nature of sexuality. Instead, and rather than legislating a different definition of consummation and adultery into the CPA, the government made vague references to civil partnerships being 'loving and caring' relationships (Women and Equality Unit 2005) to create an implication of conjugality. The reason why it is perhaps unnecessary to include adultery in civil partnerships (or, indeed, marriage) is because a spouse or civil partner can petition for divorce if the respondent has behaved in such a way that 'the petitioner cannot reasonably be expected to live with the respondent' (Matrimonial Causes Act 1973, s1(1)(b); Civil Partnership Act 2004, s44(5)(a)). This easily encompasses not only adultery but also behaviour that would fall short of the legal definition of adultery but a partner may nevertheless consider unfaithful. Consummation itself is arguably unnecessary and outdated (for a feminist critique of consummation, see Barker 2006).

The difference between civil partnership and (heterosexual) marriage that has the most concrete impact on civil partners, though, is the different treatment in relation to survivor pensions. Whereas a heterosexual spouse would have access to a spousal survivor pension relating back to the beginning of the pension contribution, a civil partner (and now a same-sex married spouse) can be lawfully prevented from accessing the benefits of any pension contributions made before 5 December 2005, when the CPA came into force (this is permitted by an exception in the Equality Act 2010, Sch 9, para 18).[11] This is arguably contrary to European Union (EU) anti-discrimination law[12] but was recently unsuccessfully challenged in an Employment Appeal Tribunal, when a man who had already retired when he entered a civil partnership challenged the pension scheme's decision that his civil partner would be entitled to a survivor's pension of only £500 per year, whereas a heterosexual spouse would have been entitled to two-thirds of his £85,000 annual pension (*Innospec Ltd and others v Walker* [2014] ICR 645). The court held that the relevant EU law did not have retrospective effect and the unequal treatment was not unlawful at the time it was done. They further held that even if they had concluded that the provision was incompatible with EU anti-discrimination law, they could not have permitted Walker's claim because to do so would 'be diametrically opposed to the thrust of the legislation … and to the apparent intention of Parliament' (at p 667). They also justified the different treatment on the basis that 'Marriage is a status which is not exactly comparable to that of civil partnership' (at p 660). This case is awaiting appeal and it will be interesting to see whether this reasoning holds up not only in the higher courts, but also in subsequent cases brought by same-sex couples who are married yet still denied equal treatment in relation to pensions, because same-sex married couples are treated the same way as civil partners for this purpose rather than as different-sex married couples.[13]

Criticisms of the Civil Partnership Act 2004 within the lesbian, gay, bisexual and transgender communities

Despite the CPA being 'a victory for the politics of compromise' (Stychin 2006: 79, and Weeks in this collection) and an undoubted improvement in the legal position of same-sex couples, there remain some criticisms of the legislation both from within the lesbian, gay, bisexual and transgender (LGBT) communities and from those who opposed the provision for religious or other (homophobic) reasons. First, like marriage before the MSSCA, civil partnership remains an institution that is defined by gender. This means that trans people who are in a civil partnership would need to get a dissolution before they are able to get a gender recognition certificate (see Renz in this collection). Second, the same criticisms that feminists and some queers[14] make of the institution of marriage apply to civil partnership precisely because it does mirror marriage to such a close extent (see Barker 2012), though these critiques were largely absent from the mainstream debates prior to the CPA being passed (Young and Boyd 2006; Auchmuty

2007). Finally, the CPA was criticised by those seeking access to marriage who considered civil partnership to be a second-class provision, drawing on the critiques of 'separate but equal' during racial segregation in the United States as an analogy to argue that this was discriminatory. For example, speaking on behalf of the Equal Love Campaign, Professor Robert Wintemute said:

> There is no longer any justification for excluding same-sex couples from civil marriage and different-sex couples from civil partnership. It's like having separate drinking fountains or beaches for different racial groups, even though the water is the same! The only function of the twin ban is to mark lesbian and gay people as inferior to heterosexual people.
>
> (Equal Love 2010)

This criticism was first made in the English courts in the case of *Wilkinson v Kitzinger* [2006] EWHC 2022 (Fam) in which the parties unsuccessfully sought a declaration that their Canadian marriage was valid in the UK rather than having it 'downgraded' to a civil partnership (para 5). They argued that:

> While marriage remains open to heterosexual couples only, offering the 'consolation prize' of a civil partnership to lesbians and gay men is offensive and demeaning. Marriage is our society's fundamental social institution for recognizing the couple relationship and access to this institution is an equal rights issue. … [Marriage and civil partnership] are not equal symbolically, when it is marriage that is the key social institution, celebrated and recognized around the world. …
>
> (Para 18)

The 'separate but equal' analogy was also made after a series of applications by heterosexual couples to get civil partnerships and by same-sex couples to get married were rejected by register offices, which led to an application to the European Court of Human Rights in Strasbourg in 2011.[15] This case is still pending but arguments made in the application draw on cases from South Africa, Canada and some jurisdictions in the United States, where 'separate but equal' provisions were strongly rejected by the courts:

> It will be very difficult for the United Kingdom to explain why, after taking all the most politically sensitive decisions voluntarily, and having gone so far to ensure equality between the two institutions, the United Kingdom should be allowed to withhold access to the traditional, public, legal institution and word 'marriage' from same-sex couples, and access to the new, public, legal institution and words 'civil

> partnership' from different-sex couples. Given that marriage and civil partnership confer virtually identical rights and obligations, how can the United Kingdom justify maintaining two different public, legal institutions, with eligibility for membership based on sexual orientation?
>
> (Para 161)

One issue that arose during the same-sex marriage debates was whether heterosexuals should be permitted to enter into civil partnerships or whether this separate institution should be phased out or abolished entirely. However, following consultation during which the vast majority of over 10,000 respondents supported neither of these options, it appears that civil partnership is here to stay for a while longer: 'Given the lack of consensus on the way forward, the Government will not be making any changes' (Department for Culture, Media and Sport 2014b: 21; and see Norrie in this collection).

The Marriage (Same Sex Couples) Act 2013

Just seven years after the first civil partnerships, the coalition government began consulting on introducing same-sex marriage in England and Wales (Equalities Office 2012). A separate consultation process was undertaken in Scotland and legislation followed (see Norrie in this collection). Similarly, while the CPA applies to Northern Ireland, as yet the MSSCA does not. One objection to the consultation in England and Wales was that there was no opportunity to disagree with the proposal itself. While the consultation did ask the question 'Do you agree or disagree with enabling all couples, regardless of their gender to have a civil marriage ceremony?' it also made clear that the consultation was 'about *how we best* remove the ban on same-sex couples having a civil marriage, not on whether this should or should not happen' (para 2.8, our emphasis). This led to a series of objections to the Bill, such as that made by Lord Forsyth:

> The process by which this Bill has been handled is inappropriate, and has left the country divided, bewildered and puzzled by something that has come out of a blue sky. That is not a proper way in which to make such a major social reform.
>
> (*Hansard*, HL Deb, 4 June 2013, col 1097)

However, the most dominant objections to the Bill were concerned with religion. From the Ministerial Foreword on the very first page, the consultation emphasised the distinction between civil marriage and religious marriage in an attempt to pre-emptively allay concerns of religious bodies that they would be compelled to marry same-sex couples. This attempt proved futile, as such claims persisted well into the parliamentary process. In the consultation, the government made clear that because 'some religious organisations … believe that marriage can only be between a man and a woman' (Equalities Office 2012: para 1.7), it would not be possible to have a same-sex marriage ceremony on religious premises, though it would be possible to have a civil marriage at a registry office followed by a religious blessing in religious premises. Because the Church of England has a common law duty to marry in their local parish church any parishioners who are legally eligible to marry, the government proposed to protect the Church from having to marry same-sex couples by providing that:

> It would not legally be possible for a Church of England minister to marry a same-sex couple on religious premises and through a religious ceremony. There would therefore be no duty on Church of England ministers to marry same-sex couples … As a result, no Church of England minister should face a successful legal challenge for refusing to conduct a same-sex religious marriage
>
> (Equalities Office 2012: para 2.11)

The idea behind the absolute prohibition was not only to reassure religious leaders, particularly the Church of England bishops who sit in the House of Lords, that they would not have to participate in same-sex marriages, but also to reflect the distinction that the government was drawing between religious and civil marriage.[16] The consultation also took the unusual step of attempting to reassure religious bodies that they need not be fearful of litigation or prosecution for hate speech or discrimination if they were to refuse to perform, or if they speak out against, gay marriages. However, neither of these reassurances was successful and these issues become a major theme of the parliamentary debates.

There were a few differences between the proposals in the consultation and the final Bill. One of these differences was that the absolute prohibition on same-sex weddings in religious premises was replaced by a provision that would allow religious bodies to choose to perform same-sex weddings if they wished to do so. Given that a similar absolute prohibition had just been removed from the CPA[17] it is slightly peculiar that the government had proposed to re-create it for same-sex marriage. Ironically, when the previous government had introduced the prohibition on religious ceremonies in the CPA in 2004, the Bishop of Oxford had objected to it on the basis that it interfered with the religious freedom of not only the couple but also the Church itself:

> As a matter of principle, it is for [religious] authorities and not for the state to decide whether or not their premises should be available to be used for registration purposes—unless there is some overriding national interest, which is very difficult to identify on this issue.
>
> (Bishop of Oxford, HL *Hansard*, 22 April 2004, cols 399–400; see also Baroness Thomas, HL *Hansard*, 22 April 2004, cols 425–26)

If the government wanted to justify such an interference with freedom of religion, which is protected under Article 9 of the European Convention on Human Rights (ECHR), it would have to demonstrate that the interference was prescribed by law, necessary in a democratic society and proportionate. Perhaps because the government realised that an absolute prohibition on religious same-sex weddings was not likely to pass the proportionality test, or perhaps because of lobbying by those religious bodies which did want to perform same-sex weddings, the Marriage (Same Sex Couples) Bill 2013 did not contain the absolute prohibition of the consultation, but instead protected religious bodies which did not want to perform same-sex weddings through creating a 'quadruple lock', which we return to below.

Another difference between the consultation and the final Bill related to the vexed subject of consummation and adultery. Initially, the proposal was that, unlike civil partnerships, these should apply to same-sex marriages but the government was going to leave it to the courts to define sex for these purposes: 'case law may need to develop, over time, a definition as to what constitutes same-sex consummation and same-sex adultery' (at para 2.16). By the time the Bill was published at second reading in the House of Commons there was no mention of consummation and adultery was confined to its heterosexual definition.[18]

The parliamentary debates: same-sex marriage in the Church of England

Introducing the Marriage (Same Sex Couples) Bill in the House of Commons, Maria Miller MP appeared to be responding to, amongst other things, the 'separate but equal' critique of civil partnerships:

> The depth of feeling, love and commitment between same-sex couples is no different from that depth of feeling between opposite-sex couples. The Bill enables society to recognise that commitment in the same way, too, through marriage. Parliament should value people equally in the law, and enabling same-sex couples to marry removes the current differentiation and distinction.
>
> (*Hansard*, HC Deb, 5 February 2013, col 125)

One sentence later she was interrupted for the first question when Sir Gerald Kaufman (Labour) asked:

> Will the right hon. Lady give the House a cast-iron guarantee that, if the Bill becomes law, no religious denomination, no place of worship and no clergyman – or equivalent in other religions – will be forced through legal action in the courts or in the European Community to carry out weddings against their wishes?
>
> (*Hansard*, HC Deb, 5 February 2013, col 125)

This exchange summarises the parliamentary debates quite well. On the one hand, those supporting the Bill emphasised the similarities between same-sex and different-sex couples and the equal value of same-sex relationships, while those opposing the Bill did not usually openly disagree with this (see Weeks, and Browne and Nash in this collection in connection with this shift).[19] Rather, the opponents pointed to alleged discrimination against others or other reasons to oppose the Bill such as those associated with the definition of marriage.[20] This mirrored the tactics deployed in relation to civil partnerships with the 'spinster sister' issue but this time the alleged discrimination was not based on an exclusion from the provision, but rather a feared over-inclusion: religious bodies would eventually be compelled to marry same-sex couples.[21] Another aspect of the civil partnership debates that was mirrored in the marriage debates was the invocation of another, similarly unpopular, measure to support the argument. In relation to siblings and civil partnerships it was inheritance tax. Those opposed to same-sex marriage drew on the twin detested spectres of 'Europe' and 'human rights',[22] arguing that the courts, whether in the UK or 'Europe',[23] would inevitably compel religious bodies to perform same-sex wedding ceremonies against their will.[24] This was not only a strategy to oppose this Bill, but also a way of making a broader point about what they see as the unacceptable influence of the supranational institutions of the EU and the Council of Europe. For example, David Davies took the opportunity to make a point about resisting rulings from the European Court of Human Rights:

> Will the right hon. Lady assure us that, if at any time in the future the European Court of Human Rights ruled that a church not wishing to conduct a gay wedding ceremony was in breach of a discrimination Act, we would defy the European Court and not try to placate it as we did over prisoner voting?
>
> (*Hansard*, HC Deb, 5 February 2013, col 128)

Because of the widespread misunderstandings of the various human rights provisions, even amongst MPs, it is difficult to tell to what extent the human rights argument was a genuine (if misguided) concern as opposed to something that was strategically deployed to support a weak opposition to same-sex marriage. In place of overt homophobia, there is a misrepresentation (whether intentional or not) of human rights law in order to create a frightening (for religious conservatives) narrative of the consequences of same-sex marriage for religious bodies. It is presented as creating a clash of rights between gay people and religious people, where people of faith inevitably lose out. For example, Lord Vinson said: 'Fifty years ago, those who criticised Christ were persecuted; today those who promote Christ are prosecuted' (*Hansard*, HL Deb, 4 June 2013, col 1078).

This was fuelled by recent cases where Christian individuals fell foul of their employer's policy on equality and inclusion and these were also invoked as a concern following from the Bill:

> The Minister has referred to the protections in the Bill, but we have already seen the case of Mr Adrian Smith, who lost his job, spent an enormous amount of money on legal fees, and suffered a 40% cut in his salary after making a private comment on a Facebook site. How, in future, are we to protect people like Mr Smith who are working in the public sector up and down the country?
>
> (Andrew Selous MP, *Hansard*, HC Deb, 5 February 2013, col 129)

'The Minister has spoken about protections for religious ministers. Can she offer the same protections to registrars?' (Duncan Hames MP, *Hansard*, HC Deb, 5 February 2013, col 129).

The facts of the cases referred to in these comments would not have been directly affected by same-sex marriage because they related to other statutes that already exist independently of same-sex marriage. Mr Smith had said that gay marriage is 'an equality too far' on his Facebook page and had in fact won his complaint against his employer for demoting him as a result of that comment (see BBC News 2012). The concern about registrars comes from the case of *Ladele v UK* (2013) 57 EHRR 8, where a registrar who was a Christian had unsuccessfully complained of religious discrimination and harassment after being asked to perform civil partnerships contrary to her religious beliefs.

Despite our focus on opposition to the Bill in Parliament, it is worth noting that many parliamentarians spoke in favour of the Bill, many from personal experience of having gay friends and family members or being gay themselves. For example, in the House of Lords Baroness Barker began her speech: 'My Lords, I declare an interest. Many years ago, I had the great good fortune to meet someone. She and I have loved each other ever since. … ' (*Hansard*, HL Deb, 3 June 2013, col 951). Toby Perkins MP, who spoke 'as a Christian' and expressed his happiness that the Minister had confirmed that teachers would not be required to 'promote gay marriage', said:

> I have never said this in political terms before, but at the end of her life my mother was gay. It was difficult for me as a young man growing up in Sheffield to think that my friends might discover that. People do not deserve to live in that way, so this is fundamentally about mutual respect (*Hansard*, HC Deb, 5 February 2013, cols 148–49).

Besides the debate between those who were for and against same-sex marriage, there were also other issues raised in parliamentary debates about the detail of the Bill, including the pensions issue, discussed above in relation to civil partnerships, that is mirrored in the MSSCA, whether heterosexuals should be able to enter into a civil partnership now that same-sex couples can get married (see, for example, Christopher Chope MP, *Hansard*, HC Deb, 5 February 2013, col 134; Simon Hughes MP, *Hansard*, HC Deb, 5 February 2013, col 167), and whether trans people should be required to seek consent from their spouse prior to a gender recognition certificate being issued (see, for example, *Hansard*, HC Com, 12 February 2013, col 58; see further, Renz in this collection).

Key Provisions of the Marriage (Same Sex Couples) Act 2013

The MSSCA provides that 'marriage between same-sex couples is lawful' (s1) and such marriages have the same legal effect as that between a different-sex couple, with all existing and future legislation from England and Wales that applies to spouses being read to include same-sex spouses unless specific exceptions are made (s11 and Sch 3). Schedule 4 to the Act specifies the exemptions as including adultery, consummation, presumption of paternity and pensions. Similarly to when the matter arose in civil partnerships, the heterosexual nature of the definitions of consummation and adultery made it too difficult to extend these to same-sex acts:

> Consummation is a concept that historically concerns the possibility of procreation, and therefore it would not make a great deal of sense to extend it to same-sex couples. In addition, the same sort of difficulties would apply to proving non-consummation of a same-sex marriage, whether by wilful refusal to consummate the marriage or because of incapacity, as apply to defining adultery between people of the same sex. Ensuring that couples understand their legal position is important, and it would be difficult to define the acts that constitute consummation of the marriage of a same-sex couple with the certainty needed for legal proceedings. (Hugh Robertson MP, *Hansard*, HC Com, 7 March 2013, col 439)

However, if a spouse in a same-sex marriage were to commit adultery with a member of the different sex, this would still constitute adultery (MSSCA, Sch 4, para 3), so 'adultery will therefore continue to mean the same for both same-sex and opposite-sex married couples, as well as sexual relations with a person of the same sex' (*Hansard*, HC Com, 7 March 2013, col 440). Under Schedule 4, the common law assumption that a spouse is the father of a child born during the marriage is excluded from same-sex marriages so a female partner will not be presumed to be the other legal parent of her wife's child (Sch 4, para 2).

Same-sex marriages will be solemnised under the same provisions as marriage between different-sex couples in the Marriage Act 1949.[25] However, there is no duty on any member of clergy or religious body to solemnise a same-sex marriage and no corresponding right of same-sex couples to have their marriage solemnised by clergy or in religious premises (s1(4)). The duty to marry parishioners only applies to members of the Church of England and Church in Wales, and so this provision, which is the first part of the 'quadruple lock', is only for these Churches (see Goddard in this collection, for further discussion of the Church of England; and Norrie in this collection, for discussion in relation to the Church of Scotland). The same section also ensures that the MSSCA does not impact on canon law by expressly stating that this can still provide that marriage is a 'union of one man with one woman' (s1(3)).

The remaining three parts of the 'quadruple lock' apply to all religious denominations. First, in order to conduct a same-sex marriage, the governing body of a religious organisation must 'opt in', preventing individual ministers from solemnising a legal same-sex marriage against the wishes of their governing body because written consent from this body is required (s4(1) inserts a new s26A(3) into the Marriage Act 1949). However, the Church of England and the Church in Wales cannot opt in without further legislation because the provision that allows for religious bodies to opt in states: 'Nothing in this section is to be taken to relate or have any reference to marriages solemnised according to the rites of the Church of England' (Marriage Act 1949, s26A(5)). Second, no individual or body can be compelled to opt in, conduct or take part in a religious same-sex wedding (s2(1)(2)). During the parliamentary debates, the Minister made it clear that the purpose of these provisions is to avoid the government interfering with the internal governance of religious bodies (Mrs Helen Grant, *Hansard*, HC Com, 5 March 2013, col 375). This avoids coming into conflict with established case law from the European Court of Human Rights, which provides that states should not seek to regulate the internal governance of religious organisations (*Hasan v Bulgaria* (2002) 34 EHRR 55) and perhaps also addresses the concerns expressed by the Bishop of Oxford (above) in relation to civil partnerships by avoiding an absolute prohibition and deferring to each governing body to decide. However, the exception might be the Church of England and Church in Wales, which remain constricted by statute and therefore would need additional legislation before they could opt to perform same-sex wedding ceremonies (on the debate within the Church of England, see Goddard in this collection).

Finally, the Equality Act 2010 has been amended to make it clear that it would not be unlawful discrimination for a religious body or individual to refuse to marry a same-sex couple in a religious ceremony (s2(5) and (6)). Therefore, as the Explanatory Notes to the Act explain (at para 35), a Church organist or individual minister who disapproves of his or her religious body's decision to opt to perform same-sex weddings could lawfully refuse to take part in a religious same-sex wedding, but civil registrars or wedding photographers could not because their role is not part of the religious ceremony and this would be unlawful discrimination (s2(4)(b)) specifically excludes civil registrars from this exemption).

The Act also allows the government to make regulations for those same-sex couples who have already contracted a civil partnership in England and Wales to convert it to a marriage (s9). The Marriage of Same Sex Couples (Conversion of Civil Partnership) Regulations 2014 came into effect on 10 December 2014. However, the process for converting has been criticised as lacking 'heart' and being more akin to taxing a car than getting married (Ball 2014; in contrast those in Scotland who are already civil partners may still marry each other: see Norrie in this volume). It must take place at a register office (reg 6(1)), except for those who are housebound, detained or seriously ill (regs 7, 8, 9). The process involves signing a 'conversion declaration' that says:

> I solemnly and sincerely declare that we are in a civil partnership with each other and I know of no legal reason why we may not convert our civil partnership into a marriage. I understand that on signing this document we will be converting our civil partnership into a marriage and you will thereby become my lawful wife [*or* husband].
>
> (reg 3(2)(b))

They must also make a declaration that each party believes all the information given to the registrar to be true (reg 3(2)(c)). The usual fee will be £45 (reg 6(1)(d)), though the government has waived this for the first year for those who contracted a civil partnership before same-sex marriage was available (reg 15).

The MSSCA has also had a positive impact for trans people, who are no longer necessarily required to nullify their existing marriage before they can acquire their full gender recognition certificate (though see Renz in this collection, for discussion and critique). Under the Gender Recognition Act 2004 (GRA), an interim certificate would be issued until the marriage or civil partnership was dissolved in order to avoid creating either a same-sex marriage or a heterosexual civil partnership following the legal change of gender (GRA, s4(3)). Schedule 5 of the MSSCA amends the GRA so that those who are in a 'protected marriage'[26] can get a full gender recognition certificate without dissolving the marriage if their partner consents to the marriage continuing (Sch 5, para 3 amending GRA, s4(2)(b)) and those who are in a civil partnership can do likewise if their partner is also transitioning (Sch 5, para 3, amending GRA, s4(2)(c)). If their partner does not consent to the marriage continuing or if they are in a 'protected civil partnership', an interim certificate will be provided until the marriage or civil partnership is dissolved as per the procedure that existed prior to the MSSCA (Sch 5, para 3, amending GRA, s4(3)).

Remaining questions

In addition to the celebrations that have occurred as a result of its passage, there are a number of remaining questions about the MSSCA and critiques of the provision, many of which are discussed at length in the chapters of this book (see below for an overview). The first is the question of the future of civil partnership as an institution and whether it will become available to heterosexual couples. Despite the government's review (noted above) there is still a case pending before the European Court of Human Rights. This Court has recently held that a civil partnership provision that was created for heterosexuals in Greece cannot exclude same-sex couples solely on the basis of their sexual orientation (*Vallianatos v Greece* (2014) 59 EHRR 12) so the outcome of this case remains a somewhat open question for the time being.

Second is the question of pension provision (discussed above in relation to civil partnerships). During the parliamentary debates on the Marriage (Same Sex Couples) Bill, this issue was raised again with the result that the Act contained a requirement for the Secretary of State to 'arrange for a review' of the differences in survivor benefits between same-sex and different-sex couples and the costs of equalising these benefits (MSSCA, s16). This review explained that:

> Given the potential for retrospective changes to create scheme deficits, successive Governments have maintained a policy presumption against making or mandating retrospective changes to pension schemes. This particularly applies when a pension has already been awarded, as there is then no scope for offsetting reductions in the benefits that have been awarded or for the member to make additional contributions.
>
> (HM Government 2014, para 2.25)

It reported that the cost of eliminating differences between surviving female spouses from a same-sex marriage or civil partnership compared with wives from a different-sex marriage, and differences between surviving male spouses from a same-sex marriage or civil partnership compared with husbands from a different-sex marriage, would be only around £0.02 billion for public sector schemes and £0.1 billion for private sector schemes (para 4.14). This would leave in place differences based only on sex because surviving men would still be treated differently (and less favourably) to surviving women (para 4.15).[27] It concluded that:

> Pensions are unique in that the consequences of actions that were taken in the past are crystallized today, and therefore reflect the inequalities of the past in today's pension outcomes. … [T]he Government will need to consider these costs and the potential impact on pension schemes along

> with the wider consequences of making retrospective changes to scheme rules.
>
> (Para 6.3)

If the government chooses not to take any action and there is no further case law, the differences will 'work their way out of the system as the number of scheme members with earlier periods of service declines' (para 2.28). However, this is a long time to wait.

Finally, there remain questions about what the impact of same-sex marriage in England, Wales and Scotland will be on jurisdictions connected with Britain (the remnants of the Empire) that do not have access to it, both within the UK (Northern Ireland is yet to permit same-sex marriages as marriage is a devolved matter) and in the British Overseas Territories. The absence of same-sex marriage in Northern Ireland is mitigated by the existence of civil partnerships there and the fact that a same-sex marriage contracted in England and Wales will be recognised in Northern Ireland, though only as a civil partnership (MSSCA, Sch 2(2)). However, this is not generally the case in the British Overseas Territories because most do not have any recognition of same-sex relationships and questions are already being asked about why British citizens are entitled to be married under the MSSCA in British consulates around the world (Sch 6) but there is no similar facility provided for those living in the British Overseas Territories, where there are no British consulates (see for example: Strangeways 2014a).[28] Citizens of the Overseas Territories are British citizens with the same status as those resident in the UK in terms of entitlement to live and work in the UK and EU, and protection under the ECHR. However, on LGBT issues generally and same-sex relationship recognition in particular, there are big differences between the laws of each of the Overseas Territories and in some cases a wide divergence from the standards set by the ECHR. While Gibraltar has recently introduced civil partnerships, the UK's MSSCA triggered a number of assurances by the various Governors of the other Territories that this legislation would not extend to them (see, for example, BVI Platinum News 2014; Strangeways 2014a). However, it necessarily raises questions. For example, despite the absence of any family recognition for same-sex couples and their children in Bermuda, the Attorney General acknowledged that Bermuda may have to 'respect the rights of a couple' who married abroad and returned home (*Bermuda Sun* 2013). A number of Bermudians have married their same-sex partner in Canada, the United States and the UK, but when they return home there is currently no legal recognition of this marriage or their status as a family. This is likely to result in litigation in the near future (Strangeways 2014c) and it will be interesting to see how the Privy Council and Strasbourg, if the cases reach them, will respond and how they might apply the margin of appreciation[29] to the UK in respect to Northern Ireland and the

British Overseas Territories now that the UK Parliament has legislated for same-sex marriage in England and Wales and the Scottish Parliament has for Scotland.

Chapter outlines

Part I of the collection – 'Towards marriage' – looks back at the recent history and charts the process towards same-sex marriage. The opening chapter 'Liberalism by stealth? The Civil Partnership Act and the new equalities agenda in perspective' is by Jeffrey Weeks, the doyen of sexuality studies in the UK and one of the academics who emerged from the Gay Liberation Front and was subsequently a founder member of Gay Left. Taking a long view, Weeks maps the political and social terrain to present in effect a 'history of the present'. His analysis focuses on changes at the political, governmental and parliamentarian level, as well as reconfigurations at the grass-roots level within the LGBT community (or communities). Arguing that the CPA and the MSCSCA reflect that 'something profound, and unexpected, had changed in the culture of Britain, and in the political possibilities around sexuality', Weeks locates the roots to this shift within a wider liberal European context and notes the distinctions here with the United States. For Weeks, 'the LGBT community had made further advances towards becoming an "ordinary" part of British society than anyone, least of all the community itself, had fully anticipated by the early 2000s'. On making this argument Weeks makes clear that 'ordinariness' is and should be understood as something distinct from 'assimilated' or 'normalised'. At the same time he engages with the increasing diversity and variety of responses to relationship recognition within the LGBT world and in doing so introduces many of the tensions and debates that are explored in more detail in subsequent chapters.

Weeks describes the recent history of law reform as being in some ways 'very British': cautiously pragmatic, incremental and respectful of tradition. The next chapter, 'Civil partnership in Scotland 2004–14, and beyond', by Kenneth McK Norrie, provides an important and timely reminder of the contingency of Britishness, for while the CPA applied to the UK as a whole, the path to equal marriage in Scotland was very different. Norrie explains the political background to the decisions of the Scottish Parliament to leave civil partnerships to Westminster but to take a very distinct approach to same-sex marriage. His account highlights the important differences between Scots and English family law, frequently overlooked by English commentators, and the significance of the distinct constitutional role of the Church of Scotland, as compared with the established Church of England. In linking same-sex relationship recognition with the politics and legal practicalities necessitated by devolution, the importance of sexuality as a key maker of national identity and indeed nation making is clear.

Norrie argues that one of the reasons why the Scots left the introduction of civil partnerships to Westminster was because of the well-funded and vocal opposition to the Scottish Parliament's repeal of the notorious Local Government Act 1988, s28 (three years before the Westminster repeal for rest of the UK); that the campaign, 'had made Scottish politicians exceptionally nervous about directly challenging what appeared to be powerful religious forces which had shown an ability to disrupt normal political debate'. The shifting terrain of conservative opposition to relationship recognition is the focus of the next chapter, 'Opposing same-sex marriage, by supporting civil partnerships: resistances to LGBT equalities', by Kath Browne and Catherine Nash. Opposition to equalities reforms may be far more marginal than in earlier times but it is frequently highly coordinated – at the same time a key argument here is that 'homophobia' is not consistent across continents. Through a detailed study of online sources, newspapers, magazines and newsletters Browne and Nash explore how arguments were structured so as to enable opposition groups to claim that they support equal rights (and were thus 'not homophobic'), while simultaneously opposing same-sex marriage. A key part of this strategy during the later equal marriage debates was acceptance of, and sometimes explicit support for, civil partnerships by groups that had previously vociferously opposed their introduction. Taking seriously and focusing on conservative opposition to equality agendas is, for Browne and Nash, not antithetical to engaging with progressive critiques of equality claims but part of moving beyond simple for/against positions.

Flora Renz teases out the tensions between binary positions in an important, but often overlooked, dimension to the law relating to civil partnerships and same-sex marriage: the impact on trans people. In 'Consenting to gender? Trans spouses after same-sex marriage' she unpicks the often ambivalent place of the 'T' in 'LGBT' both in terms of the law (and in particular the 'forced' dissolution/divorce requirements in the Gender Recognition Act 2004), but also by asking deeper questions about what the relationship can tell us about the ongoing significance of gender more widely. Consequently, while same-sex marriage means that trans people no longer need to change from one relationship category to the other to reflect their 'new' sexual orientation, Renz argues that the reformed law is still underpinned by assumptions about the vulnerability and potential exploitation of the partners of trans people and in particular of women (drawing parallels with the response of UK law to the position of divorced women in Jewish law). By revealing lingering homophobia and distrust of trans people and their identity claims, Renz identifies the extent to which 'sex/gender is far from becoming irrelevant to the concept of marriage itself'.

In Part II, 'Changing minds, changing practice? After the wedding', from different perspectives the contributors all look at the impact of the debates about relationship recognition and the legal reforms: on grass-roots social policy and practice, on institutions, and on individual lives. More removed from the explicitly political world and in distinct and varied contexts, the authors collectively engage with the relationship between law reform and shifting understandings and experiences of family and 'connectedness' (Smart 2007).

In gay and lesbian scholarship, whether from liberal or more radical perspectives, one area frequently overlooked is social work practice. Yet it is here that decisions and judgements about gay and lesbian family lives, and aspirations, have profound consequences. In 'Social work and adoption the impact of civil partnerships and same-sex marriage', Christine Cocker notes how gay and lesbian experiences are marginalised within mainstream social work policy and training and maps the, not insubstantial, progressive reforms that have taken place. But at the same time she asks critical questions about the limits to reform, the conditions of inclusion, in particular focusing on experiences of the adoption process that occurs within the shadow of the law. Locating adoption within a broader social and economic context, Cocker notes how the assessment process provides opportunities for agencies to implicitly require applicants – and also for lesbian and gay people to opt themselves – to mask aspects of their lives in order to perform according to normative ideals premised on conventional heterosexual values. The significance of civil partnerships and marriage may be formally legally marginal here, but the extent to which it informs these expectations and self-presentations is one of the unknown unexpected consequences of relationship recognition.

Despite strongly held ideological views for and against relationship recognition, we know very little about how people experience these changes individually or collectively within their families and social networks. In 'Civil partnership and ordinary marriages', Brian Heaphy considers how the possibilities enabled by legal reform are engaged with by younger generations of same-sex partners who have grown up with the relative cultural visibility and social acceptance of same-sex relationships from an early age, and who will have access to the kind of relational citizenship offered by civil partnership, same-sex marriage and associated 'equalities' legislation for most of their adult lives. Drawing on empirical research Heaphy suggests that for those who entered civil partnerships under the age of 35 it was commonly referred to as 'marriage' by the partners themselves and is spoken of and experienced as an inevitable and 'natural' choice. Understanding this as a valuing of 'ordinariness' Heaphy considers the implications of this for ways of thinking about the life-politics of marriage.

As the legal history above makes clear and as Weeks, Norrie, and Browne and Nash all subsequently note, religion has played an important role in the campaigns and movement towards both civil partnerships and ordinary marriages. In 'The Church of England and gay marriage: what went wrong?' Giles Goddard provides an insider account and reflection on the response by the Church of England. The constitutional role of this highly complex institution has always led to it claiming an authoritative status, in particular in any matters concerning marriage. Yet while its formal opposition to same-sex relationship recognition has been 'consistently negative', examined from within the story is multifaceted with contradictory stances, theological disputes with centuries old roots and, significantly, an international dimension that touches on political and cultural tensions which are critical to global conflicts that go beyond debates about equal marriage. Locating thc debates within these broader contexts, Goddard teases out the reasons why a future change of stance could be understood as part of, rather than a breach with, the institution's traditions and position within society.

Goddard's contribution emphasises and demonstrates the importance of avoiding making assumptions or crude generalisations about communities, religious or otherwise; and in this respect what he does for Anglicans, the next chapter does for lesbians. In 'Even sociologists get civilly partnered? Loving same-sex marriage and other contradictions', Yvette Taylor presents personal reflections and findings from empirical research to ask 'what does it mean to be "in love" in a time of UK – and indeed international – equalities legislation'. Central to her enquiry is class – a timely and necessary focus. While noting 'tensions and ambivalences rather than a straightforward capitalisation' Taylor traces the subtle classed readings and experiences of civil partnerships, the making of families and parenting. Going beyond simple for and against arguments, significantly here she notes the distinction between 'the moment of celebration/acceptance' and everyday ongoing struggles. And at this critical moment – when same-sex marriage is achieved at the same time as the introduction of a 'bedroom tax' – she raises questions about contemporary sexual citizenship noting its exclusions, the 'cost' of civic acceptance and its impact on intimacies and communities rarely heard either politically or in social science research where 'middle classness' is too often the unnamed norm and measure.

While for many people the most visible and justificatory moment of a civil partnership/marriage is its celebration, for family lawyers the moment of legal, familial and public recognition of a relationship attracts relatively little attention. Instead, and it may appear at best dour, their predominant concern focuses on what happens at the end of relationships (whatever the cause). Consequently it is in the final Part, 'The end of (the) marriage: dissolutions, disputes and the future', that we find most of the legal commentators in this collection, addressing the dissolution of civil partnerships, conflicts about children and disputes arising on the death of a partner.

In '"Square peg, round hole"? The legal regulation of plus-two-parent families', Chris Dietz and Julie Wallbank examine provisions under the Human Fertilisation and Embryology Act 2008 and the case law where the courts have been requested to resolve parenthood conflicts between gay fathers and lesbian mothers. Arguments in favour of same-sex relationship recognition sometimes refer to the welfare and interests of children in gay and lesbian families (McCreery 2008), but as Dietz and Wallbank note, such arguments, at best, work less well or, at worst, simply ignore families that do not confirm to a dyadic couple. And consequently gay fathers in these contexts, who are neither 'sperm donors' nor divorced heterosexual men, do not fit the dominant legal imagination. Reading judgements through an avowedly anti-assimilationist lens and drawing on the concept of 'heteronormativity', Dietz and Wallbank argue that 'challenging the traditional two-parent model and choosing to co-parent with one or more gay men and their extended family' are political choices and motivations that the law, if it is serious about recognising diversity, ought to take into account and incorporate when determining the welfare of the children caught up in these conflicts.

The parenthood disputes discussed by Dietz and Wallbank, perceived as 'private' and depoliticised, do not fit within a gay and lesbian rights paradigm. Consequently, unlike cases where people are pitted against explicit homophobia, it is not easy to take sides. In the next chapter, 'Judging the Act: civil partnerships disputes in the courtroom and the media', Daniel Monk examines three other cases that are similarly obscured; the first two arising on the death of one of the partners within a same-sex relationship, and the third on the dissolution of a civil partnership. These recent cases all required the judges to apply provisions under the CPA. Monk argues that while none of the outcomes are necessarily unjust, the ways in which the judges tell the stories and exercise their discretion indicates both the frequently unexpected impact on gays and lesbians of the terms and conditions of civil partnerships and, at the same time, the subtle impact of same-sex relationships on the institution of marriage. Central to his analysis, which also contrasts the judicial narratives with media coverage of the cases, is the continuing significance of gender as an underlying rationale and foundation of the legal recognition of the couples.

Gender is also central to the next chapter, 'Dissolution or disillusion? the unravelling of civil partnerships' by Rosemary Auchmuty. Drawing on the first available statistics and empirical research about people's experiences of dissolutions of civil partnerships, Auchmuty challenges the idea and 'modern tendency to assume an identity of interests among lesbians and gay men'. And in doing so explores why initially more men entered civil partnerships than women and also why women have dissolved their civil partnerships at a consistently higher rate. For Auchmuty, explanations are best provided by returning to feminist perspectives which she argues have been 'drowned out' by the dominant equal-rights discourse. At the same time, alongside the centrality of gender, Auchmuty, like Heaphy, finds significant generational differences in understandings and experiences of the law and expectations about relationships. And from the perspective of an earlier generation these changes are viewed with ambivalence and sometimes disappointment.

In the final chapter, 'After the wedding, what next? Conservatism and conjugality', Nicola Barker picks up on many of the themes from earlier chapters to look to the future and to imagine how family law might develop. In doing so she engages critically with some of the premises and motivations that brought about civil partnership and equal marriage. In particular, taking seriously Prime Minister David Cameron's statement that 'I don't support gay marriage despite being a Conservative. I support gay marriage because I'm a Conservative', Barker locates equal marriage within a broader conservative politics premised on traditional social values and austere anti-welfare economics. Linking this with the future are proposals, made by both conservative opponents and progressive commentators, for a move away from the conjugal couple as the only privileged relationship in order to recognise siblings, carers and other alternative family forms. Avoiding simple answers and recognising the sometimes contradictory pull to such propositions, Barker enables us to think of civil partnerships and same-sex marriage as the possible beginning of an expansion of relationship recognition and, as such, the end of conjugality as the foundation of law's notion of family. In this way she echoes most of the other contributions in recognising that current law is not only experienced in complex and contradictory ways but that in an uncertain social and political context its very purpose and meanings are open to debate.

Notes

1 Part 8, s1, para 295A(i)(a)(i).
2 *Fitzpatrick v Sterling Housing Association Ltd* [1999] UKHL 42, [2001] 1 AC 27, and later as spouses: *Ghaidan v Godin-Mendoza* [2004] UKHL 30, [2004] 2 AC 557.
3 The Relationships (Civil Registration) Bill (Bill 36, 2001–2) introduced in the House of Commons by Jane Griffiths MP, and the Civil Partnerships Bill 2002 (Bill 41, 2001–2) introduced in the House of Lords by Lord Lester.
4 See, for example, Baroness Buscombe, HL *Hansard*, 25 January 2002, col 1737.
5 Ibid., 1738.
6 The response to the consultation document (Women and Equality Unit 2003a) was surprisingly positive with 83 per cent of respondents in England and Wales supporting the proposed civil partnership (Women and Equality Unit 2003b: 9).
7 The Bills would have provided only a limited set of provisions for civil partners, in contrast to the government's comprehensive mirroring of marriage in the CPA, and also differed from marriage in some key ways regarding dissolution of relationships.
8 Per Baroness Scotland, HL *Hansard*, 22 April 2004, col 387.
9 Baroness Scotland, HL *Hansard*, 22 April 2004, col 322.
10 See, for example, Baroness O'Cathain, *Hansard*, HL Deb, 24 June 2004, vol 662, col 1363; Edward Leigh MP *Hansard*, HC Deb, 9 November 2004, vol 426, col 731.
11 Recent statistics indicate that 27 per cent of pension schemes rely on the Equality Act 2010, Sch 9, para 18 to treat civil partners differently than spouses and, of those, two-thirds restrict civil partner survivor benefits to contributions made after 2005: HM Government 2014, para 3.28.
12 See Robert Wintemute's opinion in Application in *Ferguson and Others v United Kingdom* (lodged with the European Court of Human Rights on 2 February 2011)

available at: http://equallove.org.uk/wp-content/uploads/2011/02/equalloveapplicationtoechr.pdf [accessed 10 August 2014], pp. 13–14, fn. 5.

13 However, it should be noted that even within different-sex married couples surviving wives and surviving husbands are still treated differently in some circumstances. Surviving same-sex partners who are in certain types of pension schemes are treated the same as surviving husbands from different-sex marriages, in that their benefits are calculated based on service accrued since 1988. This is still less favourable than the benefits given to surviving wives because there is still a process of 'gradual evolution' towards equalising the benefits (HM Government 2014: para 2.27). For more detail on the differences between the different types of pension schemes and their impact on different couples and surviving spouses, see HM Government 2014.

14 Queer is a complex concept with lots of, often contradictory, meanings but here it refers to an identity and politics that marks resistance to perceived mainstream gay and lesbian identities.

15 *Ferguson v the United Kingdom*. For further information see Equal Love (2010).

16 The Church of England has, of course, vehemently denied that such a distinction exists: Church of England (2012: 1).

17 An amendment to the CPA had just been implemented in December 2011 to remove the prohibition on civil partnerships taking place in religious premises but the prohibition on religions ceremonies during the actual registration of the civil partnership remains (Equalities Office 2012: para 1.10).

18 This was discussed during the Committee Stage of the Marriage (Same Sex Couples) Bill but in the Minister's view the provision of divorce on the basis of unreasonable behaviour was adequate if 'adultery' had occurred in a same-sex marriage (see *Hansard*, HC Com, 12 February 2013, col 5). The Minister nevertheless declined the opportunity of reforming divorce for different-sex couples to remove adultery (ibid.: col 6).

19 There were, however, comments in the House of Lords about how same-sex and heterosexual couples are distinct and so should be treated differently (see, for example, Lord Anderson: 'the Bill seeks to make equal that which is not equal': *Hansard*, HL Deb, 3 June 2013, col 966), about the 'destabilising and confusing effect on children and the existing concept of family' (Lord Vinson, *Hansard*, HL Deb, 3 June 2013, col 1077), and about same-sex marriage harming the institution of marriage, particularly in terms of declining rates of marriages amongst heterosexuals in countries that had introduced same-sex marriage as though there were a causal effect (see, for example, Lord Waddington, *Hansard*, HL Deb, 3 June 2013, col 960), but also in terms of 'the "what next?" factor' (Lord Brennan, *Hansard*, HL Deb, 3 June 2013, col 1070) with suggestions that it might lead to polygamy.

20 For example, Jim Dobbin said: 'For the first time in history, a Government have proposed a Bill that will change the very nature of marriage in law. … The Bill proposes to change the definition and therefore the meaning of marriage in the interests of equality. … This is not a Bill that has equality at its heart. In honesty, it is a Bill that dilutes the meaning of marriage' (*Hansard*, HC Deb, 5 February 2013, col 151; see also Lord Dear, *Hansard*, HL Deb, 3 June 2013, col 942).

21 This is despite the Church of England having accepted during Committee Stage that the provisions of the Bill regarding the position of the Church were 'generally okay' (Rev. Alexander McGregor, *Hansard*, HC Com, 12 February 2013, col 27), though the Catholic Church remained unconvinced (at col 33).

22 There is a vocal group of people within the Conservative Party who would like to, in the language of Theresa May, 'scrap the Human Rights Act', and 'pull out of

the European Convention on Human Rights' (see Wallace 2014). This group appears to have become dominant in the party after both Dominic Grieve and Kenneth Clarke, who were the most vocal supporters of the Convention, were sacked during the recent cabinet reshuffle (see Chapman 2014). For an academic analysis of the backlash against human rights in conservative circles in the UK, see Marks (2014).

23 No distinction was made between the Court of Justice of the European Union and the European Court of Human Rights, which were instead usually referred to as the 'European Court' or simply just the EU or 'Europe'.

24 Other MPs objected to such assertions: 'The Coalition for Marriage and some Churches have deliberately and consistently misinterpreted the Government's intentions by pretending that we were forcing Churches to marry same-sex couples. That was never the intention of the Government, and I and other colleagues would never have supported the Bill had it been so' (Margot James MP, *Hansard*, HC Deb, 5 February 2013, col 163).

25 In addition, marriages entered into overseas between a same-sex couple will be recognised as marriages (s10).

26 A protected marriage is a marriage under the laws of England and Wales or outside the UK (Sch 5, para 14, amending GRA, s25), thus excluding Scottish and Northern Irish marriages because marriage is a devolved matter in Scotland and Northern Ireland. Likewise, a protected civil partnership is a civil partnership under the laws of England and Wales.

27 Removing the sex inequality would cost significantly more: £2.8 billion to public sector schemes and £0.3 billion to private sector schemes (HM Government 2014: para 4.16).

28 Same-sex marriages may also take place in a military chapel. Unlike other religious premises, military chapels are usually owned by the Crown rather than the religious body (Explanatory Notes, para 51). MSSCA, s6 allows same-sex couples to marry in these chapels as long as the ceremony is not in accordance with the rites of the Church of England or Church in Wales. The chapel would need to be licensed under the new Marriage Act 1949, s70A to perform same-sex weddings and the individual minister could still lawfully decline due to the exception inserted into the Equality Act 2010, but where a minister is willing to register the chapel and perform the ceremony, a same-sex marriage can be contracted in military chapels. This may be a route to same-sex marriage in the Overseas Territories, where there is a local regiment of the British military, but no embassy for consular marriage.

29 The margin of appreciation is a tool used by the European Court of Human Rights to give states some leeway to legislate for local conditions, values, concerns and so on, rather than applying a fixed standard across the very diverse 47 member states of the Council of Europe. It is not unlimited and once more states begin to legislate for same-sex marriage it is likely to narrow but at present it is quite a wide margin on the issue of same-sex marriage given the lack of consensus amongst states on this matter.

References

Auchmuty, R. 2007. 'Out of the Shadows: Feminist Silence and Liberal Law' in Munro, V.E. and Stychin, C.F. (eds) *Sexuality and the Law: Feminist Engagements* (Abingdon: Routledge-Cavendish).

Ball, James. 2014. 'Gay Marriage Conversion Process Has No "Heart", Say Same-Sex Couples', *Guardian*, 23 July http://www.theguardian.com/society/2014/jul/23/gay-marriage-civil-partnership-conversion-process-couples [accessed 20 August 2014].

Barker, N. 2006. 'Sex and the Civil Partnership Act: The Future of (Non)Conjugality?' *Feminist Legal Studies* 14(2), 241–59.

——2012. *Not the Marrying Kind: A Feminist Critique of Same-Sex Marriage* (Basingstoke: Palgrave).

——2014. 'Why Care? "Deserving Family Members" and the Conservative Movement for Broader Family Recognition' in Wallbank, J. and Herring, J. (eds) *Vulnerabilities, Care and Family Law* (Abingdon and New York: Routledge).

Barnett, L. 2007. 'Mother is First Lesbian Guilty of Bigamy', *TimesOnline*,10 July 2007, http://www.timesonline.co.uk/tol/news/uk/crime/article2051926.ece [accessed 25 August 2014].

BBC News. 2012. 'Facebook Gay Wedding Comment Man Wins Demotion Case' http://www.bbc.com/news/uk-england-manchester-20357131 [accessed 18 August 2014].

Bermuda Sun. 2013. 'Gay Marriage: Challenges Ahead for Government', *Bermuda Sun*, 21 June 2013 http://bermudasun.bm/Content/NEWS/News/Article/Gay-marriage – challenges-ahead-for-Government-/24/270/67698 [accessed 1 August 2014].

BVI Platinum News. 2014. 'UK Will Not Force BVI to Accept Same Sex Marriage – Governor', *BVI Platinum News*, 20 January 2014 http://www.bviplatinum.com/news.php?articleId=1390223634 [accessed 1 August 2014].

Chapman, J. 2014. 'We Must Pull Out of Euro Human Rights Rules, May Tells the PM: It's the Only Way We Can Get Rid of Foreign Criminals, She Says', *Mail Online*, 11 August 2014 http://www.dailymail.co.uk/news/article-2722361/We-pull-Euro-human-rights-rules-May-tells-PM-It-s-way-rid-foreign-criminals-says.html [accessed 13 August 2014].

Church of England. 2012. *A Response to the Government Equalities Office Consultation 'Equal Civil Marriage' – from the Church of England* https://www.churchofengland.org/media/1475149/s-s%20marriage.pdf [accessed 25 August 2014].

Coalition for Marriage, 2013. 'Summary of the Aidan O'Neill Legal Opinion on Gay Marriage and Liberty of Conscience' http://c4m.org.uk/downloads/legalopinionsummary.pdf [accessed 21 May 2014].

Collier, R. 1995. *Masculinity, Law and the Family* (London: Routledge).

Department for Culture, Media and Sport. 2014a. *Civil Partnership Review (England and Wales): a Consultation* (January).

——2014b. *Civil Partnership Review (England and Wales) – Report on Conclusions.*

Equal Love. 2010. 'Legal Challenge to Ban on Gay Marriage & Straight Civil Partnerships', 25 October 2010 http://equallove.org.uk/2010/10/legal-challenge-to-ban-on-gay-marriage-straight-civil-partnerships/ [accessed 10 August 2014].

Equalities Office. 2012. *Equal Civil Marriage: A Consultation.*

HM Government. 2014. *Review of Survivor Benefits in Occupational Pension Schemes* (June).

Marks, S. 2014. 'Backlash: the Undeclared War Against Human Rights', *European Human Rights Law Review*, 4: 319–27.

McCreery, P. 2008. 'Save Our Children/Let Us Marry: Gay Activists Appropriate the Rhetoric of Child Protection', *Radical History Review*, 100: 186–207.

Odysseus Trust. 2002. 'Civil Partnerships Bill: Press Release', 8 February 2002 http://www.odysseustrust.org/civil_partnerships/press.html [accessed 31 March 2008].

Polikoff, N. 2000. 'Recognizing Partners but Not Parents/Recognizing Parents but Not Partners: Gay and Lesbian Family Law in Europe and the United States', *New York Law School Journal of Human Rights*, 17: 711–51.

Smart, C. 2007. *Personal Life* (Cambridge: Polity).

Stonewall. 2003. 'Stonewall Response to: Civil Partnership – A Framework for the Legal Recognition of Same-Sex Couples', August http://www.stonewall.org.uk/documents/Stonewall_response_August_2003.doc [accessed 25 August 2014].

——2004a. 'Parliamentary Briefing: Civil Partnership Bill, House of Lords Second Reading', 22 April http://www.stonewall.org.uk/documents/Lords_Second_Reading_Apr_2004.doc [accessed 23 June 2006].

——2004b. 'Parliamentary Briefing: Civil Partnership Bill, House of Lords Report Stage 24 June 2004', 1 July http://www.stonewall.org. uk/documents/Lords_Report_June_04.doc [accessed 22 July 2007].

——2004c. 'Parliamentary Briefing: Civil Partnership Bill, House of Commons Second Reading', 12 October http://www.stonewall.org.uk/documents/oahq_ Commons_Second_Reading_Sep_2004.doc [accessed 22 July 2007].

Strangeways, S. 2014a. 'Island Misses Out on UK's Gay Marriage Move', *The Royal Gazette*, 2 July http://www.royalgazette.com/article/20140702/NEWS/140709937 [accessed 2 July 2014].

——2014b. 'Lawyer Sees Possible Route to Gay Marriage In Bermuda', *The Royal Gazette*, 3 July http://www.royalgazette.com/article/20140703/NEWS/140709882 [accessed 1 August 2014].

——2014c. 'A Violation of My Rights: Gays Consider Legal Challenge over Marriage Recognition', *The Royal Gazette*, 10 July http://www.royalgazette.com/article/20140710/NEWS/140719982 [accessed 1 August 2014].

Stychin, C. 2006. 'Not (Quite) A Horse and Carriage: The Civil Partnership Act 2004', *Feminist Legal Studies*, 14(1): 79–86.

Walker, P. 2007. 'Woman Admits Bigamy in Same-Sex Partnership', *Guardian*, 9 July http://www.theguardian.com/society/2007/jul/09/gayrights.uknews [accessed 25 August 2014].

Wallace, M. 2014. 'The Motivations of May's Attack on Strasbourg', *Conservative Home*, 12 August http://www.conservativehome.com/thetorydiary/2014/08/the-motivations-of-mays-attack-on-strasbourg.html [accessed 13 August 2014].

Women and Equality Unit. 2003a. *Civil Partnership: A Framework for the Legal Recognition of Same-Sex Couples* http://www.womenandequalityunit.gov.uk/research/civ_par_con.pdf [last accessed 1 April 2008].

——2003b. *Responses to Civil Partnership: A Framework for the Legal Recognition of Same-Sex Couples* http://www.womenandequalityunit.gov.uk/publications/CP_responses.pdf [last accessed 1 April 2008].

——2005. *Civil Partnership Act 2004 – Frequently Asked Questions* http://www.womenandequalityunit.gov.uk/lgbt/faq.htm [last accessed 1 April 2008].

Young, C. and Boyd, S. (2006) 'Losing the Feminist Voice? Debates on the Legal Recognition of Same Sex Partnerships in Canada', *Feminist Legal Studies*, 14: 213–40.

Part I

Towards marriage

Chapter 2

Liberalism by stealth?

The Civil Partnership Act and the new equalities agenda in perspective

Jeffrey Weeks

Introduction

It is far easier for historians and social scientists to forecast the past than foretell the future. Few at the beginning of the 2000s would have confidently predicted the rise and rise of same-sex marriage as a, if not the, defining cause in lesbian, gay, bisexual and transgender (LGBT)[1] politics and cultures in the next 15 years, certainly in what we still call the West, but also in other parts of the world, from South Africa to Argentina and Uruguay. And even fewer would have foreseen its rapid implementation.

When my colleagues Brian Heaphy, Catherine Donovan and I produced our book *Same Sex Intimacies* in 2001 (Weeks et al. 2001), based on research conducted in the mid-1990s, civil partnerships and equal marriage seemed a distant prospect in Britain, despite government promises. Opposition appeared unrelenting, especially in the House of Lords and parts of the press. When we were writing it the Thatcher government's poisoned gift to the LGBT community, Section 28 of the Local Government Act 1988, with its notorious rejection of 'pretended family relations', was still on the statute book in England and Wales, though the Westminster government had tried to repeal it (and the Scottish government had successfully done so in 2000 in the teeth of fierce opposition, see Norrie in this collection). And yet barely a dozen years later a Conservative prime minister sponsored and forced through a government bill, carried with Labour Party votes, to allow equal marriage, over the heads of his disgruntled grass-roots and socially conservative backbencher MPs, though by now a majority of Tory peers did support it in the House of Lords. Whatever the qualifications critics might wish to make about the limitations of the legislation, there can be no doubt that something profound, and unexpected, had changed in the culture of Britain, and in the political possibilities around sexuality. This was acknowledged by David Cameron himself when he greeted the first same-sex couple to get married in the early minutes of 29 March 2014 (the day same-sex marriage was legalised in England and Wales) with the reflection that history had been made, in a very British way (Boffey 2014). Same-sex marriage had been recuperated for the national tradition. And in retrospect we can see that the Civil Partnership Act 2004 (CPA), approved by Parliament ten years before in 2004, and more crucially its successful implementation from late 2005, was a crucial marker, and perhaps a decisive staging post, in the shift of attitudes towards same-sex activities and forms of existence.

Soon after the introduction of civil partnerships I wrote an article suggesting that the act was a 'very British compromise' whereby LGBT people were accorded access in effect to most if not all marriage privileges by calling it something else; which in turn was a classic example of what I called 'liberalism by stealth', making progressive changes under cover of cautious pragmatism (Weeks 2011). I want now to revisit and partly revise some of the arguments I made then in the light of what has happened since, focusing in particular on two key features: the politics of sexual reform as implemented by the Blair and subsequent Brown governments; and developments in the LGBT world itself to which in many ways the legislative changes were a response. I will suggest that the New Labour reforms had more radical implications than many saw at the time; and that the LGBT community had made further advances towards becoming an 'ordinary' part of British society than anyone, least of all the community itself, had fully anticipated by the early 2000s.[2]

The politics of sexual reform

The success of civil partnerships and same-sex marriage, especially in Europe, has been propelled by the emergence of a policy consensus amongst national and transnational political elites, and of highly effective political organisation by LGBT campaigners in often close linkage with policy-makers (Kollman 2013). We can see this at work in Britain where the work of the premier lesbian and gay campaigning organisation Stonewall in careful lobbying for change was secured when its chief executive, Angela Mason, moved to the Cabinet Office Equalities Unit and became a key architect of the CPA (Weeks 2007). Although there were other campaigners pushing for change from the outside (Grice et al. 2013; Tatchell 2014), Stonewall was effectively working on the inside, advising on the drafting of legislation.

The Danish recognition of same-sex registered partnerships in 1989 in a real sense established the pattern, both in its initial gradualism and in its methods, which characterised the European as opposed to the American path. While in the USA campaigners began by focusing on judicial action and popular mobilisation for full and equal same-sex marriage, social-democratic Denmark, followed by the rest of Scandinavia, started with limited recognition (excluding, for example, same-sex adoption of children), using tried and trusted lobbying and parliamentary processes. Once recognition of registered partnerships were embedded, recognition of same-sex marriage followed, and only later were full parenting rights conceded (Rydsröm 2011).

The legislation that established PACS (*pacte civil de solidarité*) in France in 1999 followed classic republican traditions and protocols by not recognising the separate cultural identities of lesbians and gays (Borillo 2001; Fassin 2001; Johnston 2008), and was opposed by republican absolutists of left as well as right. It allowed civil unions for heterosexual and homosexual couples alike, and was clearly demarcated from marriage, whose legal status was not affected. The partners initially remained individualised, no new legal entity was created and no challenge was offered to the permanence of sexual difference or traditional rights of inheritance ('filiation'), which left-wing and right-wing conservatives saw as essential to the symbolic and social order. In the event, by 2009, 92 per cent of the new civil unions were contracted by heterosexual couples (*Washington Post* 2009). Same-sex marriage in France, when it came in 2013, engendered the same oppositional coalition, though opposition from the left was now more muted, but could now be justified as a working through of republican values of equality. That did not, however, stop opposition to equal marriage becoming a major symbolic rallying point for Catholic and far-right conservatism.

In the Netherlands radical changes initially came about through what Waaldijk (2001a: 440) called the 'law of small changes', an incrementalism that fitted in easily with the tradition of pillarisation that assumed the co-existence of different rights claims in a complex plural society, and was committed to recognising them. The introduction of same-sex civil partnerships and then of marriage in the early 2000s therefore seemed a logical next step in Netherlands' famous liberalism – though it characteristically did not lack critics who felt that same-sex marriage represented merely a sexual settlement that normalised conservative norms, and in a growing climate where acceptance of gayness had become a symbol for the far right as well as the left of national modernity against the perceived Muslim and fundamentalist threat (Hekma 2005).

In the USA, on the other hand, same-sex marriage became a key battle-front in the so-called 'culture wars', a battle that was as much about the current and future direction of society as a whole as the particular rights of LGBT people. Judicial battles, beginning in Hawaii in 1990, led to exhaustive appeals, attempts to declare same-sex marriage unconstitutional, battles in some states to legislate for equality, popular initiatives and further appeals, up to the Supreme Court (Kandaswamy 2008; Klarman 2013). The process proved long-drawn out, exhaustive and exhausting, but by December 2014, 35 US states plus the District of Columbia within the USA recognised same-sex marriage.

The trend across many different countries towards the legal acceptance of same-sex unions took different forms, and confronted different challenges and opportunities within different national traditions. This is not unusual, but precisely because it fundamentally impacts on such a traditionally key subject as marriage, and behind that the complex patterns of family law, kin, the rearing of children, the transmission of property and other inheritance rights, the debates over same-sex relationships have a way of casting a glaring light on the nature of society and cultural attitudes. They mark out the legacies of the past, the confusions of the present, but also the possibilities for the future: about what sort of society we want to live in, as the American debate clearly underlined.

Within this wider framework, the experience of the UK is especially revealing. For a long time, it was classically hesitant in pursuing the legalisation of same-sex partnerships – or indeed any liberalisation of attitudes towards homosexuality (Bailey-Harris 2001). Between 1967 and 1994, despite the emergence of a lively LGBT politics and community, the only significant legal shift in England and Wales had been negative – Section 28. Yet within a very short period at the beginning of the new millennium a series of legal reforms belatedly modernised British sexual law, culminating symbolically in the CPA. From notoriously in the 1950s having the most authoritarian legal regulation, and moral censure, of sexual unorthodoxy in the Western world, by 2010, when Labour left office, it had amongst the most liberal laws and attitudes, in what was in danger of becoming one of the most secular and tolerant of countries (Weeks 2007).

The legislative changes of the early 2000s signified a formal move to homosexual equality: an equal age of consent, equality in the armed services and in relation to immigration, the repeal of repressive legislation directed specifically at lesbians and gays, such as Section 28 of the Local Government Act 1988, and the offence of 'gross indecency', equality in relation to adoption and employment protection, and in the delivery of goods and services, as well as the granting of new rights to transgendered people through the passing of the Gender Recognition Act in 2004, all culminating in the Equality Act 2010 which encoded equity for all the recognised categories of difference and disadvantage, including LGBT people. This was an unprecedented series of reforming changes, the most significant concerning sexuality since the 1960s, and probably the most decisive in modern British history. The groundwork for legislative action had in many ways been laid down in a number of key court cases, but what is striking in historical perspective is that unlike earlier reforming efforts the legal reforms were the results of government initiatives, using the full panoply of legislative powers, including use of the Parliament Act 1911 to force legislation through when opposed in the House of Lords, signalling a break with the fiction that such changes should be a matter of individual conscience votes in response to private members' initiatives, as had happened in the 1960s (Weeks 2007).

The goal of equality between heterosexuals and LGBT people had been signalled by Tony Blair as long ago as 1994, before he had become prime minister, but had not featured prominently in the early years of the post-1997 Labour government (Weeks 2004). Nor was there any formal or explicit linking of these changes as part of a single project. They were presented as pragmatic adjustments to change, a modernisation of archaic and discriminatory laws. While the majority of Conservatives generally voted against, and the House of Lords was difficult, often blocking government proposals, there was at first no sense of a coherent drive or battle for equality within the government: this came only in the last stages of the New Labour project, as the wheels were coming off other ambitions. Like many other features of New Labour governance, this was liberalism by stealth rather than confrontation. Yet the changes were potentially radical, and constituted, I would argue, some of the most profoundly important and lasting achievements of the Blair government. Blair certainly thought so, even as subsequent commentators on his government tended to ignore them. He saw the CPA as an example of a new paradigm in social policy: 'what you did in your personal life was your choice, but what you did to others was not' (Blair 2010: 582; compare his comments in a broadcast interview, Coles 2014).

The CPA itself (which applied to the whole of the UK, unlike the later same-sex marriage legislation) went significantly further than had been signalled in the earlier consultation, largely the result of the work of the Cabinet Office's Equalities Unit and discreet lobbying rather than popular mobilisation. In effect, it enacted a new legal status that was practically identical with civil marriage (for its provisions, see Richards 2014). Ministers, of course, consistently reiterated that the government was not endorsing same-sex marriage, and this was subsequently upheld in a judicial decision, *Wilkinson v Kitzinger* [2006] EWHC 2022 (Fam). In part this position was obviously a way of avoiding divisive debates such as had taken place in the USA and elsewhere, and which had threatened at one stage to block parliamentary progress in the UK. From this point of view, the introduction of civil partnerships can be seen as a characteristically pragmatic way of adjusting to changing social realities without challenging traditional forms, and without as a nice consequence arousing too much political hostility – a very British compromise. Although conservative religious organisations and pro-family groups voiced strong opposition, they were by now very much minority voices, and the legislation had a decent modicum of cross-party support as it went through Parliament, at least from the majority of Labour and Liberal Democrats, backed by a minority of Tories. What especially diminished religious opposition was that what seemed to be on offer was a marriage-like arrangement separate from but parallel to civil marriage, which had long existed. The Established Church, while refusing blessings and use of its churches, eventually came round to *de facto* acceptance, even for its clergy (as long as celibacy was maintained) – to the extent that when the debate on same-sex marriage raged a decade later, some Church leaders saw civil partnerships an acceptable alternative to the equal marriage proposals that they opposed.

From another perspective the introduction of civil partnerships can be seen as part of the Europeanisation of British social legislation, and the impact especially of a new emphasis on human rights, symbolised by the enshrining of the European Convention on Human Rights into British law (see Waaldijk 2001b). The UK government had already been pressured by the European Court of Human Rights to concede various forms of equality, regarding spousal rights in housing, pensions and the like, and there was a clear logic in going further (Bell 1998). In one area, however, Britain went beyond European norms. At first the legislation in other EU countries explicitly excluded equal adoption and fostering rights – until 2005, even Belgium's granting of same-sex marriage excluded these. Children, childcare, parenting remained a last taboo. With the passage of the Adoption and Children Act 2002, granting equal rights on adoption and parenting to heterosexual and non-heterosexual couples alike before the recognition of civil partnerships, England and Wales unexpectedly leapt ahead. This suggests that the pragmatism displayed in the implementation of the new policy was underpinned at least implicitly by a developing set of values about relationships, whether they were heterosexual or non-heterosexual – as the quote from Tony Blair above suggests.

Despite the modest claims made for it, the British legislation had an ideological colouring that fitted into a wider social agenda. It was fully in line with the residual communitarian commitments that underpinned the government's social philosophy, which stressed the importance of strengthening family and community life as a way of combating societal dissolution and the weakening of social capital (compare Etzioni 1995). In practice, the emphasis was increasingly on supporting parents, especially those facing poverty, regardless of their marital status (Williams 2004), but marriage-like arrangements as a focus of both rights and responsibilities remained a powerful, if elusive, talisman for key members of the Blair government. From this perspective, the granting of strong guaranteed rights and agreed responsibilities to same-sex couples who entered legal partnerships fulfilled communitarian principles about building stable relationships (which up to this point in the wider debate initiated by Etzioni and his followers had signally ignored same-sex relationships) whilst not immediately undermining the legal and symbolic status of marriage. Prime Minister David Cameron was later to deploy similar arguments to support equal marriage from a Conservative position. Diversity in relationships was no longer seen as a problem, but instability in relationships was, especially if it contributed to wider social disorder. As Blair went on to say: 'a distinction came about between attitudes to human beings (non-discriminatory in race, gender or sexuality) and attitudes to social order (we need to impose it)' (Blair 2010: 582).

At the same time as the right to enter a civil partnership was seen as offering a new positive freedom by many, it was seen by others as potentially a new form of regulation, which produced new types of subjects, the legalised and legitimised couple. The American philosopher Judith Butler (2004: 104) had critically remarked on the dangers of the 'normalizing powers of the state' defining same-sex marriage as the right way to live for lesbians and gays, and for many radical critics civil partnership and related legislation carried with it the danger of separating off the respectable gay from the unrespectable, the stable couple from the promiscuous, and of imprinting new normativities onto the LGBT community.

There is no doubt that the Blair government was anxious to support marriage-like relationships. This was in the context of a continuing decline in the numbers of people who got married, the high divorce rates, amongst the highest in Europe, the large number of children born to single mothers, and a sense of uncertainty about changing sexual and family mores and patterns. However, there is no evidence of any ulterior or Machiavellian regulative zeal from the government. What you saw was what you got. Its ultimate preoccupations were not about stigmatising relationships it disliked – its general tone in relationship to consensual activities, whether heterosexual or same-sex, was broadly permissive – but about supporting types of relationship that they believed worked. Fiona Williams argued at this time that 'A new normative family is emergent, which … revolves around the adult couple whose relationship is based on their parenting responsibilities, and whose priorities are rooted in work, economic self-sufficiency, education and good behaviour' (2004: 244). It is easy to see how this model could fit in closely with simultaneously supporting strong lesbian and gay relationships, especially when they embraced parenting experiences, which was a major preoccupation of the New Labour government between 1997–2010.

Whilst acknowledging the significance of the Blair model of social policy, it is important not to see this in reductive terms, and to try to fit everything together too neatly into a preordained explanatory framework. This is particularly important when considering the impact of wider moves towards neo-liberal restructurings of the economy and society (Stedman Jones 2012). It has been tempting for radical critics of initiatives such as civil partnerships to attempt to place them within the frameworks they are familiar with: we live in neo-liberal climate; the Blair government supported neo-liberal economic reforms; therefore, civil partnerships must be a manifestation of neoliberal sexual governance (Richardson 2004). Civil partnerships may indeed express values which are complementary to a form of neo-liberalism governance, but they are also rooted, I have argued, in a form of communitarianism, and beyond that an older social democratic tradition based on a combination of mutuality, self-sufficiency, individual freedom and strong communal values. I am reminded of Anthony Crosland's famous encomium in the late 1950s to a modern European-style social democracy, characterised by 'the cultivation of leisure, beauty, grace, gaiety, excitement, and of all the proper pursuits, whether elevated, vulgar or eccentric, which contribute to the varied fabric of full private and family life'. In the blood of socialists, he argued, 'there should always run a trace of the anarchist and the libertarian, and not too much of the prig and the prude' (quoted in Weeks 1991: 181). Models of a tolerant, consensual, relaxed social democratic society – Scandinavian countries are obvious models – underpin these developments as much as neo-liberal rationalism. It is therefore difficult to agree with those critics, both from queer and leftist quarters, who have argued that new citizenship claims, including same-sex marriage, are complicit with neo-liberal strategies (Brandzel 2005). The USA, the most neo-liberal of states, has been on an official level the most hostile of all Western nations to same-sex citizenship rights, while the European country most hostile to globalisation, and to Americanisation, France, pioneered partnership rights, via PACS, and subsequently same-sex marriage. Neo-liberalism, I suggest, had little to do with it. More important were developments and shifts within the wider social world, including the changing patterns of relations, which in a sense made marriage less crucial than in the past as an anchor of social life. Most important of all were profound changes in the constituency the reforms addressed: the LGBT world itself.

The changing lesbian, gay, bisexual and transgender world

Whatever the motives of the political elite, a, if not the, crucial actor in this drama is the LGBT movement/community/social world itself. This had undergone profound transformations since the 1970s when the modern lesbian and gay movements had first emerged. By the early 2000s, I would argue, the LGBT world was no longer a single social movement in any meaningful sense, if it had ever been, though it gave rise to a variety of campaigns and many forms of informal and formal organisations. Nor was there necessarily a strong sense of community embracing all participants. Many of those identifying with the LGBT world were deeply sceptical about the romantic notion of community existing in any meaningful sense. Yet there could be little doubt that there were ties of values, identity, memories and common narratives, and a sense of belonging that linked people together across differences and diversity. It was a social world in the broadest sense, which had some elements of an ethnic identity, perhaps a common sexual ethos (Blasius 1994), and a shared history of an oppressive past, some of it not so distant. But it was also increasingly shaped by a rapidly evolving society. The LGBT community had become part of a complex, pluralistic multi-culture. The all-embracing movement of many activists' hopes had morphed into a dense network of sometime warring, but closely interlinked, loosely organised but emotionally and sexually intertwined civil society groupings, engaged in a continuous conversation about the meanings and possibilities, hopes and desires, of an ever-growing counter-public, offering a public discourse on personal life (Plummer 1999). And a profound shift in common preoccupations had occurred: from an embattled movement primarily concerned with asserting identity against a hostile sexual order to a world increasingly concerned with the possibilities of everyday life, and especially of relationships. It was becoming a social and cultural presence that governments, especially self-declared progressive governments, could not ignore. LGBT people were now everywhere!

Within this complex social world some were highly critical of the very idea of state recognition of LGBT relationships. Feminist critiques of marriage had a deep influence within lesbian and gay politics and these had become an embedded aspect of LGBT life (Barker 2013). Queer critiques of same-sex marriage, particularly strong in the USA, and echoing the feminist critique, in effect argued that marriage could never be freed of its 'heteronormative' anchoring, an institution that underpinned the dominance of heterosexual values and inequality between men and women. Queer analysis, Brandzel (2005: 195) argued, suggests that 'marriage is a mechanism by which the state ensures and reproduces heteronormativity, and absorbing certain types of gay and lesbian relationships will only further this process'. Marriage, Warner (1999: 82) wrote, 'sanctifies some couples at the expense of others. It is selective legitimacy.' Which is why social conservatives and queer theorists could both oppose same-sex marriage: conservatives because it confers legitimacy on the illegitimate, because it normalises the abnormal; radicals because it elevates one type of same-sex relationships over others, it normalises a particular type of couple relationship against the subversive and transgressive possibilities that sexual radicalism had aspired to.

Catherine Donovan, a British scholar far removed from the ideological divides of North America, and writing explicitly as a lesbian and a feminist, expressed similar fears very clearly in relation to the British context:

> I am against same-sex marriage (or any same-sex partnership legislation) for two main reasons. First, the place in UK society of marriage as a privileged legal and emotional contract reinforces inequalities between people depending on the way they organize and live their personal lives. Second, I believe that the model of love represented by marriage should not be held up unquestionably as the idea to which we should all aspire (Donovan 2004: 25).

When Catherine Donovan, Brian Heaphy and myself were researching together for our book *Same Sex Intimacies* in the mid-1990s (Weeks et al. 2001), we found that these sorts of sentiment were widely echoed. The interviewees portrayed in the book wanted their differences respected whilst claiming equal rights as a simple matter of justice. Yet while there was a widespread belief that non-heterosexual people had as much right to marriage as heterosexuals, and most people wanted some form of legal recognition for lesbian and gay relationships on grounds of equal citizenship, that did not necessarily mean that they themselves intended to seize the opportunity. The major reason for this was a strong sense that lesbian and gay relationships had genuine strengths and possibilities over and above what the law and convention allowed. Many were highly critical of traditional marriage and wanted nothing to do with it (Weeks et al. 2001: 192–94). Most of the self-defined LGBT people we interviewed believed that they had unique opportunities to lead more egalitarian lives than their heterosexual fellow citizens, precisely because they were excluded from the gendered and hierarchical relationships that traditional marriage represented. Friendship was especially valued as an egalitarian relation that often provided an alternative to the traditional family, which had excluded LGBT people. What was a matter of necessity in an era of oppressive legal codes and endemic prejudice had become normative within the LGBT community itself in more liberal times and, as many suggested, including liberal sociologists of intimacy such as Anthony Giddens (1992), a model for heterosexual society.

Given this background, it is not surprising that LGBT people on the whole were initially sceptical about the merits of same sex marriage or legalised partnerships in so far as they replicated traditional marriage. The sort of conservative justification for same-sex marriage put forward by Sullivan (1995) and similar gay conservatives especially in the USA, that it would mark the full integration of lesbians and gays into conventional society, found little favour amongst those we interviewed, though there was some support for marriage on other grounds. An online survey of mainly LGBT people drawn from 27 countries, reporting in 2006, found strong support for equal rights, and for same-sex marriage on these grounds (Harding and Peel 2006). A smaller qualitative study at the same time, however, found attitudes towards marriage 'more messy' than the debates tend to assume (Clarke et al. 2006: 155). Instead we found an interesting duality. On the one hand, there was a conscious desire for formal equality with the heterosexual majority in the whole range of citizenship rights, from benefit entitlements to care responsibilities, up to and including marriage. On the other hand, there was a widespread reluctance to simply 'mimic' straight society (Weeks et al. 2001: 193). If this was the case, then same-sex marriage hardly seemed to be the right way forward.

Two experiences, however, pushed the other way. The first was the absence of parenting rights, both amongst lesbians who had formerly been in heterosexual marriages, and lesbians and gay men who wanted to parent, which had led to a long lasting and difficult campaign for parenting rights (Hanscombe and Forster 1983; Griffin and Mulholland 1997; Harne and Rights of Women 1997). The second was the experience of the HIV/AIDS epidemic, especially amongst gay men, where there was a multitude of personal experiences of partners of people living with AIDS being denied anything remotely like partnership rights (Heaphy et al. 1999; Weeks et al. 2001: 17–19). Both experiences underlined the denial of full citizenship to lesbian and gay people (Watney 1994: 159–68), especially regarding care and relational rights.

So although there had been little popular pressure for change (see Shipman and Smart 2007), when in December 2005 it finally became possible in Britain for same-sex couples legally to confirm their relationships under the CPA, many same-sex couples appeared to welcome it with open arms, and there was an early rush to local registry offices. Though carefully not officially deemed same-sex marriage, the legislation was deliberately framed by the government in parallel terms to heterosexual marriage. The only significant differences, ironically given the obsessive cultural tradition of defining LGBT people solely by their sexuality, concerned the absence of sexuality: unlike heterosexual marriage, sexual consummation was not required to complete the partnership, and adultery could not provide evidence for the dissolution of the union (Richards 2014). Many in the gay community ignored these subtle distinctions, and decided to call it marriage anyway, and took up the offer with enthusiasm. During the first nine months over 30,000 lesbians and gays took advantage of the new legislation, with at first twice as many men entering civil partnerships as women, a pattern that was common in most jurisdictions. The legislation allowing civil partnerships, especially when linked to the Adoption and Children Act 2002, which allowed same-sex couples the same rights as heterosexual couples, gave same-sex couples in Britain as many, if not more, rights as in other countries in Europe even though it still denied the formal title of marriage to same-sex couples.

Towards equality?

Governments and legislators may seek to develop and shape new normative frameworks, but there can never be a one to one fit between intention and effect, and the unintended effects of state action are usually more potent than the intended in relation to sexual and intimate life – which is why governments are usually reluctant to do anything that looks too obviously like moral engineering, or to go further than they need to. Piecemeal moral engineering is about as far as British governments tend to go, though in this case, as we have seen, the CPA was part of a much wider package of reform. But there was an inherent logic in the reforms themselves that suggested further change, even as commentators, politicians and some activists seemed to think this was a firm settlement. Radical critiques of the new civil partnerships ranged from rejection of any legislative framework for same-sex relationships through a desire to see new legal rights for all types of relationships, including polyamorous ones, to a rejection of the separation of marriage and civil partnerships. Why should LGBT people and heterosexual couples not have civil partnerships? The legislation of an equal but different status for LGB people soon hit a logical problem with T people. Under the Gender Recognition Act 2004 the trans person could now gain legal status in his or her new gender, thus creating a same-sex couple if they were heterosexually married. But if they wished to maintain a legal bond, they had to divorce and then enter a civil partnership for the basic reason that same-sex couples were not allowed to marry (see Renz in this collection). In other words, by essentialising both the heterosexual/homosexual binary (based on the assumption that LGB people were distinct from heterosexual people and required different legal provisions) and gender (assuming an absolute divide between men and women), the CPA was in danger of storing up legal tangles (Hines 2013). Even though there was an immediate government reluctance, echoed by Stonewall, to further immediate change, civil partnerships inexorably pointed to the logic of equal marriage.

This shift reflected new stirrings on the ground. Despite all the earlier hesitations, when the opportunity arose, people rapidly lost their inhibitions. For most people who in these early days entered into a civil partnership the motives have been less political than pragmatic. For them civil partnerships were already marriages in all but name, and from the start had been using the language of 'weddings' and 'marriage' almost universally. In practice new meanings and realties were being created as LGBT people formulated their own norms of acceptable behaviour, and articulated their rationales and motivations for seeking legal recognition of partnerships. Three forms of legitimisation became common, which we can broadly label: rights, commitment and recognition.

The rights agenda resonates with the larger claims to full equality that had become the prime motivation of LGBT activism. The new entitlements were considerable, and provided a very material motivation to enter a civil partnership, especially with regard to pension rights and inheritance. The reforms of the early 2000s had embedded certain rights claims and underlined a new legitimacy. As one leading and long-standing lesbian and feminist critic of marriage said to me at the time, we would be fools not to enter a civil partnership.

Important as the rights and accompanying responsibilities were, the underlying motivations were often more abstract, above all reflecting the desire to signify commitment (compare Lewis 2001: 124ff.). Long before civil partnerships seemed likely, gay couples had been finding various ways of marking commitment: from the exchange of rings and gifts, celebrating significant events such as date of first meeting or first sex, birthdays or Christmas, to participating in full-scale commitment ceremonies (Lewin 1998; Weeks et al. 2001: 127–32). Even for those of an ardently secular disposition, the affirmation of commitment was a critical moment. For many, civil partnership involved a firm commitment to traditional monogamy – 'forsaking all others'. For others, however the really important commitments were emotional, with sexual monogamy a matter of negotiation rather than prescription (Heaphy et al. 2004). Affirming commitment and love in the civil partnership may have been an intensely private experience, but it had a necessary public resonance: public recognition of a private transaction, but also public recognition of LGBT citizenship, a second coming out. Here getting married was a 'fateful moment' (Giddens 1992) which disorders previous life narratives, and requires new scripts, a reshaped life story and new possibilities.

The third key element is recognition. The denial of legal rights for same-sex unions can be seen, in Nancy Fraser's famous phrase as one of the 'injustices of recognition' that mark contemporary society (Fraser 1997; see also Adkins 2002: 27ff). The bringing of LGBT people into full citizenship is therefore not a trivial act. In the end, if it is to mean anything, it must also entail confronting the forces that have inhibited full recognition. The goal of legitimising civil partnerships or same sex-marriages, I suggest, is better seen as a form of struggle for recognition than a ruse of power. Within a very short time in the LGBT community within the UK, as elsewhere, civil partnerships were becoming rapidly normalised as one option amongst others: not the only or necessary choice, but a new possibility among many. They were in danger of becoming ordinary possibilities for LGBT people, which in the end it would be impossible for an increasingly social liberal society to deny (Heaphy et al. 2012).

It is this discourse of ordinariness that seems to me the crucial shift that has taken place in the LGBT world. It is not the same as assimilation or normalisation. It may disappoint radical advocates of transgression or an alternative sexual order. But in a quiet way, the very meanings of formal relations are being transformed, as conservative critics of same-sex marriage fully recognise (see essays in de Waal 2013). We are in the midst of a major transformation of intimate life – and civil partnerships and equal marriages are crucial components of this historic shift.

Notes

1 By the early 2000s LGBT had become generally acceptable as the acronym for what had earlier simply been called lesbian and gay politics and community, and I have used it throughout this article – though occasionally omitting the T when a piece of legislation or policy did not apply to transgender people.

2 I have used Weeks (2011) as the starting point of this essay to suggest the rapidly shifting nature of the changes that have taken place, and to open a dialogue with my earlier interpretation.

References

Adkins, L. (2002) *Revisions: Gender and Sexuality in Late Modernity* (Open University Press).

Bailey-Harris, R. (2001) 'Same Sex Partnership in English Family Law', in Wintermute, R. and Andenaes, M. (eds) *Legal Recognition of Same-Sex Partnerships*, 605–22.

Barker, N. (2013) *Not the Marrying Kind: A Feminist Critique of Same Sex Marriage* (Palgrave Macmillan).

Bell, M. (1998) 'Sexual Orientation and Anti-discrimination Policy: The European Community', in Carver and Mottier 1998, 58–67.

Bernstein, E. and Schaffner, L. (eds) (2005) *Regulating Sex: The Politics of Intimacy and Identity* (Routledge).

Blair, T. (2010) *A Journey* (Hutchinson).

Blasius, M. (1994) *Gay and Lesbian Politics: Sexuality and the Emergence of a New Ethics* (Temple University Press).

Boffey, D. (2014) 'I Now Pronounce You Wife and Wife: Same-Sex Couples Can Marry at Last', *Observer*, 30 March, 1.

Borrillo, D. (2001) 'The "*Pacte Civil de Solidarite*" in France: Midway Between Marriage and Cohabitation', in Wintermute, R. and Andenaes, M. (eds) *Legal Recognition of Same-Sex Partnerships*, 475–92.

Brandzel, A. L. (2005) 'Queering Citizenship? Same-sex Marriage and the State', *GLQ: A Journal of Lesbian and Gay Studies* 11 (2), 171–204.

Butler, J. (2004) *Undoing Gender* (Routledge).

Carver, T. and Mottier, V. (eds) (1998) *Politics of Sexuality: Identity, Gender, Citizenship* (Routledge).

Clarke, V., Burgoyne, C. and Burns, M. (2006) 'Just a Piece of Paper? A Qualitative Exploration of Same Sex Couples' Multiple Conceptions of Civil Partnership and Marriage', *Lesbian and Gay Psychology Review* 7 (2), 141–61.

Coles, R. (2014) 'Gay Rights: Tying the Knot?', radio programme, BBC Radio 4, broadcast on 19 and 23 March 2014.

De Waal, A. (ed.) (2013) *The Meaning of Matrimony: Debating Same-Sex Marriage* (Civitas).

Donovan, C. (2004) 'Why Reach for the Moon? Because the Stars aren't Enough', *Feminism and Psychology* 14 (1), February, 24–29.

Duncombe, J., Harrison, K., Allan, G. and Marsden, D. (eds) (2004) *The State of Affairs: Explorations in Infidelity and Commitment* (Lawrence Erlbaum Associates).

Etzioni, A. (1995) *The Spirit of Community: Rights, Responsibilities and the Communitarian Agenda* (Fontana).

Fassin, E. (2001) 'Same Sex, Different Politics: "Gay Marriage" Debates in France and the United States', *Public Culture* 13 (2), 215–32.

Fraser, N. (1997) *Justice Interruptus: Critical reflections on the Post-socialist Condition* (Routledge).

Giddens, A. (1992) *The Transformation of Intimacy: Sexuality, Love and Eroticism in Modern Societies* (Polity Press).

Grice, A. et al (2013) *Same Sex Marriage: The Road to Equality* (Independent Print Limited).

Griffin, K. and Mulholland, L. (eds) (1997) *Lesbian Mothers in Europe* (Cassell).

Hanscombe, G. and Forster, J (1983) *Rocking the Cradle: Lesbian Mothers. A Challenge in Family Living* (Sheba Feminist Publishers).

Harding, R. and Peel, L. (2006) '"We do"? International Perspectives on Equality, Legality and Same-Sex Relationships', *Lesbian and Gay Psychology Review* 7 (2), 123–40.

Harne, L. and Rights of Women (1997) *Valued Families: The Lesbian Mothers' Legal Handbook* (Women's Press).

Heaphy, B., Donovan, C. and Weeks, J. (2004) 'A Different Affair? Openness and Nonmonogamy in Same Sex Relationships', in Duncombe, J., Harrison, K., Allan, G. and Marsden, D. (eds) *The State of Affairs: Explorations in Infidelity and Commitment* (Lawrence Erlbaum Associates), 167–84.

Heaphy, B., Smart, C. and Einarsdottir, A. (2012) *Same Sex Marriages: New Generations, New Relationships* (Palgrave Macmillan).

Heaphy, B., Weeks, J. and Donovan, C. (1999) 'Narratives of Love, Care and Commitment: AIDS/HIV and Non-Heterosexual Family Formations', in Aggleton, P., Hart, G. and Davies, P. (eds) *Families and Communities Responding to AIDS* (UCL Press), 67–82.

Hekma, G. (2005) 'How Libertine is the Netherlands?: exploring Contemporary Dutch Sexual Cultures', in Bernstein, E. and Schaffner, L. (eds) *Regulating Sex: The Politics of Intimacy and Identity* (Routledge), 209–24.

Hines, S. (2013) *Gender Diversity, Recognition and Citizenship* (Palgrave Macmillan).

Johnston, C. (2008) 'The PACS and (Post)Queer Citizenship in Contemporary Republican France', *Sexualities* 11 (6), December, 688–705.

Kandaswamy, P. (2008) 'State Austerity and the Racial Politics of Same-Sex Marriage in the United States', *Sexualities* 11 (6), December, 706–25.

Klarman, M. J. (2013) *From the Closet to the Altar: Courts, Backlash and the Struggle for Same-sex Marriage* (Oxford University Press).

Klesse, C. (2006) 'Heteronormativity, Non-monogamy and the Marriage Debate in the Bisexual Movement', *Lesbian and Gay Psychology Review* 7 (2), 162–73.

Kollman, K. (2013) *The Same-Sex Unions Revolution in Western Democracies: International Norms and Domestic Policy Change* (Manchester University Press).

Lewin, E. (1998) *Recognizing Ourselves: Ceremonies of Lesbian and Gay Commitment* (Columbia University Press).

Lewis, J. (2001) *The End of Marriage? Individualism and Intimate Relations* (Edward Elgar).

Plummer, K. (1999) 'The Lesbian and Gay Movement in Britain: Schism, Solidarities and Social Worlds', in Adam, B. D., Duyvendak, J.-W. and Krouwel, A. (eds) *The Global Emergence of Gay and Lesbian Politics: National Imprints of a Worldwide Movement* (Temple University Press), 133–57.

Richards, S. (2014) *Civil Partnership and Marriage (Same Sex Couples) Act 2013* (Emerald Guides).

Richardson, D. (2004) 'Locating Sexualities: From Here to Normality', *Sexualities* 7 (4), 391–411.

Rydström, J. (2011) *Odd Couples: A History of Gay Marriage in Scandinavia* (Aksant).

Shipman, B. and Smart, C. (2007) '"It's made a huge difference": Recognition, Rights and the Personal Significance of Civil Partnership', in *Sociological Research Online* 12 (1), January, http://www.socresonline.org.uk/12/1shipman.html.

Stedman Jones, D. (2012) *Masters of the Universe: Hayek, Friedman, and the Birth of Neo-Liberal Politics* (Princeton University Press).

Sullivan, A. (1995) *Virtually Normal: An Argument about Homosexuality*, London: Picador.

Tatchell. P. (2014) 'Same-Sex Marriage – This is How We Won It', *New Statesman*, 28 March, online at http://www.newstatesman.com/politics/2014/03/it-was-long-fight-equal-marriage-finally-it-s-here.

Waaldijk, K. (2001a) 'Small Change: How the Road to Same-Sex Marriage Got Paved in the Netherlands', in Wintermute, R. and Andenaes, M. (eds) *Legal Recognition of Same-Sex Partnerships*, 437–64.

Waaldijk, K. (2001b) 'Towards the Recognition of Same-Sex Partners in European Union Law: Expectations Based on Trends in National Law', in Wintermute, R. and Andenaes, M. (eds) *Legal Recognition of Same-Sex Partnerships*, 635–52.

Warner, M. (ed.) (1999) *The Trouble with Normal: Sex, Politics and the Ethics of Queer Life* (The Free Press).

Washington Post (2009) http://www.washingtonpost.com/wp-dyn/content/article/2009/02/13/AR2009021303365.html [accessed 7 August 2014].

Watney, S. (1994) *Practices of Freedom: Selected Writings on HIV/AIDS* (Rivers Oram Press).

Weeks, J. (1991) *Against Nature: Essays on History, Sexuality and Identity* (Rivers Oram Press).

Weeks, J. (2004) 'Labour's Loves Lost? The Legacies of Moral Conservatism and Sex Reform', in Steinberg, D. L. and Johnson, R. (eds) *Blairism and the War of Persuasion: Labour's Passive Revolution* (Lawrence & Wishart).

Weeks, J. (2007) *The World We Have Won: The Remaking of Erotic and Intimate Life* (Routledge).

Weeks, J. (2011) 'A Very British Compromise? Civil Partnerships, Liberalism by Stealth and the Fallacies of Neo-Liberalism', in Jones, J., Grear, A., Fenton, R. A. and Stevenson, K. (eds) *Gender, Sexualities and Law* (Routledge).

Weeks, J., Heaphy, B. and Donovan, C. (2001) *Same Sex Intimacies: Families of Choice and other Life Experiments* (Routledge).

Williams, F. (2004) *Rethinking Families* (Calouste Gulbenkian Foundation).

Wintermute, R. and Andenaes, M. (eds) (2001) *Legal Recognition of Same-Sex Partnerships: A Study of National, European and International Law* (Hart Publishing).

Chapter 3

Civil partnership in Scotland 2004–14, and beyond

Kenneth McK. Norrie

Introduction

Exactly ten years separates the passing by the UK Parliament of the Civil Partnership Act 2004, which brought civil partnership to Scotland, and the passing by the Scottish Parliament of the Marriage and Civil Partnership (Scotland) Act 2014, which opened marriage to same-sex couples in Scotland; exactly 15 years separates the (re)establishment of the Scottish Parliament in 1999 and the Independence Referendum in 2014. The political judgment made in 1999 that devolution would kill the aspiration to independence stone dead has proved as misconceived as the political judgment in 2004 that civil partnership would satisfy any demand for same-sex marriage. The new political structures within the UK established by devolution rendered it inevitable that the development of civil partnership would play out very differently in Scotland and in England, but the existence of two distinct legal systems, on separate developmental paths, long pre-dates devolution.

Scottish family law has always been based on very different perceptions of family life from English family law and these differences reflect profound historical, social and (particularly) religious dissimilarities between the two nations. We in Scotland have no concept, for example, of parental consent to marriage, revealing a different view of both the nature of the parent–child relationship and of marriage (and avoiding the difficulties English law will face when parents refuse consent due to non-acceptance of their child's sexual orientation). That marriage is a more secular contractual relationship in Scotland than it is in England is shown by the facts: (i) that marriage contracts have always been enforceable in Scotland but are (generally speaking) unenforceable in England (Scherpe, 2012); and (ii) that divorce has been available in Scotland for 300 years longer than in England. The grounds laid down in the (English) Matrimonial Causes Act 1973 by which a marriage is voidable leaves the Scots lawyer utterly bemused. The differences in both the rules of annulment and of divorce are traced to the very different religious histories of the two countries.

The Reformation was caused by separate pressures in Scotland and England, and led to very different forms of church (and, before the Union and after devolution, state) governance. Scotland adopted a Presbyterian model for its national church (the Church of Scotland, or "the Kirk"), which is membership-led and without a hierarchy of vicars, rectors, bishops and the like. Its more puritan doctrines are illustrated well by the fact that divorce – following the biblical precedents – was accepted in Scotland immediately after the Reformation while the reformed English church continued to adhere to Catholic doctrine concerning the sanctity (and therefore irreversibility) of marriage. The flattened, non-hierarchical, structure of the Kirk, which is to be compared with the retained Catholic hierarchy within the established Church of England, had political as well as legal consequences: the King became the Supreme Governor of the Church of England but, like everyone else, a mere member of the Church of Scotland. (Indeed it was the efforts of King Charles I to turn himself from member to master of the Church of Scotland that triggered what is usually, rather oddly, referred to as the "English" Civil War.) And it affected social attitudes: the social democracy that is ascendant in present-day Scotland, which has resisted the individualism of most of the rest of the UK, has long historical roots.

Devolution offered the opportunity for Scottish family law to take a very different route from that in England, though in the two jurisdictions same-sex relationship recognition has followed a similar path, responding to similar social pressures. The *28th British Social Attitudes Report* (National Centre for Social Research, 2010: table 2.6) shows a continuous fall in the number of people in the UK who consider same-sex relationships to be always or mostly wrong (48 per cent in Scotland and 46 per cent in England in 2000; 40 per cent in both Scotland and England in 2005; and 27 per cent in Scotland and 29 per cent in England in 2010), together with a concomitant rise in the number of those who consider same-sex relationships to be not wrong at all (29 per cent in Scotland and 34 per cent in England in 2000; 35 per cent in Scotland and 37 per cent in England in 2005; and 50 per cent in Scotland and 44 per cent in England in 2010). The Scottish Parliament has been quick to respond to this change in social attitudes. The Scotland Act 1998 itself included prevention of discrimination on the ground of sexual orientation in its definition of "equal opportunities", and one of the Scottish Parliament's earliest pieces of legislation was the Adults with Incapacity (Scotland) Act 2000 which contains the first explicit statutory inclusion in the UK of same-sex couples in a provision dealing with families. Since then no legislative provision passed by the Scottish Parliament concerning couples has failed to include same-sex couples on the same terms. The civil partnership proposals in 2003–4 were never going to be resisted by the Scottish Parliament.

Why Westminster?

The Civil Partnership Act 2004 is, of course, an Act of the UK Parliament at Westminster, and it provides three separate civil partnership regimes: one for England and Wales, one for Northern Ireland and one for Scotland. Differences between the three parts reflect the existing differences in the marriage laws in these three jurisdictions. Yet civil partnership is a matter that falls clearly within the authority of the Scottish Parliament: family law is not one of the areas that the Scotland Act 1998 reserved to Westminster. As such, the first question to ask in relation to Scotland is this: Why does the 2004 Act contain a "Part 3: Civil Partnership in Scotland" at all?

Shortly after the UK Government proposed a system of civil partnership registration for same-sex couples in England and Wales (Department of Trade and Industry, Women and Equality Unit, 2003), the Scottish Executive (as the Scottish Government was then known) announced that it would seek the agreement of the Scottish Parliament to include Scottish provisions in the UK Bill. A consultation paper was then published (Scottish Executive, 2003), in which a number of difficulties were identified that would follow if England and Wales introduced civil partnership but Scotland did not: Scottish couples who registered their partnership in England would be treated as civil partners for reserved matters (including tax, benefits and pensions) but not for devolved matters (such as succession, property sharing and dissolution); if Scottish civil partnership were substantially different from English civil partnership (for example in eligibility to enter such a relationship), some Scottish couples might be recognised for devolved but not for reserved matters. The simplest solution, the consultation paper suggested, was to provide a civil partnership registration scheme in Scotland, equivalent to the English system.

The Scottish Parliament was therefore invited to pass a motion giving its permission for the UK Parliament to legislate on a devolved matter. The official line was that this was desirable in order to ensure that the reserved consequences of marriage, such as tax and social security, could be extended to civil partnership at the same time as the non-reserved consequences, but would also ensure consistency between the two jurisdictions (Scottish Executive, 2003: [4.2]–[4.6]). The same argument might, of course, be made in relation to same-sex marriage, which similarly involves a mix of both devolved and reserved consequences, but by the time same-sex marriage was on the agenda Scotland had elected a Scottish Nationalist Government, and there was never any question of that Government using the legislative consent motion process for an issue so central to domestic social policy. One of the inherent tensions in the devolutionary settlement is illustrated here: the UK Parliament, legislating for England and Wales, does not distinguish between devolved and reserved matters and so domestic English debate at Westminster continues to have consequences for Scots (and Northern Irish) law.

One of the explanations for the Scottish Parliament's willingness to allow Westminster to act on its behalf is that, though in its second four-year session by 2004, the Scottish Parliament was still finding its feet, and the Scottish Executive was at that time a coalition government – comprising the Scottish Labour Party as the dominant, and the Scottish Liberal Democrats as the junior, partners. This meant that the Scottish Government at that time had very strong political connections to the (Labour) UK Government. (These connections of course came to an end in 2007 when the coalition was replaced by the Scottish Nationalists, and even more profoundly in 2010 when the Labour Government was replaced by a UK coalition dominated by the Conservative Party, whose support in Scotland shows no sign of recovering from its Thatcherite crash.)

But there is a deeper reason beyond these close governmental links that explains the Scottish Parliament's willingness to contemplate Westminster legislating for Scotland, a reason that traces its roots (like the Scottish Tory collapse) back to the Thatcher era. In 1988 the UK Parliament passed the Local Government Act 1988, Section 28 of which prohibited local authorities throughout the UK from "promoting homosexuality as a pretended family relationship". Both the Labour Government in the UK, elected in 1997, and the Labour/Lib-Dem Coalition in Scotland, elected in 1999, very early indicated that "Section 28" was to go, and this was effected in Scotland in 2000,[1] three years before the British Parliament managed to do so for the rest of the UK.[2] However, notwithstanding that the overwhelming number of MSPs from both the coalition Government and the SNP opposition favoured repeal, opposition took a surprising and disturbingly extra-parliamentary form. A wealthy businessman and Evangelical Christian, Brian Soutar, who owns and operates the Stagecoach group of companies, joined forces with the Roman Catholic Church and mounted a vicious scare-campaign against the repeal of Section 28. Souter funded the so-called "Keep the Clause campaign" to the tune of £1 million,[3] which was used to conduct a private "referendum" on the matter (though in fact the campaign could not even get the correct name of the statute on the ballot paper). Catholic priests instructed their flocks how to vote, and posters appeared across Scotland explicitly associating homosexuality with child abuse: the narrative presented by the Keep the Clause campaign was that Section 28 was all about protecting children.[4] Many opponents to Section 28 simply ignored this "referendum" but it is a sobering thought that, from an electorate of around three million, just over one million people in Scotland "voted" to keep Section 28 on the statute book. To its credit, the Scottish Executive went ahead with its repeal, with only the Conservatives (very much a minority party in Scotland) and a handful of nationalists voting to retain it.

The repeal of Section 28 did little to voting patterns, and the same (Lib–Lab) coalition was re-elected to the Scottish Parliament for its second session in 2003, but there is little doubt that the Keep the Clause campaign had made Scottish politicians exceptionally nervous about directly challenging what appeared to be powerful religious forces, which had shown an ability to disrupt normal political debate. It was against that background that the decision had to be taken when the UK Government announced its Civil Partnership Bill for England and Wales (and Northern Ireland) whether the Scottish Parliament would take the responsibility that the Scotland Act 1998 had given it in this central family law matter or would allow Westminster to legislate on its behalf. The convenience argument (which is not without merit) won, though the suspicion has long remained that the infant Scottish Parliament simply did not have the courage to take on the issue, so soon after the bruising Section 28 fight. In any case the Scottish Parliament passed the necessary motion and the UK Parliament extended its Civil Partnership Act 2004 to Scotland.

The Civil Partnership Act 2004 in Scotland

The policy objective for Scottish civil partnership was the same as for English civil partnership: to replicate so far as possible the marriage (and divorce) rules for this new legal institution, and the differences between the Scottish and the English parts of the Act reflect the fact that the matrimonial laws of the two jurisdictions, as we have already seen, have always been substantially different. This policy objective was achieved in the Scottish part by three distinct drafting strategies: (i) replicating in the 2004 Act itself those family law statutes concerning the creation and termination of the marital relationship; (ii) amending existing legislation that gave legal consequences to marriage; and (iii) creating entirely new statutory rules applicable to civil partners for those consequences of marriage that continue to be governed by the common law. The most important of the last mentioned is Section 131, which puts into statutory form for civil partners the ancient common law rule that the surviving spouse of a person who dies domiciled in Scotland has an indefeasible claim to part of the deceased's estate.

Since the Civil Partnership Act 2004 came into force, Scotland has not seen the litigation experienced in England involving individuals unwilling to accept the moral, social and legal equivalence of marriage and civil partnership, and the development of the law has been driven by subsequent legislation, politically designed to further the original objective of making civil partnership as much like marriage as possible.

Differences between marriage and civil partnership

Though the UK Act went noticeably further than most other European jurisdictions that introduced civil partnership in equiparating the institution with marriage, in neither Scotland nor England is civil partnership completely identical to marriage. In Scotland there are two major structural respects (other than the obvious difference in gender-mix) in which the two institutions were, until 2014, treated differently: civil partnership, unlike marriage, was designed to be an entirely secular institution, and an entirely sex-free institution. Civil partnership for its first ten years could be created only by a district registrar and registration was prohibited in religious premises (a matter explored more fully below). The sexual aspects of marriage were deliberately excluded too (and indeed remain so, even after the 2014 amendments). Adultery, though still a ground for divorce, was not made a ground to dissolve a civil partnership – though all the other grounds for divorce are replicated. And the only ground upon which a marriage in Scotland is voidable and open to retrospective annulment – incurable impotency at the date of the marriage – was not extended to civil partnership. So while marriage remains even today a relationship with both religious overtones and sexual undertones, civil partnership was designed as a relationship with legal consequences created by a state official without any religious involvement at all, and without any implication of sexual fulfilment. To many people this is an attractive blueprint for the legal regulation of personal relationships in the modern age but, as we will see, it is a model followed only to a limited extent as marriage has developed.

There were also a couple of important areas where the decision was made to treat civil partnership differently from marriage. There is some difference in the calculation of pensionable service in relation to occupational pension schemes, which is an area where the laws of Scotland and England are identical – and is reserved to Westminster (and Scots law on the matter will therefore be reviewed under the terms of Section 16 of the (English) Marriage (Same Sex Couples) Act 2013 rather than the Marriage and Civil Partnership (Scotland) Act 2014). Other than that, the most important difference between marriage and civil partnership in the Scottish part of the 2004 Act concerned adoption of children. The Adoption (Scotland) Act 1978 restricted couple-adoption to married couples, as did the equivalent English legislation until the Adoption and Children Act 2002 allowed in that jurisdiction joint adoption by any couple, of whatever gender-mix, so long as the applicants are "living as partners in an enduring family relationship".[5] This was amended in the English part of the Civil Partnership Act 2004 so that spouses and civil partners could jointly adopt, as well as couples in an enduring family relationship. No equivalent amendments were made to the Scottish adoption legislation, on the only partly persuasive ground that Scottish adoption law was at that time under review and that the matter of extending capacity to adopt was better dealt with within the context of a comprehensive restructuring of adoption law (Scottish Executive, 2003: [6.40]). So while civil partners in England and Wales were able to adopt from the commencement date of the Civil Partnership Act 2004, civil partners in Scotland had to wait until the Adoption and Children (Scotland) Act 2007 came into effect in September 2009.

Errors in the Civil Partnership Act 2004

The drafting strategy adopted, for all three UK jurisdictions, was to amend each individual statute that provides consequences for married couples rather than to enact a general amending provision such as "wherever 'spouse', 'husband', 'wife' or cognate terms appear they shall be read to include civil partners". It was all but inevitable from that drafting strategy that errors and omissions would be made, requiring subsequent amendment.

By far the most serious error in relation to Scots law was discovered in 2012, by which time the 2004 Act had been in force for almost seven years. For it was not noticed until that point that the secondary legislation that allows courts to dispense with third-party evidence in non-contested divorces[6] had not been extended to the dissolution of civil partnerships. This was a problem because courts since civil partnership came in had been happily granting dissolutions without such evidence in non-contested cases, just as they do in non-contested divorces. By the time the error was discovered, some 145 dissolutions had been granted without third-party evidence, giving rise to an exceptionally nice legal problem: is a decree granted by a court acting beyond its powers completely void, in which case the couples are still empartnered (and any subsequent registration or marriage is invalid), or merely voidable, in which case the couple are free until such time as their decree of dissolution is reduced? Emergency legislation was passed,[7] but it was not made retrospective since the Scottish Government took the view that the decrees were merely voidable, and that anyone who had acted on the basis that they were now single would be personally barred (or "estopped", in the English term) from challenging their dissolution; in any case the Government felt that it could not use secondary legislation to render valid any existing decree that might be invalid, but that primary legislation would be necessary.[8] Section 27 of the Marriage and Civil Partnership (Scotland) Act 2014 backdates the secondary legislation to the date the Civil Partnership Act 2004 came into effect, thereby retrospectively validating all such potentially invalid decrees. This is an inelegant solution to a problem that inevitably arises when the law has two institutions doing the job of one. There is an important lesson here that will need to be remembered when the decision comes to be taken whether to retain civil partnership or to abolish that institution as unnecessary now that same-sex couples have the right to marry.

Place of registration

The location where marriage ceremonies may take place has never been a big deal in Scotland, where the control mechanism has traditionally lain more in who is authorised to celebrate the marriage rather than where it can be done. This can be seen by comparing the lengthy provisions in the (English) Marriage (Same Sex Couples) Act 2013 on the registration of premises with the equally lengthy provisions in the Marriage and Civil Partnership (Scotland) Act 2014 on the authorisation of celebrants. Questions like the one that troubled the Supreme Court in 2013, whether Scientology was sufficiently a "religion" that its premises could be used for marriage ceremonies,[9] would not arise in Scotland, where religious marriages have always been able to be solemnised anywhere agreed to by the parties and the celebrant. Civil marriages could originally be solemnised only in the registration office of the relevant local authority, but since 2002 local authorities have been able to approve any place as suitable for marriage solemnisation, other than a place associated with a religion the doctrines of which would be inconsistent with civil marriage.[10]

The Civil Partnership Act 2004 gave rather greater protection to religious organisations, by prohibiting the use of any "religious premises", whether or not the religion in question adhered to doctrines inconsistent with civil partnership.[11] But this created an inconsistency between civil marriage in Scotland and civil partnership. The response of the Scottish Government was to amend the 2002 Regulations for civil marriage and bring in the more restrictive rule applicable to civil partnership.[12] It is a paradox that legislation designed to liberalise the law of personal relationships thus led directly to a reduction rather than an increase in the choices available to couples getting married. And there was a bigger paradox to come, for the English provision limiting place of registration of civil partnership was repealed in the Equality Act 2010, but the identical Scottish provision was not – mainly it would seem because it was a late amendment from an English peer and then the whole of that Act was rushed through just before the dissolution of the Westminster Parliament for the 2010 General Election. The end result was to leave Scotland with a restrictive rule, designed to be consistent with English law, but which English law has since dropped. The Marriage and Civil Partnership (Scotland) Act 2014[13] attempts to resolve the conundrum by repealing all the rules about local authority authorisation of places, for both civil marriage and civil partnership, but maintaining the prohibition on either being in a religious place: the effect is to shift the burden from the local authority to the district registrar to determine whether a place is religious.

Unregistered same-sex couples

An ever-increasing gap between Scottish and English family law is found in the way that informally cohabiting couples – cohabitants – are treated in the two jurisdictions. The primary aim of the Civil Partnership Act 2004 was, of course, to deal with formalised relationships but the Act's failure to amend the law of cohabitation meant that same-sex couples continued after the 2004 Act came into force to be treated less well than opposite-sex couples who did not formalise their relationship with the state. The interpretative obligation imposed by the House of Lords in *Ghaidan v Godin-Mendoza*[14] to include same-sex couples within the concept of "living together as husband and wife" only partly assuaged the problem because some legislation remained very gender-specific. But two years after the Civil Partnership Act 2004, the Scottish Parliament passed the Family Law (Scotland) Act 2006, the major effect of which was to create new financial remedies at the termination of cohabitation, either by death or by separation. This goes far beyond what English law has yet been able to achieve for cohabitants and, perhaps, reflects a discomfort in Scotland with hierarchies of relationships that has not fully evolved in England. The provisions in the 2006 Act were, of course, applied to same-sex as well as opposite-sex cohabitants,[15] and the 2006 Act also took the opportunity to extend to same-sex couples existing cohabitation provisions that had not been so extended by the Civil Partnership Act 2004. Interestingly, and perhaps presaging the ending of civil partnership, the Marriage and Civil Partnership (Scotland) Act 2014 repeals all statutory references to same-sex couples "living together as if civil partners", and replaces them with references to "two people ... living together as if they were married to each other".[16]

The Marriage and Civil Partnership (Scotland) Act 2014

Showing a confidence and maturity that was, perhaps, less evident in 2004, the Scottish Parliamentary debates on the Bill that became the Marriage and Civil Partnership (Scotland) Act 2014 contain very few references to the equivalent English legislation. No longer was the aim to do as the English were doing, but instead was to provide a marriage and civil partnership regime consistent with existing Scottish principles. As in England the main opposition came from religious organisations, but that opposition was far less strident than it had been during the "Section 28" debates – not least because the most prominent Roman Catholic cleric in Scotland, Cardinal Keith O'Brien, was forced to resign in early 2013 due to allegations of sexual impropriety with other priests. The final vote in favour of same-sex marriage (105 to 18[17]) was substantially greater in Scotland than in England and Wales (where at the Third Reading in the House of Commons the Marriage (Same Sex Couples) Bill passed with 366 MPs in favour to 161 against).[18]

The headline effect of the Marriage and Civil Partnership (Scotland) Act 2014 is, of course, to open marriage to same-sex couples but it also amends marriage law in a number of interesting and useful ways. First, the existing common law rule that a wife cannot be convicted of "reset" (receiving stolen goods) if the husband is the thief is simply abolished,[19] removing from Scots law the last vestige of a wife's duty to obey her husband. Second, the rules relating to impotency are limited to marriages involving opposite-sex couples,[20] with the consequence that there is no ground upon which a same-sex marriage will be voidable and open to retrospective annulment.[21] Third, the Registrar General for Scotland is given new powers to ensure that religious or belief bodies that seek to provide marriage celebrants meet certain prescribed requirements.[22] Fourth, the concept of "religious marriage" is extended to include "religious or belief" marriages. The inclusion of belief marriages (and belief civil partnerships) was designed to accommodate humanist ceremonies, though it removes what had been a rather pleasing paradox in Scotland that the Humanist Society Scotland was prescribed by the Registrar General for Scotland as a religious body in order to allow humanist celebrants to solemnise marriages. (This could not happen in England, for humanists have no "places of worship" – a matter irrelevant in Scotland.) In truth of course, we have always had belief marriages – we call them religious marriages – and the most logical thing to do (other than require all marriages to be civil) would have been to subsume religious marriage into the more general category of belief marriages. Politically, however, this was simply not practicable within an Act that was already irritating most mainstream religious bodies almost beyond endurance.

In addition to these changes to marriage law the Scottish legislation – as its title suggests and in sharp distinction from the English legislation – contains comprehensive amendments to civil partnership too.

The "religification" of civil partnership

The primary change to civil partnership effected by the 2014 Act was to remove its one great saving grace: its immunity from religious involvement. Originally designed as a strictly secular institution, civil partnership could not be registered by anyone other than a district registrar, nor at any religious venue. Now, however, religious officials are to be allowed to effect their registration. In the name of equality with marriage, civil partnership is made equally vulnerable to religious interference. This is madness. Once we allow religious bodies to effect the creation of our relationships, we invite them to tell us how to live our lives, and such bodies are unlikely to decline the invitation. The history of religion is the history of powerful bodies of men (and the gender-specificity here is deliberate) taking it upon themselves to lay down rules of sexual and familial behaviour – not only for their own followers but for the whole of society.

The result is that same-sex couples in Scotland will be able to choose one of four mechanisms for formalising their relationship in law: (i) religious or belief marriage, solemnised by a religious or belief celebrant; (ii) civil marriage, solemnised by a district registrar; (iii) religious or belief civil partnership, registered by a religious or belief celebrant; or (iv) civil registration of civil partnership, effected by a district registrar. (The limitation of choice for opposite-sex couples to civil or religious/belief marriage only is no substantive deprivation and requires no expenditure of sympathy.)

Conversion of civil partnership to marriage

It is likely that many of the same-sex couples who have since 2005 registered their civil partnership in order to formalise in law their relationship would have preferred to marry, had that option been available to them. The Marriage and Civil Partnership (Scotland) Act 2014 allows for same-sex couples who are in a civil partnership (registered either before or after marriage became available to them) to convert that partnership into a marriage. The Act provides two methods of conversion, neither of which involves divorce. First, there is to be an administrative process the details of which are contained in regulations made by the Scottish Ministers.[23] Second, the civil partners may, quite simply, marry each other: in other words, an exception has been created to the otherwise universal rule that a person in a civil partnership is ineligible to marry.[24] (It may be noted that the equivalent English legislation provides only an administrative process for conversion[25] – civil, but not religious, conversion.) There is, however, no mechanism for converting ("downgrading"?) a marriage into a civil partnership.

Accommodating religious opposition

The debates in the Scottish Parliament were far less strident than the debates in the media (or the UK Parliament), perhaps because parliamentary opponents realised from an early stage that they would lose the primary argument – and were more realistic in that assessment than their English counterparts. Opponents in both jurisdictions sought instead a number of amendments, such as to confer a right of conscientious objection to district registrars, a right of school teachers to teach that same-sex marriage is wrong, a right of service providers to discriminate between opposite-sex and same-sex marriage, and a specific statutory provision exempting expressions of opposition to same-sex marriage from the hate crime legislation. In Scotland, unlike in England, all of these amendments failed and the only concession made to religious sensitivities was that any religious or belief body that wishes to provide civil partnership celebrants or marriage celebrants for same-sex couples must seek authorisation to do so; and there is an explicit statutory statement that no religious or belief body is obliged to seek any such authorisation.[26] The Equality Act 2010 already provides religious bodies with a right to refuse to offer public services in a non-discriminatory fashion, but the protections for individuals are necessarily different and an additional protection is provided by an amendment by the UK Parliament to the 2010 Act (which is reserved to Westminster), allowing any individual member of a religious or belief organisation that has sought prescription as a body empowered to register civil partnerships (or solemnise same-sex marriages) to refuse as an individual to do that which his or her body permits.[27] As Wintemute (2014: 224) comments:

> The challenge for human rights law … [is] to allow the religious individual to participate to the greatest extent possible in public life, while ensuring that particular manifestations of their religious beliefs do not have the effect of imposing their beliefs on others.

It is unlikely that the amendments to the 2010 Act fully meet that challenge. Though described as a conscience clause, it is to be noted that this protection of conscience works only in one direction and any person who belongs to a body that disapproves of same-sex relationships cannot be authorised as a celebrant even when he or she, as an individual, welcomes as a matter of conscience same-sex relationship recognition.

It is not just the church minister who can claim a conscientious objection, but anyone who might otherwise be expected to participate in the solemnities of the occasion, such as the organist or choirmaster – though the right does not extend to those involved in the celebratory elements, such as the chauffeur or the hotel waiter whose employers have contracted to provide such services to a same-sex couple. Exactly where to draw the line between solemnisation and celebration will not always be clear, and it is not out of the question that the courts will interpret the exemption expansively.[28] The conscientious objection need not be based on any official religious doctrine: it is the individual's self-defined belief that is protected, irrespective of its basis. This is a major widening of existing exemptions from the requirements in the Equality Act 2010, as illustrated in the Supreme Court's decision in *Bull v Hall*,[29] where Lady Hale pointed out that the 2010 Act exemptions (then applicable) were deliberately restricted to institutions protecting their own doctrinal positions, and that this represented a carefully calibrated balance between the equality imperative and the need to give some recognition to religiously traced requirements to discriminate.[30] The amendments to the 2010 Act necessitated by the Marriage and Civil Partnership (Scotland) Act 2014 to allow opposing members of supporting churches to continue to discriminate for their own self-defined reasons threatens to disrupt that carefully struck balance.

The position of the Kirk in Scotland, Scotland's "national church", is very different from the position of the Established Church of England in England (see Goddard in this collection) and there was no need to make any special provision for the Kirk which is, therefore, as open as any other religious organisation to decide that it will, in future, offer marriage services to same-sex couples. It is interesting to note that, in its response to the Scottish Government's consultation on the Bill, the Church of Scotland, while opposing the opening of marriage to same-sex couples on doctrinal grounds, nevertheless explained the process by which its doctrines on the matter could be changed (Church of Scotland, 2011: [6]–[8]). This was very different from the doctrinal objections of the Church of England, which founded on the definitional argument that it is not open to a legislature to change the nature of church doctrine (Church of England, 2012: [8]), and reflects the membership-led governance of the Kirk: as Kirk membership changes its views, so too does church doctrine. (This approach is found with other non-hierarchical denominations, such as the Scottish Methodists, who similarly contemplated that its membership might change its current opposition to same-sex marriage.) Nor was there any need to exempt members of the clergy of the national church from the obligation to solemnise marriages[31] because in Scotland there is no such obligation. The Kirk's opposition to same-sex marriage reflected its earlier opposition to civil partnership, though it is noticeable that its response to the marriage consultation expressed opposition only to religious civil partnership (see Browne and Nash in this collection). In 2009 the Kirk established a Special Commission to determine whether being in a civil partnership was compatible with the ministry; this Commission reported in 2011,[32] recommending a further two-year period of reflection, and the General Assembly in 2013 voted in favour of allowing the training and ordination of civil partners (that is to say, of gay and lesbian people).[33] A gradual accommodation of same-sex relationships seems to be the route that the Kirk is on.

The future of civil partnership

From 2014, therefore, there are two institutions in Scotland, marriage and civil partnership, both available to same-sex couples, though only marriage is available to opposite-sex couples. This position is surely unsustainable, giving as it does more options to the former than to the latter. Both the UK Government and the Scottish Government have recognised this unsustainability. The Scottish legislation does not contain, as the equivalent English legislation does,[34] a statutory obligation to review the continued operation of civil partnership, but the Scottish Government announced before the 2014 Act was passed that such a review would nevertheless take place. It is likely that there are two primary models for the future, which might be called the Dutch model and the Scandinavian model. The former, which seems to be the preferred option of the main LGBT campaigning group in Scotland (the Equality Network), would involve maintaining both marriage and civil partnership, but opening civil partnership to opposite-sex couples.[35] The latter option would involve closing civil partnership registrations for the future while retaining existing civil partnerships until such time as they naturally die out.

Each option has some attractions, but the Dutch model has far more serious disadvantages than the Scandinavian model. Choice is of course a good thing, but four different means for registering one's relationship with the state smacks of overindulgence. In any case, and more substantively, choice is valuable and real only if there is a practical difference in the options available. Given that marriage for same-sex couples is now virtually identical in its consequences to civil partnership, any choice between these two separate institutions (even when open to all) is illusory. A choice only of a name – "marriage" or "civil partnership" – is a choice without substance.

A more practical objection to the Dutch model is that it is not efficient law reform to have two institutions doing the job of one. At the moment we require two sets of legislation, two sets of forms to be designed, two sets of approvals of celebrants, two sets of opt-ins, two registers of (non-registrar) celebrants: mistakes will inevitably be made, as we in Scotland have already seen with the expedited divorce provisions, mentioned above. Any amendment of the law will require twice the effort in legislative drafting than if we had only one institution doing one job: there are costs involved in this even without the risk of error.

After its review of civil partnership, the UK Government decided that the lack of consensus justified retaining the present situation. The Scottish review is taking place as this chapter is being written and might well come to a different conclusion, leading to intriguing possibilities of registered relationships having a different range of consequences depending upon whether they were registered in Scotland or in England. The fear of the inevitable complexities that would give rise to was decisive in the original decision to allow Westminster to extend its Civil Partnership Act 2004 to Scotland. The present, independence-seeking Nationalist, Scottish Government is more sanguine about such complexities, seeing them as the unavoidable consequence of the devolutionary settlement. That settlement is unlikely to survive in its present form much beyond 2014 – not with standing the outcome of the Independence Referendum held in September 2014 – and so there is no guarantee that the Scots, faced with the question of keeping or abolishing civil partnership, will do as they did in 2004 and simply follow the English lead.

If it is accepted that only one institution is necessary, then (for reasons of international recognition if no other) that institution must be marriage. The best approach would be to build upon the attractive aspects of civil partnership and use that institution – as originally designed – as a model from which to effect improvements in the law of marriage (letting civil partnership itself gradually wither). This process has already started: the removal of the sexist reset rule came about when it was realised that not only could it not be applied to same-sex couples but that, in truth, there was no good reason to keep it for opposite-sex couples either. The limitation of impotency to annulments of opposite-sex marriages might well prove so anomalous that it is finally scrapped for all marriages – and the exclusion of all sexual considerations from civil partnership continues to provide a role model that marriage must, surely, adopt eventually (see Barker in this collection). Cohabitation is now defined in terms of its similarity to marriage and no longer to either marriage or civil partnership. The influence was in the other direction with the unfortunate imposition on civil partnership of the marriage rules relating to religious involvement, but that may simply be the price that needs to be paid to ensure parity between the two institutions. The anomaly would, in any case, be very short lived if the Dutch approach were rejected and the Scandinavian embraced. Civil partnership would be an institution that, having acted as a bridge to the ultimate goal of gender-neutral marriage, had served its function and could now be dispatched to an honourable place in history.

Notes

1 Ethical Standards in Public Life etc (Scotland) Act 2000, s 34.
2 Local Government Act 2003, sched 8 para 1(1).
3 See "Soutar to Bankroll Clause Referendum" *BBC News* (28 March 2000): http://news.bbc.co.uk/1/hi/scotland/693172.stm [accessed 2 December 2014].
4 See "A Mother's Anger at 'Keep the Clause' Campaign" *Herald* (Glasgow, 26 February 2000).
5 Adoption and Children Act 2002, s 144(4).
6 Civil Evidence (Scotland) Act 1988, s 8(3A), disapplied in relation to non-contested divorces by the Sheriff Court Rules 1993 (rule 33A.66–75) and the Rules of the Court of Session (rule 49.80A-I).
7 Evidence in Civil Partnership and Divorce Actions (Scotland) Order 2012, SSI 2012/111.
8 Executive Note, attached to the Evidence in Civil Partnership and Divorce Actions (Scotland) Order 2012.
9 *R (on the Application of Hodkin) v Registrar General of Births, Deaths and Marriages* [2013] UKSC 77.
10 Marriage (Approval of Places) (Scotland) Regulations 2002, SSI 2002/260.
11 Civil Partnership Act 2004, s 6 (for England and Wales), s 93 (for Scotland).
12 Marriage (Approval of Places) (Scotland) Amendment Regulations 2005, SSI 2005/657.
13 Marriage and Civil Partnership (Scotland) Act 2014, ss 21 and 24(10) and (11).
14 [2004] UKHL 30, [2004] 2 AC 557.
15 See for example *Savage v Purches* 2009 SLT (Sh Ct) 36.
16 2014 Act, s 4(3) and (4). The English legislation does the same.
17 Voting breakdown was as follows: SNP voted 56 to 7; Labour voted 33 to 3; Lib-Dems voted 5 to 0; Conservatives voted 7 to 8; Greens voted 2 to 0; Independents voted 2 to 0.
18 Voting breakdown: Labour 194 to 4; Conservatives 124 to 134, Lib Dems 43 to 4; others 5 to 9. SNP MPs do not vote in purely English/Welsh votes.
19 2014 Act, s 7.
20 2014 Act, s 5(1).
21 Adultery is explicitly stated in s 5(2) to be unaffected by the Act, so a marriage, whether same-sex or opposite-sex, can be terminated by divorce if one of the parties had (heterosexual) sexual intercourse outwith marriage, but not if the sexual activity were homosexual. It is the same under the English legislation.
22 2014 Act, s 12(2)(b).
23 Marriage Between civil partners (procedure for change and fees) (Scotland) regulations 2014 (SSI 2014/361). For details, see Norrie "Converting Civil Partnerships into Marriages" (2015) 133 *Greens Fam.* L.B.4.
24 2014 Act, s 11.
25 Marriage (Same Sex Couples) Act 2013, s 9. The Marriage of Same Sex Couples (Conversion of Civil Partnership) regulations 2014 (SI 2014/312) allows, however, religious and other ceremonies to follow the conversion process.
26 2014 Act, ss 12–15 (for marriage) and s 25 (for civil partnership). An amendment to strengthen this provision so that religious bodies cannot be forced "by any means, including by enforcement of contract or a statutory or other legal

requirement" to do so was defeated. The English Act, in s 2, was amended (in the House of Lords) in precisely this way.

27 Equality Act 2010, Sch 3(5) para 25B (as Inserted by The Marriage and Civil Partnership (Scotland) Act 2014 and Civil Partnership Act 2004 (Consequential Provisions and Modifications) order 2014, SI 2014/3229).

28 In *Doogan v Greater Glasgow and Clyde Health Board* [2013] CSIH 36 the Court of Session held that the conscientious objection clause in the Abortion Act 1967 had to be interpreted widely enough to include all those who felt their own beliefs compromised by the activity in question. The Supreme Court, however, overruled this ([2014] UKSC 68) and held instead that the conscience clause extended only to those who take part in a 'hands on' sense.

29 [2013] UKSC 73.

30 [2013] UKSC 73, [8], [38].

31 As found in the English Marriage (Same Sex Couples) Act 2013, s 1(4).

32 *Special Commission on Same Sex Relationships and the Ministry* (Church of Scotland, May 2011).

33 Not all parishes were happy with this result, and it is reported that a congregation in Stornoway has as a result left the Kirk for the more traditionalist Free Church of Scotland: see "Church of Scotland Responds to Congregation's Vote to Leave", *Stornoway Gazette*, 20 May 2014.

34 Marriage (Same Sex Couples) Act 2013, s 15.

35 As well as the Netherlands, Belgium, France and New Zealand adopted this model. But the analogy is not exact, for all of these countries started with a civil partnership regime that was available to all couples, and opening marriage extended the same range of options to same-sex couples. In the UK it is opposite-sex couples who (now) have limited options.

References

Church of England, *Response to the Government Equalities Office Consultation "Equal Civil Marriage"* (London, 2012).

Church of Scotland, *Response to the Scottish Government's Consultation "Registration of Civil Partnerships; Same Sex Marriage"* (Edinburgh, 2011).

Department for Trade and Industry, Women and Equality Unit, *Shared Lives: A Framework for the Legal Recognition of Same-Sex Couples* (London, 2003).

National Centre for Social Research 2010, http://ir2.flife.de/data/natcen-social-research/igb_html/pdf/1000001_e.pdf. [Accessed 3 March 2014].

Scherpe, Jens, *Marital Agreements in Comparative Perspective* (Oxford, Hart, 2012)

Scottish Executive, *Civil Partnership Registration: A Legal Status for Committed Same-Sex Couples in Scotland* (Edinburgh, 2003)

Wintemute, Robert, "Accommodating Religious Beliefs: Harm, Clothing or Symbols, and Refusals to Serve Others" (2014) 77(2) *Modern Law Review* 223–253.

Chapter 4

Opposing same-sex marriage, by supporting civil partnerships

Resistances to LGBT equalities

Kath Browne and Catherine Nash

Introduction

Whilst many speak of battles being won around lesbian, gay, bisexual and transgender (LGBT) equalities, the debates regarding same-sex marriage and the implementation of equalities legislation suggests that there continues to be strong resistances to sexual and gendered rights. Scholarship on the political and social activism of the Christian right, as well as on the conservative right more broadly, has detailed the depth and breadth of the ongoing resistance to LGBT equalities. Much of this research is focused on the USA, documenting how the oppositional approaches taken by US organisations have shifted (Herman, 1997) and demonstrating the geographical specificity of various resistances (Nash and Browne, 2014; Browne and Nash, 2014).[1]

In this chapter, we focus on the various forms these resistances to LGBT equalities can take. This is important because while we might assume that opposition to LGBT equalities is now understood as 'marginal' or in 'the minority' in places such as Great Britain, these groups continue to organise co-ordinated and at times somewhat effective resistances to LGBT equalities, particularly during the implementation phase.[2] These resistances suggest that 'homophobia remains not just alive but aggressively kicking' (Weiss and Bosia, 2013: 7). Therefore, alongside considerations of 'the world we have won' (Weeks, 2007) and the emergence of various homonormativities (critiques of the normalisations of gay men and lesbians that see equalities as reiterating norms, rather than critiquing them), it remains important to examine how heteronormativities[3] continue to be asserted and manifest in ways that are different in different places and times. The core argument of this chapter is that the modes of resistance and the discourses deployed by those who seek to 'protect' marriage as a 'union of one man and one woman' are shaped by and are reflective of an element of Great Britain's contemporary political and cultural context. This challenges Weiss and Bosia's (2013: 6) contention that homophobia is imposed consistently across continents. Key in the British context is the consultation about, and eventual passing of, same-sex marriage legislation in 2014 *after* same-sex civil partnerships had been in place for some ten years and had appeared to gain a wide degree of acceptance.

The chapter will first outline some of the key claims about the importance of marriage equality by proponents of same-sex marriage, before moving on to argue for a complementary focus on those groups seeking to maintain heteronormative privileges through the institution of marriage. The chapter will then explore the specific constitution of resistances to LGBT equalities, focusing on data collected through online sources (see Tables 4.1 and 4.2) as well as newspapers, magazines and newsletters. We begin by considering the centrality of the marriage debate in this historical moment. We then explore in-depth how arguments were structured so as to enable opposition groups to claim that they support equal rights (and were thus 'not homophobic'), while simultaneously opposing same-sex marriage. In particular, we focus on these groups' 'support' of civil partnerships rather than same-sex marriage to deflect criticisms of homophobia and bigotry, and show how critical engagements with a politics of marriage equalities are (re) presented by those who seek to maintain marriage as a 'union of one man and one woman'.

Same-sex marriage debates

The debates surrounding the passage of same-sex marriage legislation are important sites of legal and symbolic contestations around sexual citizenship, which have, as Kitzinger and Wilkinson (2004: 132) argue, always been 'intensely political' (Bell and Binnie, 2000; Weeks et al., 2001). Scholarly discussions about the implications of same-sex marriage for gays and lesbians have tended to argue about the possibilities and potentialities of gay and lesbian assimilation into dominant, normative values and the related concerns about what might be included in these homonormativities (Duggan, 2002). Feminist critiques have also engaged with questions about whether same-sex marriage might challenge (or queer) the institution of marriage itself (Auchmuty, 2004; Barker, 2012; Bell and Binnie, 2000; Butler, 2004). Taking these arguments in turn, we will consider how they are intertwined with contemporary resistances to LGBT equalities in order to highlight our assertion that engagements with LGBT equalities gains have sparked certain forms of resistances we consider under the term 'hetero-activism'.[4] We then explore the enactment of civil partnerships in the UK and Northern Ireland as a specific context for the emergence of these movements.

Those that seek to challenge institutional homophobia and the 'defence of the family' right wing often look to establish the importance of same-sex marriage in gaining equality (Bevacqua, 2004; Bolte, 1998; Calhoun, 2000; Kitzinger and Wilkinson 2004; Rauch, 2004; Saavedra, 2004; Sullivan, 1995). Literature in this area contends that same-sex marriage and civil partnerships advance the rights of lesbians and gay men by offering equality in terms of equal rights and responsibilities. These are part of a politics of recognition that allows gay and lesbian relationships to be regarded as being on an equal footing with heterosexual relationships (see, for example, Bolte, 1998; Calhoun, 2000; Rauch, 2004; Sullivan, 1995). For some, the right of gays and lesbians to marry will provide momentum for the promotion of broader rights for all LGBT people (Kitzinger and Wilkinson, 2004). The 'gay liberal reformists', as they are termed (Bell and Binnie, 2000), regard same-sex marriage as ensuring LGBT equality with heterosexuality and that gays and lesbians will have the same legal rights as straight people.

For others, the institution of same-sex marriage is just the starting point to effect a more substantial transformation in the 'flawed' institution of marriage as a whole (Bevacqua, 2004: 38). This includes dissolving distinctions between heterosexuality and homosexuality, challenging the naturalised, gendered power imbalances in heterosexual marriages, removing the emphasis on 'proper families' for reproduction and even contesting the very conceptualisation of 'family' itself (Bolte, 1998; Calhoun, 2000; Duggan and Hunter, 1995). Rather than being assimilationist then, 'same-sex marriage is held as capable of undermining the most solid of social structures ("the family") by infiltrating it and exposing its contradictory logics from within' (Bell and Binnie, 2000: 57; Bevacqua, 2004; Saavedra, 2004). It is unsurprising then that these arguments about the undermining of the meanings of 'family' and 'marriage' through the implementation of same-sex marriage are also used by those opposed to LGBT equalities as a key reason that same-sex marriage is what they term a 'slippery slope' to moral decay (see also Nash and Browne, 2014).[5]

Those who critique same-sex marriage on the grounds that it privileges and normalises 'marriage' as a pre-eminent social institution also draw on feminist interventions that condemn same-sex marriage as merely reproducing heterosexual, gendered family structures while overlooking the need to continue to agitate for the human rights of the individual (Auchmuty, 2004; Barker, 2012; Card, 1996; Davis, 2005; Donovan, 2004; Rauch, 2004; Spade, 2011; Warner, 1999). Some queer theorists also contend that as certain gay men and lesbians become assimilated into capitalist hegemonic structures, they no longer offer the same critique of normativity through their existence as a sexual and gendered alternative set of experiences and practices (Davis, 2005; Halberstam, 2005). In this view same-sex marriage is always and already normative and patriarchal, and indeed same-sex marriage has become a key feature defining homonormativity (Auchmuty, 2004; Davis, 2005; Donovan, 2004; Duggan, 2002; Halberstam, 2005). Those who engage in same-sex marriage can also be considered to be mimicking heterosexuality such that we are not looking at how 'heterosexuals might not live best' or the ways that 'lesbians and gays might live better' (Auchmuty, 2004: 124).

For some, the same-sex marriage battle is not one that we should fight. Rather, there is a call for the abolishment of the institution of marriage itself

(Card, 1996; Donovan, 2004). Feminists have long contested the patriarchal model of heterosexual marriage, critiquing the impoverishment, vulnerability and abuses of women (see Bernard, 1973; Greer, 1970; Wollstonecraft, 1792/1929). In this context, Auchmuty argues, '200 years of feminist agreement that marriage permits, even encourages oppression makes the institution of marriage untouchable and irredeemable in the eyes of many women, including myself'. She contends that in the USA, it is usually gay men advocating an agenda based on same-sex marriage because they have not encountered the difficulties with the institution of marriage that women have 'save it excludes them' (2004: 105).

In this context, the recuperation of what was once radical and transgressive, that is, all lives that existed outside the heterosexual ideals of opposite sex marriages and reproduction, allows conservative agendas around commitment, public sex and 'proper' partnerships to be re-established. This can give rise to a problematic binary between the 'good gay' and 'bad gay' where properly lived gay lives are those appropriately enfolded into monogamous, middle-class and child-centred marriage and constituting the acceptable form of relationship (Bell and Binnie, 2000; Davis, 2005). Bell and Binnie (2000: 61) contend that these hierarchisations of relationships and the sex negative links between monogamy and marriage, suggest it is 'unlikely' that same-sex marriage offers anything other than assimilation. In other words, as Davis (2005: 24) puts it, same-sex marriage does not embrace 'the multiple ways we have learned to love and fuck each other'. These arguments, and those of organisations such as Against Equality (Conrad, 2010, 2014), are also taken up by those resisting LGBT equalities. As we will show later in the chapter, they are reiterated and reproduced in ways that support the argument for keeping 'traditional marriage', particularly through the assertion that 'gay people don't want it'.

Butler (2004), whilst recognising the problems related to same-sex marriage, also argues that there are substantial psychic and social problems arising from *not* recognising same-sex unions (see also Auchmuty, 2004; Bourassa and Varnell, 2002). Yet, she remains ambivalent about same-sex marriage, as do many others. In a similar vein, recent discussions about civil partnerships and same-sex marriages, drawing on empirical evidence, have found a messiness not easily reducible to straightforward questions of assimilation or transgression. There is a complex array of perceptions, meanings, lived experiences, citizenships and implications of same-sex marriage for those agitating for it or seeking to engage with it. Smart (2008), for example, notes that lesbian and gay couples are aware of the political, social and cultural ramifications of their decisions to formally commit. The move between for/against is a core tenet of this book, and here we wish to raise awareness of the tensions arising from the queer/homonormative critique of marriage and how agitation for same-sex marriage can mobilise resistances to LGBT equalities more broadly.

Civil partnership to marriage

The specific political context of the 1980s and 1990s in Britain was decidedly more hostile to LGBT people with legislation such as Section 28 of the Local Government Act 1988, banning the promotion of 'pretended family relationships' in schools and other local authority schemes for people under 16. However, as Auchmuty (2004: 119) contends, 'the legal [and we could add political] world of the 21st century is very different from that of the 20th century'. LGBT equalities gained traction over the last decade, culminating in the Equality Act 2010. We now need to account for a very different political context in Britain, one that arguably has achieved legislative equality for 'all gay men and lesbians' (see also Cooper, 2004; Stychin, 2003; Richardson and Monro, 2010). One of the key ways in which legislative equality in the UK was achieved was through the passage of the Civil Partnership Act 2004.

Stonewall, a lesbian, gay and bisexual lobby group that operates across Britain, asserted that civil partnerships are marriage in everything but name. Kitzinger and Wilkinson (2004: 133), however, regarded this nomenclature as creating 'a symbolic separation of same-sex couples from the hallowed institution of "marriage"', a situation they liken to apartheid and interracial marriages. Auchmuty (2004: 102) argued that it is marriage, rather than civil partnerships, that has a symbolic significance that 'confers upon the individuals the highest social status and approval'. In a similar vein, Butler (2004) contends that the use of varying names and different rights simultaneously recognises and excludes gays and lesbians from the institution of marriage, a move that paradoxically pleases both the right-wing fundamentalists and radical critics of the institution of marriage (Thorpe, 2005).

There was little organised and mobilised opposition to the Civil Partnership Act 2004 (see Weeks in this volume) although the Church of England did oppose it quite vigorously (see Goddard in this volume). However, in 2011–13, there was a large, co-ordinated and concerted opposition mounted to the Marriage (Same Sex Couples) Bill 2013 that also galvanised a broader collective opposition to LGBT equalities that had been predominantly vocalised through individual court cases grounded in claims of religious freedoms (see Cooper and Herman, 2013). In 2011–12, consultations on same-sex marriage re-ignited opposition from organisations, such as Society for the Protection of Unborn Children (SPUC), which had argued against homosexual teaching in schools in the 1980s and 1990s, but whose activisms prior to this debate had focused predominantly on abortion.

Table 4.1 provides a summary of an analysis of 49 online groups and websites engaged in opposition to LGBT equalities in 2012 in the UK. As Table 4.1 indicates, same-sex marriage became the predominant focus for opposition to LGBT equalities. In some cases, new groups were founded to combat the proposed legislation (e.g. Coalition for Marriage), while in other

Table 4.1 Issues addressed by groups opposed to LGBT equalities

Issue	*No.*	*Organisations*
Same-sex marriage	38	SPUC, Family Education Trust, Coalition for Marriage, Network of Sikh Organisations, Scotland for Marriage, Thomas Moore Institute, The Catholic Union of Great Britain, Evangelical Alliance, CARE, Christian Concern, Orphans of Liberty, BNP, Christian Institute, Anglican Mainstream, Opus Dei, Core Issues, Christian Legal Centre, Christian Medical Fellowship, True Freedom Trust, Affirming the Faith, Civitas, Jubilee Entre, Lovewise, Marantha, Theos Think Tank, Voice for Justice, The Lawyers for Christian Fellowship, Centre for Social Justice, Alliance Defending Freedom, Love for Life, Affinity, Centre for Policy Studies, Young Britons Foundation, Liberty League, UKIP, Conservative Christian Fellowship, Reform, Challenge Team
Gay education (including, but not limited to, sex education)	6	SPUC, Scotland for Marriage, Orphans for Liberty, BNP, International Healing Foundation, NARTH
Sex education	14	SPUC, Family Education Trust, Scotland for Marriage, The Catholic Union of Great Britain, Evangelical Alliance, Opus Dei, Christian Medical Fellowship, Christian Concern, The Christian Institute, Anglican Mainstream, Campaign to Protect Children, Challenge Team UK, Lovewise, Voice for Justice UK
Gay parenting/ same-sex parenting, adoption/fostering	17	SPUC, Family Education Trust, CARE, Orphans of Liberty, BNP, The Christian Institute, NARTH, Opus Dei, Christian Legal Centre, Christian Medical Fellowship, Lovewise, Maranatha, Theos Think Tank, Voice for Justice UK, The Lawyers Christian Fellowship, Centre for Social Justice, Young Britons Foundation
Public policy, legislation	5	Family Education Trust, CORE Issues, Trust Freedom Trust, Liberty League, Evangelical Alliance
Family structure	3	Family Education Trust, CARE, Centre for Policy Studies
LGBT rights/gay rights	8	The Catholic Union of Great Britain, Evangelical Alliance, Orphans for Liberty, BNP, The Christian Institute, International Federation for Therapeutic Choice, CORE, True Freedom Trust
LGBT rights versus religious rights, liberty versus LGBT rights	11	Opus Dei, International Federation of Therapeutic Choice, Christian Legal Centre, Civatas, Jubilee Centre, Theos Think Tank, Voice for Justice UK, The Lawyers Christian Fellowship, Redeemed Lives, Alliance Defending Freedom, UKIP
Gay/LGBT identity	9	Christchurch London, People Can Change, Cru, Association for Christian Councillors, PATH, Live In Christ, Courage, Christian Medical Fellowship, Core Issues

Table 4.1 (continued)

Issue	*No.*	*Organisations*
Gay reparative therapy	13	Anglican Mainstream, NARTH, International Federation for Therapeutic Choice, Core Issues, Living Waters UK, Christian Medical Fellowship, True Freedom Trust, Redeemed Lives, Live in Christ, PATH, Association of Christian Councillors, JONAH, People Can Change
HIV/health	3	NARTH, Protection of Conscience Project, Family Education Trust
Trans, gender identity	5	Protection of Conscience, NARTH, Christchurch London, True Foundation Trust, Parakaleo
Gay bullying	2	Alliance Defending Freedom, International Healing Foundation

cases organisations refocused their activism as is the case of the Society for the Protection of Unborn Children (SPUC). Many organisations were also issue-based and loosely categorised around so-called 'cultures of life', which included asserting the heterosexual family as the 'bedrock' of society.

Nonetheless, the key issue for groups opposed to LGBT equalities solidified around opposition to same-sex marriage. There can be little doubt that the same-sex marriage debates galvanised oppositions to LGBT equalities in Great Britain, which received significant support; for example, the coalition for marriage petition was signed by over 600,000 people, despite eventually being defeated in both the House of Commons and the House of Lords. It is important to note that 161 MPs in the House of Commons and 148 peers in the House of Lords voted against same-sex marriage (as opposed to 366 and 390, respectively, voting in favour). This is a significant minority that illustrates the importance of resistances to LGBT equalities, even where the Bill was seen as having an 'easy passage' through both houses.

What was clear from our data is that there was a major shift in how resistances to homosexuality have been framed. In the 1990s, homosexuals were largely cast as morally dangerous to children; a position used to support the passage of the infamous Section 28 of the Local Government Act 1988. But as we can see from Table 4.2, and as we have argued elsewhere (Nash and Browne, 2014), in developing arguments in opposition to same-sex marriage, organisations framed their concerns as a consideration of 'the best for society' and framed these concerns in ways that sought to privilege certain relationships (i.e. monogamous, heterosexual) over others – what we are calling hetero-activism. These organisations challenged accusations of homophobia and bigotry by arguing that these labels were used to close down debate and silence opposition. Disputing or deflecting accusations of homophobia is key for these organisations, particularly in contexts such as the UK where 'homophobia' is becoming increasingly unacceptable and associated

Table 4.2 Reasons for opposing same-sex marriage

Reason	*No.*
Marriage is between one man and one woman, basis of society	15
Protects children/best environment/marriage is about children/procreation as key	14
Redefines marriage, not a state role	11
Leads to polygamy or incest, love and commitment not enough	11
Schools	10
Ordinary people don't support it, 'evidence' that people don't want it, no mandate	9
Civil partnerships are enough	8
Loss for individuals/freedoms/discrimination on religious grounds	7
Not a priority/costly	6
Religious protections won't work and churches will be made to perform ceremonies/EU will interfere	5
Will lead to demands for more	4
Undermines marriage	4
Not bigoted or homophobic, marginalises the majority	3
Gay people don't want it	2
Adultery isn't part of the Bill	2
Gay relationships are non-monogamous	2
Started with decriminalisation	2
The more its tolerated, the more it proliferates	1
Homosexuality is morally wrong	1
Gay relationships are different/gay sex is wrong	1
Massive change not incremental	1
Rejected by most worldwide	1
Will lead to disestablishment	1
It's too early	1
European Convention on Human Rights doesn't support it/gay marriage not a human right	1

with extremisms. Thus, whilst Weiss and Bosia (2013) seek further theorisations of homophobia, there is also a need to explore how those opposing LGBT equalities are contesting the term itself. While a full exploration of this is beyond the scope of this chapter, it is sufficient to note that reclaiming and redefining homophobia is central to contemporary debates on same-sex marriage in places such as Britain.

One important way that opposition to LGBT equalities are manifest in the British context is through supporting 'civil partnerships', while contesting same-sex marriage. As Table 4.2 illustrates, this was the key focus for eight groups engaged in opposing same-sex marriage. Thus, these groups are not necessarily 'rewriting history' in now supporting civil partnerships, but their use of equality to contest accusations of homophobia and bigotry marks a shift in the ways in which LGBT rights are contested (see also Nash and Browne, 2014).

Equality not parity: opposing the Marriage (Same Sex) Act 2013 by supporting civil partnerships

Our focus for this section is on how civil partnerships are used to contest same-sex marriage. This was a strong theme that emerged from the data, showing that it is a prominent feature of the UK debate. The availability of this argument to hetero-activists is specific to contexts such as Britain because it instigated a form of civil union instead of same-sex marriage and then sought to implement same-sex marriage later. Other themes (such as basis of society, protection of children) are explored elsewhere (see Nash and Browne, 2014; Browne and Nash, 2014).

We start with UKIP (United Kingdom Independence Party), a right-wing political party that has gained popularity in the past five years because of its opposition to the European Union and its stance on European migration. It now receives regular invitations to appear in mainstream media outlets such as BBC Radio 4 and *Newsnight* on BBC Two, and spokespeople for the party are regularly asked to comment on current political debates. In 2014, UKIP won a historical victory in the UK European elections, topping the polls ahead of the two key parties, Labour and the Conservatives. UKIP has an LGBT wing known as 'Lgbtq in UKIP'. The group's slogan is 'Britain Should be Out and Proud'. It's comments in relation to same-sex marriage focus on contending that some form of 'special rights' were being created for LGBT people through the enactment of same-sex marriage legislation. In November 2012, David Coburn of UKIP's National Executive Committee clarified the party's policies and positions with regard to LGBT issues:

> The party fully supports the existing concept of civil partnerships. Coburn stated, 'UKIP's stance on gay marriage is simple: we entirely, wholeheartedly support equal rights for couples regardless of their sexuality and we believe this has been achieved through the introduction of civil partnerships, which UKIP supported.'
>
> (UKIP)

As this quote demonstrates, Coburn can both 'wholeheartedly support equal rights' while not giving support to same-sex marriage. Some form of civil partnerships allows for this somewhat paradoxical claim. UKIP is able to throw its support behind civil partnerships and thus espouse some form of 'equality' for LGBT people but is able to stand against same-sex marriage, which it elsewheres seeks to define as a 'special right'. By maintaining this 'support', it seeks to move itself away from accusations of homophobic bigotry. It is interesting that in the discourse of 'special rights', civil partnerships could be seen as 'special rights', and marriage understood as removing these 'special' conditions. In other words, UKIP neglects to see civil partnerships as 'special' in its opposition to 'gay marriage'. Here 'special' exists in opposition to a normative heterosexuality.

The Coalition for Marriage, a coalition of groups opposed to LGBT equalities, was established as a not-for-profit company to specifically contest the Marriage (Same Sex Couples) Bill 2013. In its words, its mission was to 'support traditional marriage and oppose any plans to redefine it' (2013).[6] As with UKIP, the Coalition's stance supports 'equality' but not parity, which the Coalition associates with 'bland uniformity' and 'state imposed sameness'. Using this reasoning, civil partnerships offer 'all the legal benefits' and 'equality', but asking for marriage 'redefines' it:

> Civil partnerships already provide all the legal benefits of marriage so there's no need to redefine marriage.
>
> Same-sex couples already have equality. All the legal rights of marriage are already available to same-sex couples through civil partnerships. Equality doesn't mean bland uniformity or state-imposed sameness. If the Government genuinely wants to pursue equality, why is it banning heterosexual couples from entering a civil partnership? Same-sex couples have equal rights through civil partnerships, but they don't have the right to redefine marriage for everyone else.
>
> (Coalition for Marriage, 2012)

The Coalition for Marriage's support for civil partnerships, but opposition to marriage sets same-sex couples as different but equal. It goes beyond this to seemingly argue that straight couples should have civil partnerships, whilst continuing to oppose same-sex marriage. It appears to imply that if this legislation was about equality, heterosexual couples would be given access to civil partnerships.[7] However even if this were understood to be the case, it is unlikely there would be support for same-sex marriage.[8] Instead, the assertion that same-sex couples have all they 'need' in terms of equivalent rights acts to shield these groups from accusations of being discriminatory. By focusing on rights as utility, the symbolic rights of marriage are ignored.

One approach framing resistances to the redefinition of marriage is to position same-sex relationships as completely distinct from heterosexual partnerships because of the supposed gender 'complementarity' of man/woman relationships. Given this supposedly pivotal difference, enacting different legislative provisions is sufficient rather than including same-sex relationships under the umbrella of 'marriage', which should be reserved for those relationships that have distinctive man/woman components. Differences between relationships forms can be maintained through civil partnerships, and this is similar to contentions by scholars (Auchmuty, 2004; Kitzinger and Wilkinson, 2004). This ensures that those groups which oppose same-sex marriage can logically support essentially the same protections provided by civil partnerships, by seeing rights as utility. They can simultaneously contest same-sex marriage and the symbolic rights associated with marriage. However, at the same time, claims about the equality and parity of civil partnerships are contested by this very same assertion of difference: 'Marriage and civil partnerships have been designed for two very different types of relationship and should be kept distinct' (Christian Medical Fellowship). Central to discourses that claim it is 'best for society' to ensure marriage is limited to heteronormative couples is the possibility of procreation. This is key to the 'difference' of marriage. Keeping civil partnerships and marriage distinct renders some relationships not only different but also 'better' than others. In the assertion of difference, civil partnerships are not transgressive in the sense envisaged by scholars who see them as different to marriage (e.g. Auchmuty, 2004).

Lord Singh, head of the Network of Sikh Organisations, is reported as saying that the proposed reforms represented 'a sideways assault on religion'. 'It is an attempt by a vocal, secular minority to attack religion', he told BBC Radio 4's *Today* programme. Sikhs believe in marriage as the union of a man and a woman and that changing the definition was an attack on the English language. He said: 'We have total respect for gays and lesbians and we are delighted that there is a Civil Partnership Act. We believe that this gives gays and lesbians everything they need' (Ross, 2012).

Here Lord Singh is simultaneously claiming 'respect for gays and lesbians' and assuring us that we have 'everything we need', whilst also characterising same-sex marriage as an 'assault' on religion. The 'delight' at civil partnerships is contrasted with the 'attack' of same-sex marriage both on religion and the English language. So whilst the 'minority' can have 'everything they need', they cannot contest or be provided with an opportunity to challenge normative heterosexual relations and marriage as a 'union of a man and a woman'. The redefinition is seen as an affront to language itself, because these groups believe that marriage cannot be redefined. Thus, same-sex/gay marriage is an impossibility and marked linguistically by the use of scare quotes around gay marriage to indicate their scepticism regarding the concept itself. Civil partnerships do not need such grammatical additions.

One opposition group, the Evangelical Alliance, which claims to represent two million 'Evangelical Christians' and is based in the UK but operates within a broader global network, denies any 'inferiority' of 'single sex relationships' and asserts that they are partnerships, which are different from marriage as a 'matter of objective fact and common understanding'. These 'facts' and 'understanding' draw both on the supposed neutralities of 'facts', evoking 'natural laws' of procreation, but also societal 'common' understandings.

> Abiding single sex relationships are in no way inferior ... Parliament has not called partnerships between persons of the same-sex marriage, not because they are considered inferior to the institution of marriage but

> because, as a matter of objective fact and common understanding, as well as under the present definition of marriage in English law, and by recognition in European jurisprudence, they are indeed different. Civil partnerships already confer all the rights and benefits of marriage on same-sex couples.
>
> Same-sex couples can already obtain all the legal benefits of marriage by entering a civil partnership. Despite many requests to government for an explanation as to why gay marriage is necessary given that no further rights can be conferred that are not already available nor any injustices corrected, no answer of significance has been received. Indeed the government minister responsible for the proposed redefinition of marriage herself informed us that the only justification for the measure was 'to meet an emotional need of some same-sex couples'.
>
> There are many emotional needs in the world but we do not, cannot and should not legislate for them, especially when doing so affects a multitude of other people for whom the meaning of marriage is settled, appreciated and unchangeable.
>
> (Evangelical Alliance)

The question of equalities is addressed through 'rights and benefits' without challenging 'common understandings' or engaging in redefinitions of 'marriage' as properly reserved for man/woman relationships. More importantly, this is not about the inferiority of 'abiding' (read normative) same-sex relationships, rather that they are different. Any redefinition of marriage to include same-sex has no justification beyond 'emotional need' and such a redefinition would have a profound effect on 'other people'. This supports claims about the fixity of the meaning of marriage as 'unchangeable'. As such equality is achieved through difference rather than sameness and importantly protecting 'other people', for whom read heterosexual people.

An increasingly potent argument used by those who oppose LGBT equalities is that 'the public' has been duped by politicians, the media and the 'gay lobby' into supporting a course of action that will unwittingly lead to the demise of marriage. In the British context, this argument was supported by specific critiques of methodologies that failed to acknowledge the presence of civil partnerships:

> The public don't want it.
>
> Seven in ten people want to keep marriage as it is. Other polling which purports to show public support for gay marriage fails to tell respondents that equal rights are already available through civil partnerships. When people are told this crucial fact, most people say keep marriage as it is.
>
> (Coalition for Marriage)

Contesting the way the public opinion questions are framed is specific to the British context, that is the ways in which civil partnerships in 2004 were purported to be marriage in everything but a name. It is argued that 'people' and the 'public' are being manipulated into redefining marriage through a 'failure' to explain the benefits of civil partnerships and the potential risks to marriage itself. When polling was undertaken by those opposing same-sex marriage, the result were (unsurprisingly) very different:

> Polling has shown that 70 per cent of the population support the view that marriage should remain an exclusive commitment between a man and a woman (Marriage Survey, ComRes, 23–24 February 2012).
>
> The Coalition for Marriage petition against redefining marriage has gained more than half a million signatures in little over two months and is still growing while the rival petition is relatively small (currently outnumbered 10:1). This effectively demonstrates the overwhelming preference of the British public to preserve the historic definition of marriage as between one man and one woman.

Controlling the data and presenting this in a way that supports arguments in opposition to same-sex marriage, illustrates the importance given to the 'right research' by those opposing marriage. Having competing (and supposedly authentic) research is regarded as key to ensuring opposition groups and their spokespeople are regarded as rational, reasonable people who deserve to be listened to, rather than homophobes who are both 'behind the times' and 'on the wrong side of history'. Presenting factual contemporary data thus does more that support their argument; it allows those who oppose LGBT equalities to position themselves as having a 'reasonable debate', rather than an irrational 'rant'.

The data used by opposition groups also draws on queer and critical arguments made against marriage, by theorists and others who oppose the disciplining normativities of marriage more broadly. This claim that some gays and lesbians did not want same-sex marriage supports opposition groups' assertions that there is 'equality in difference' and that gay people are content with civil partnerships. However, the nuanced insights regarding the possibilities of marriage reiterating oppressions and social injustices are reshaped into a very different rhetoric:

> Many gay people don't want it.
>
> Polling shows that only a minority of gay people (39 per cent) believe gay marriage is a priority. And according to the Government only 3 per cent of gay people would enter a same-sex marriage. A number of gay celebrities and journalists are themselves opposed to gay marriage. Latest official data shows that only 0.5 per cent of households are headed by a same-sex couple. Not all of them want, or will enter, a

> same-sex marriage. So, why is such a monumental change being imposed throughout society?
>
> (Coalition for Marriage)

The opposition group Coalition for Marriage employs data that suggests that because few gays and lesbians themselves seem to want to marry, it should not be 'imposed' on 'society' (read heterosexual society) as a whole. Of course, the declining marriage rates for heterosexual marriages do not produce a related conclusion that because fewer heterosexuals want them that we should remove marriage. Nonetheless, the evidence here of a lack of support for same-sex marriage amongst gays and lesbians is deployed in a particular way, one that ignores the reasons 'gay people' might be hesitant and critical about marriage. This hesitancy is read as a reason to preserve marriage as the 'union of one man and one woman', rather than a dismantling of the institution itself. Instead, the institution of civil partnerships is presented as 'enough' for 'gay people':

> As the gay Labour MP Ben Bradshaw has stated: 'This is not a priority for the gay community, which already won equal rights with civil partnerships. We've never needed the word "marriage"' (*Daily Mail*, 14 April 2012). It is clear from a recent opinion poll that many gay people are not seeking 'gay marriage', not least because they consider that its imposition will polarise society and result in increased public homophobia. It needs to be noted that many 'gay marriage' campaigners do not speak for the majority of gay people in the UK, many of whom do not want 'gay marriage' because they entered into civil partnerships which they regard as wholly appropriate. The survey also revealed that fewer than half of gay people accept Stonewall's main argument for same-sex marriage, that a legal distinction between civil partnerships and same-sex marriage perpetuates discrimination.
>
> (Evangelical Alliance)

This quote from the Evangelical Alliance contests Stonewall's assertion of discrimination, arguing that 'gay people' themselves do not see civil partnerships as discriminatory. In this way the Evangelical Alliance opposition to same-sex marriage cannot be regarded as discriminatory'. Indeed, it is in the pursuit of same-sex marriage that homophobia will increase, due to the creation of a polarised society. Fault for this is laid only with gay people seeking marriage. These two quotes draw attention to how queer arguments are reused and recuperated by opposition groups in order to oppose same-sex marriage. Contestations of 'gay marriage' are seen as supporting a position of difference and the maintenance of marriage as solely between a man and a woman.

Conclusion

In this chapter we have demonstrated that resistances to LGBT equalities are not confined to 'other places' and that they continue to be manifest where the battles for legislative equalities have seemingly been 'won'. These resistances are spatially manifest, such that the focus on same-sex marriage by these groups has to be understood within the historical and geographical specificity of Britain. This placing is central to understanding how these oppositions are constituted.

Specifically, we chose to focus on how civil partnerships, introduced to very little opposition in 2004 (Weeks in this volume), and hailed as 'marriage in all but name', were redeployed by those opposed to the Marriage (Same-Sex Couples) Act 2013 and the Marriage and Civil Partnership (Scotland) Act 2014. Civil partnerships were used as a tool to illustrate apparent acceptances of some form of equalities and to challenge accusations of bigotry. Civil partnerships were used in this way because they are not marriage and this enabled a somewhat paradoxical position where equality can be claimed and yet equalities legislation resisted. This served the key purpose of distancing groups from accusations of homophobia. After all how can one be homophobic and support an institution that offers 'marriage in all but name'? Moreover, and reworking arguments presented by some queer and sexualities theorists, 'gay people don't want it' either.

The arguments discussed in this chapter lend themselves to LGBT activisms that argue the opposite, that is that same-sex relationships are not different to heterosexual ones, instead they are the same. This is what Miceli (2005) identifies in the US context between the Christian right and 'Gay Social Movement organisations' as opposing frames that polarise strategies. Yet assertions of 'sameness', and political agitation around sameness have been critiqued as normalising and normative, re-creating the oppressive structures of marriage (Barker, 2012), as well as more broadly reiterating neoliberal, raced, classed and gendered orders (see, for example, Richardson, 2005; Spade, 2011).

We contend that it is important to pay attention *both* to the ways in which homonormativities are manifest through gay (and lesbian) equalities, *and* to resistances to LGBT equalities. Such a theoretical and political strategy moves beyond the for/against same-sex marriage debates and forces a nuanced consideration of the multiple ways in which sexualities and genders are spatially policed. This requires paying attention to forces both between 'us' and against 'us', but refuses to create a homogeneous 'us' in order to undertake this task. Instead, what we are pushing for is a multilayered, spatially (and temporally) informed engagement with normativities that incorporates, but also moves beyond, the lives, activisms and politics of LGBT people.

Notes

1 Scholarship has also explored various legal challenges to LGBT equalities legislation in the North American and UK contexts (Cooper and Herman, 2013; Miceli 2005; Nicol and Smith, 2008; Rayside, 2008; Smith, 2008; Stychin, 2009).

2 We use Great Britain, because this research investigated England, Scotland and Wales. Scotland had different legislative processes to the passage of its Marriage and Civil Partnership (Scotland) Act 2014; however, the consultation and passage of this and the Marriage (Same Sex Couples) Act 2013 by the Westminster Parliament were in similar timeframes. Moreover, the opposition worked both across Britain and there were also specific organisations that focused only on Scotland. We use the UK to discuss the Civil Partnership Act 2004, which included both Scotland and Northern Ireland (see Norrie in this volume).

3 Heteronormativity is the normalisation of gender within male and female as opposites meant to come together in heterosexual relationships. This is particularly pertinent for these discussions as the groups who are opposing LGBT equalities, as it is not just sexualities that are opposed, but also gender normativities. In part this is because homosexuality is seen to come from gender transgression, so the fear of not being 'properly gendered' is central.

4 We thank Dr Miriam Smith, York University, for coining the term 'heteroactivism' in our discussions about a research bid related to this project. Whilst the label 'Christian right' is useful in a US context, in our work we are contesting the location of resistances solely there (see Nash and Browne, 2014; Browne and Nash, 2014). Heteroactivism names the processes that promote heterosexualities as morally superior to other sexual/gender identities and the 'best for society' (see Nash and Browne, 2014).

5 The extent to which this similarity knowingly uses queer/academic sources is hard to tell. At times explicit reference is made to academic material, in order to undermine mainstream arguments, whilst at other times the links and similarities cannot be traced through these channels.

6 There was a related but separate organisation to contest same-sex marriage legislation in Scotland, due to the different legislative processes

7 This is reminiscent of Norman Tebbit's comments in the civil partnership debates, which sought to give civil partnerships to sisters and other family relations, as a way to contest the passing of the Bill in 2004. This, similar to these debates, seeks to contest accusations of homophobia.

8 Consultations regarding the future of civil partnerships in Great Britain are taking place as we write this in 2014.

References

Against Equality. 2014. http://www.againstequality.org [accessed 12 March 2014].

Auchmuty, R. 2004. Same-sex marriage revived: Feminist critique and legal strategy. *Feminism & Psychology*, 14, 1: 101–26.

Barker, N. 2012. *Not the marrying kind: A feminist critique of same-sex marriage*. London: Palgrave Macmillan.

Bell, D. and Binnie, J. 2000. *The sexual citizen*. Cambridge, UK: Blackwell.

Bernard, J. 1973. *The sociology of community*. Glenview, IL: Scott, Foresman.

Bevacqua, M. 2004. Feminist theory and the question of lesbian and gay marriage. *Feminism & Psychology*, 14, 1: 36–40.

Bolte, A. 1998. Do wedding dresses come in lavender? The prospects and implications of same-sex marriage. *Social Theory and Practice*, 14, 1: 111–32.

Bourassa, K. and Varnell, J. 2002. *Just married: Gay marriage and the expansion of human rights.* Madison: University of Wisconsin Press.

Browne, K.A. and Nash, C.J. 2014. Resisting LGBT rights where 'we have won': Canada and England. *Journal of Human Rights* (Special Issue, eds A. Langlois and C. Wilkinson), 13, 3: 322–336.

Butler, J. 2004. *Undoing gender.* New York: Routledge.

Calhoun, C. 2000. *Feminism, the family, and the politics of the closet: Lesbian and gay displacement.* New York: Oxford University Press.

Card, C. 1996. Against marriage and motherhood. *Hypatia*, 11, 3: 1–23.

Christian Medical Fellowship (2012) Publications page.

Coalition for Marriage (2012) Coalition for Marriage front page.

Coalition for Marriage. (2012) 10 Reasons Why the Government is Wrong to Redefine Marriage.

Conrad, R. 2010. *Against equality: Queer critiques of gay marriage.* Lewiston, ME: Against Equality Publishing Collective.

——2014. *Against equality: Queer revolution, not mere inclusion.* Oakland, CA: Ak Press.

Cooper, D. 2004. *Challenging diversity: Rethinking equality and the value of difference.* Cambridge, UK: Cambridge University Press.

Cooper, D. and Herman, D. 2013. Up against the property logic of equality law: Conservative Christian accommodation claims and gay rights. *Feminist Legal Studies*, 21, 1: 61–80.

Davis, H. 2005. The difference of queer. *Canadian Women's Studies*, 24, 2–3: 23–27.

Donovan, C. 2004. I. Why reach for the moon? Because the stars aren't enough. *Feminism & Psychology*, 14, 1: 24–29.

Duggan, L. 2002. The new homonormativity: The sexual politics of neoliberalism. In R. Castronovo and D.D. Nelson (eds) *Materializing democracy: Toward a revitalized cultural politics.* Durham, NC: Duke University Press.

Duggan, L. and Hunter, N.D. 1995. *Sex wars: Sexual dissent and popular culture.* New York: Routledge.

Evangelical Alliance (2012) Response Document.

Greer, G. 1970. *The female eunuch.* London: MacGibbon & Kee.

Halberstam, J. 2005. *In a queer time and place: Transgender bodies, subcultural lives.* New York and London: New York University Press.

Harding, R. and Peel, E. 2006. 'We do'? International perspectives on equality, legality and same sex relationships. *Lesbian & Gay Psychology Review*, 7, 2: 123–40.

Herman, D. 1997. *The antigay agenda: Orthodox vision and the Christian right.* Chicago: University of Chicago Press.

Kitzinger, C. and Wilkinson, S. 2004. The rebranding of marriage: Why we got married instead of registering a civil partnership. *Feminism & Psychology*, 14, 1: 127–50.

Miceli, M.S. 2005. Morality politics vs. identity politics: Framing processes and competition among Christian right and gay social movement organizations. *Sociological Forum*, 20, 4: 589–612.

Mitchell, M., Dickens, S. and O'Connor, W. 2009. *Same sex couples and the impact of legislative change.* London: National Centre for Social Research.

Nash, C.J. and Browne, K. 2014. Best for society? Transnational opposition to sexual and gender equalities in Canada and Great Britain. *Gender, Place and Culture.* DOI: 10.1080/0966369X.2014.885893.

Nicol, N. and Smith, M. 2008. Legal struggles and political resistance: Same-sex marriage in Canada and the USA. *Sexualities*, 11, 6: 667–87.

Peel, E. and Harding, R. 2004. Civil partnerships: A new couple's conversation. *Feminism and Psychology*, 14, 1: 41–46.

——2008. Editorial introduction: Recognizing and celebrating same sex relationships: Beyond the normative debate. *Sexualities*, 11, 6: 659–66.

Rauch, J. 2004. *Gay marriage: Why it is good for gays, good for straights, and good for America*. New York: Times Books.

Rayside, D.M. 2008. *Queer inclusions, continental divisions: Public recognition of sexual diversity in Canada and the United States.* Toronto: University of Toronto Press.

Richardson, D. 2005. Desiring sameness? The rise of a neoliberal politics of normalisation. *Antipode* 37, 3: 515–35.

Richardson, D. and Monro, S. 2010. Intersectionality and sexuality: The case of sexuality and transgender equalities work in UK local government. In Y. Taylor, S. Hines and M.E. Casey (eds) *Theorisizing Intersectionality and Sexuality.* Basingstoke: Palgrave Macmillan.

Ross. T. 2012. 'Muslims and Sikhs attack Cameron's Gay Marriage Plan' *The Telegraph* (19 March 2012) http://www.telegraph.co.uk/news/uknews/9154043/Muslims-and-Sikhs-attack-Camerons-gay-marriage-plan.html [Last accessed 1st November 2014].

Saavedra, M. 2004. Same-sex marriage under Capricorn's tropic. *Feminism & Psychology, Special Feature on Marriage II*, 14, 1: 47–51.

Shipman, B. and Smart, C. 2007. 'It's made a huge difference': Recognition, rights and the personal significance of civil partnerships. *Sociological Research Online*, 12,1, http://www.socresonline.org.uk/12/1/shipman.html [Last accessed 1st November 2014].

Smart, C. 2008. 'Can I be bridesmaid?' Combining the personal and political in same sex weddings. *Sexualities*, 11, 6: 761–76.

Smith, M.C. 2008. *Political institutions and lesbian and gay rights in the United States and Canada*. New York: Routledge.

Spade, D. 2011. *Normal life: Administrative violence, critical trans politics and the limits of law.* Cambridge, MA: South End Press.

Stychin, C.F. 2003. *Governing sexuality: The changing politics of citizenship and law reform*. Oxford: Hart.

——2009. Faith in the future: sexuality, religion and the public sphere. *Oxford Journal of Legal Studies*, 29, 4: 729–55.

Sullivan, A. 1995. *Virtually normal: An argument about homosexuality.* New York: Alfred A. Knopf.

Thorpe, J. 2005. Redrawing the borders of the nation: Gender, race, class and same-sex marriage discourse in Canada. *Canadian Woman Studies*, 24: 2–3.

UKIP (no date) UKIP Policies: Response to Government Consultation on Same Sex Marriage.

Warner, M. 1999. Normal and normaller: Beyond gay marriage. *GLQ: A Journal of Lesbian and Gay Studies*, 5: 119–71.

Weeks, J. 2007. *The world we have won: The remaking of erotic and intimate life.* New York: Routledge.

Weeks, J., Heaphy, B. and Donovan, C. 2001. *Same sex intimacies: Families of choice and other life experiments.* London, Routledge.

Weiss, M.L. and Bosia, M.J. 2013. *Global homophobia: States, movements, and the politics of oppression*. Urbana: University of Illinois Press.

Wollstonecraft, M. 1792/1929. *A vindication of the rights of woman.* Boston: Peter Edes.

Chapter 5

Consenting to gender?

Trans spouses after same-sex marriage

Flora Renz[1]

Introduction

The new and widely celebrated advances in lesbian, gay and bisexual (LGB) rights made by the introduction of same-sex marriage also affected the rights of trans people. The Marriage (Same Sex Couples) Act 2013 amends the Gender Recognition Act 2004 (GRA), which allows a person to legally change their gender, as indicated on their birth certificate, by obtaining a Gender Recognition Certificate (GRC). The new changes made to the GRA were supposed to remedy existing discrimination affecting the marriage rights of trans people.[2] Previously, in the original version of the GRA, a GRC was granted as long as the following conditions were fulfilled: the applicant is over the age of 18; has medical evidence supporting their diagnosis with gender dysphoria; has lived in their "new" gender for two years prior to the application and continues to do so for the rest of their life; and is not currently married or in a civil partnership (GRA, ss.1–3). An applicant who is married or in a civil partnership at the time of his or her application can only obtain an "interim" GRC which is valid for six months, to give the applicant time to dissolve his or her relationship. Additionally and also related specifically to the context of marriage, the GRA amends the Matrimonial Causes Act 1973 to the effect that non-disclosure about the fact that one has obtained a GRC makes marriages voidable,[3] again highlighting the fundamental role gender plays in official understandings of marriage. The Marriage (Same Sex Couples) Act 2013 removes the "divorce" requirement for pre-existing relationships and instead applicants who are in a legally recognised relationship at the time of their application now need to show evidence of their spouse's consent before they can obtain a full, rather than an interim, GRC. However, this does not change the fact that not disclosing the existence of a GRC makes an otherwise valid marriage voidable. The GRA as a whole clearly suggests a causal link between sex/gender and sexuality, which means that a change of one's sex also leads to a change of one's sexuality. Without the availability of same-sex marriage this meant that trans people had to change from one relationship category to the other to reflect their "new" sexual orientation.

In this chapter I will be making three suggestions related to this change. First, that trans people's gender identity is perceived as "inauthentic" and "deceptive", essentially as an attempt to deceive their supposedly vulnerable cisgender[4] partners. Second, the gay marriage amendment to the GRA in many ways mirrors the amendments made in 2002 to the Matrimonial Causes Act 1973 to resolve the problem of the *agunah* in Jewish divorces. Lastly, comparing the two legal interventions seems to suggest that the government in both scenarios feels that the women involved in these marriages need additional legal protection as they are vulnerable and perhaps even being exploited by their partners. In the context of the GRA this actually implies lingering homophobia and distrust of trans people and their identity claims.

To theoretically engage with this legal change Foucault's work on the concept of governmentality can help to highlight the intersections between discriminatory practices affecting trans people today, and now redundant case law and the construction of moralistic concerns about the way people should behave and express their (gender) identity. The GRA specifically encourages individuals to express gender identity in ways that adhere to normative presumptions about sex and gender. Namely that both – sex and gender – should be binary to perpetuate a fixed sex/gender dichotomy. Although gender reassignment/confirmation surgery is not an official requirement for a legal change of gender under the GRA, many charities and support groups advise potential applicants that for a successful application they need to at least express a desire to undergo surgery.[5]

In its original form, the GRA was clearly aimed at preserving marriage as a purely heterosexual union by requiring couples who would be considered to be of the same sex, after one partner obtained a GRC, to dissolve their relationship (GRA, s.4(3)). As this legal provision shows, there are no explicit sanctions or punishments attached to failing to meet the standards of the GRA, but instead the implicit sanctions are a denial of rights, such as the right to marry, and formal legal recognition. Originally a lack of a GRC would have had a more far-reaching impact but at present it is possible to change most forms of identification, such as passports and driving licences, with "only" a doctor's report confirming that a change of gender is permanent (GOV.UK, 2014).

From legal controls to medical certificates such as those required in the GRA, as well as for passports, trans people are seen by law-makers as needing extra control and regulation due to the fact that their very existence highlights the artifice of the sex/gender binary and of heteronormativity.[6] This finds its most recent expression in the new spousal consent amendment to the GRA, which is supposed to remedy discrimination against trans people but in fact exposes the deeply problematic heteronormative foundation of the GRA.

Regulating sex/gender

Following Mitchell Dean (2010), I am suggesting that a theory of governmentality can help problematise regulation, be it legal or otherwise, by highlighting some of the unwritten rules and norms that are the foundation of regulations. Based on this, a governmentality analysis seems particularly appropriate in the context of legal rules which by themselves rarely contain explanations of their intended, never mind unintended, outcomes. Given that previous case law was highly transphobic, this approach is especially relevant in the case of the GRA, which at first glance suggests a clear break from the highly discriminatory decisions reached in earlier cases. There seem to be obvious connections between the transphobic norms at the heart of judicial decisions in previous cases and the supposedly more "progressive" piece of legislation in force now.

Governmental techniques of regulation aim to encourage specific behaviour in accordance with, sometimes contradictory, but nevertheless political, norms or objectives (Dean, 1996: 217). While governmental techniques may stem from the government itself, they are not synonymous with it and occur in a wide variety of contexts that are not necessarily associated with the explicit work of governing a country. These techniques are often not considered to be political themselves (Miller and Rose, 2008: 200). Interpreted this way, the GRA is not just a largely administrative legal framework for recognising gender identity, but rather a piece of governmental technology that is linked to clearly political rationalities and specific truths about gender, sexuality and family life. That is not to say that the GRA is the effect of a direct implementation of a consistent rationality. It is, however, to suggest that, to quote Miller and Rose, this law has "a meaning and effect" (2008: 200) on people which is highly political.

For the purposes of day-to-day social interaction, trans people's physical or aesthetic outside appearance is likely to be of greater importance than their legal status when it comes to the determination of their gender identity by others. By and large people categorise others based on their appearance, whereas official documents, especially birth certificates, are only visible to a select few. Indeed, Schilt and Westbrook (2009: 443) suggest that in most social interactions trans people's ability to pass as cisgender is more important than the specifics of their "private bodies"; however, they also concede that this may not hold true in all contexts. Schilt and Westbrook argue that primarily during sexual encounters, or in sexualised settings, gender determination relies less on outward appearance. Due to the fact that the GRA, and specifically the parts of it that relate to legally recognised relationships, deal with such sexualised settings, may partially explain some of the tensions and more problematic requirements inherent within the GRA; for instance, that non-disclosure about the fact that one has obtained a GRC makes marriages voidable.[7] As such it is important to keep in mind that the GRA was passed mainly as a response to case law that dealt with questions about the validity of marriages, specifically *Goodwin v United Kingdom (28957/95)* [2002] Fam Law 738. The GRA is always focused on regulating the exact nature of people's sex/gender and sexuality.

Furthermore, Westbrook and Schilt (2014: 34) suggest that in the context of legal regulations such as gender recognition, a more stringent standard of gender determination may also apply, even when the specific law does not deal with sexualised settings or issues. Following this logic Schilt and Westbrook argue that this is due to the fact that the determination of sex/gender can, and in the context of law and public policy often does, also take place on the level of the "imaginary"; for example, by focusing on imagined or hypothetical scenarios involving trans people that rarely correspond to reality and as such often involve a fear of the unknown or a lack of comprehension: "Imagined interactions and legal or policy decisions, in contrast, often demand more explicit, officially defined criteria. Such a focus on developing explicit criteria for determining gender has grown alongside new surgical possibilities for gender transitions" (Schilt and Windsor, 2014: 36). Exactly this imaginary determination seems to have been the case in the debates about the GRA, both in 2003 and in the more recent same-sex marriage debates, which often involved references to hypothetical scenarios. To provide just one example of these imaginary determinations, Lord Chan suggested that most applicants would not undergo any type of surgery and as such there would be "reports of outrage by women protesting against the use of their toilets by people possessing gender recognition certificates as women who have male genitalia" (*Hansard*, HL Deb (2003–4), vol 655, col 1308). That this scenario is not based on any kind of factual evidence does not seem to have prevented legislators from taking it into consideration. Indeed much of the debate around both the GRA and the new amendment to it seems to be based more on stereotypes and moral panics, which means that the resulting legislation, even when beneficial to LGB individuals in general, often discriminates against trans people in an attempt to officially regulate their expressions of identity and sexuality. Overall, trans people, specifically those who are, or want to be, in legally recognised relationships, face a much higher scrutiny of their identity claims and their conduct, then cisgender people in the same position.

How to regulate the problem of the Agunot?

A similar example of governmental and legal intervention in the context of intimate relationships would be the legal regulation of the granting of the *get* in Jewish divorces. This situation shows some interesting parallels to the recent amendment to the GRA, primarily that they designate one spouse as inherently vulnerable. Under Jewish law a divorce can only be finalised once the husband grants his wife a *get*, effectively "a bill of divorcement" (Miller,

1997–98: 2). Without the *get* the parties remain married, even if a civil divorce has been finalised (Katzenberg and Rosenblatt, 1999). This process normally runs parallel to a civil divorce and is ideally unproblematic. However, in some cases husbands have made the granting of the *get* conditional upon financial payments, more favourable conditions in the divorce, or custody of children. As the lack of a *get* means that the wife cannot remarry under Jewish law, she becomes an *agunah* – a chained wife, whose future children's marriages are also restricted. This effectively allows for husbands to put pressure on their wives during divorce proceedings and shifts the power balance in favour of the husband (Freeman, 1999). An example for this would be a case like *Brett v Brett* (1969), in which a judge intervened on behalf of a wife whose husband refused to grant her a *get* unless she lowered her demand for maintenance payments.

After extensive lobbying and requests from the Jewish community, the government intervened in these marriages due to the lack of a consistent response by the rabbinical courts. This was done in the form of the Divorce (Religious Marriages) Act 2002. The Act gives courts the power to make the granting of a decree absolute conditional on the prior dissolution of the religious marriage. This means that although this is not a perfect solution, as it only prevents the wife being coerced into a less favourable settlement as long as the husband wants a civil divorce, it nevertheless seems to have reduced the number of women becoming *agunot* (AHRC, 2011). The government here essentially intervenes in relationships, which would otherwise be considered private, to encourage specific types of behaviour that are considered to be desirable in this case, to quote Helen Reece, "divorcing responsibly" and with minimal conflict (Reece, 2003).

Michael Freeman argues that the government was justified to intervene in these specific marriages due to several key reasons: (i) the *get* rules specifically discriminate against women and states have an obligation to essentially even the playing field between the two parties 2001: 372); (ii) "blackmail", which according to him is what the *get* leads to, is a crime and as such the state has an interest to intervene to protect the "victims"; (iii) law reform has a clear symbolic value, especially when targeted at a specific group of people, in this case women perceived as particularly vulnerable (Freeman, 2001: 381).[8] Particularly the issue of symbolism raises some interesting question in regards to the recent amendments to the GRA, such as who the state considers deserving or in need of legal protection.

Questions of authenticity and the heterosexual nature of marriage

While many governmental programmes rely on technologies of self-regulation rather than legal sanctions; governing through the encouragement of particular forms of subject and identity formation seems to find a particularly obvious expression in state attempts to regulate gender and sexuality (Valverde, 2009: 91). As such the denial of legally recognised relationships for same-sex couples pre-2004 privileges and favours heterosexuality in the same way that the lack of legal recognition for trans people privileges and favours cisgender people. Trans people are not breaking the law by refusing to adhere to normative modes of gender expression but the refusal to grant legal recognition to non-binary gender identities encourages and implicitly privileges certain types of gender expression, that is those that match traditional male/female norms. As Dan Irving suggests, allowing for a legal recognition process can effectively discourage challenges to the status quo by discouraging certain types of behaviour in return for (limited) rights and freedoms (2008: 39). In this case this means that allowing trans people to obtain legal recognition in a gender other than the one they were assigned at birth, as long as they meet strict guidelines and fall within the normative gender binary, may prevent a challenge to the gender binary more generally which could occur if there was no legal recognition at all.

In the case of the GRA the regulation of identity seems to be based around several key concerns. First, the GRA is based on the assumption that gender is, and should be, binary and ideally static rather than manifold and fluid. As such applicants have to promise they will live in their gender for the rest of their lives and gender "options" are limited to male and female. Although particularly the promise to live in one's gender permanently is unlikely to be legally enforceable (Grabham, 2010), this nevertheless serves to restrict access to GRCs to those who are willing and able to at least nominally adhere to this mode of gendered existence.

The second and more crucial issue, at least for the purposes of this discussion, underpinning much of the law in this context, seems to be concerns about "fraud" or the "inauthenticity" of trans people and their gender identity. This issue has led some commentators to suggest that this is in fact a thinly veiled excuse for homophobia (Sharpe, 2002: 66). As a result of this logic, Alex Sharpe argues, trans people are often expected to explicitly define themselves as heterosexual. Homosexual desire is a factor that could indicate that a trans person is "inauthentic", that is not really trans but a homosexual person trying to gain access to marriage or deceive their partner. For example, in the pre-GRA case of *Corbett v Corbett* [1971] P 83, April Ashley, formerly Corbett, was described by Ormrod J as a "female impersonator" rather than as a woman throughout the proceedings. He refused to accept her identity despite the fact that she had undergone gender reassignment surgery; instead he insisted Ashley was actually a homosexual man. In addition to a description of sex as unchangeable and binary, Ormrod J also argued that marriage is an institution that is based on (biological) sex and not gender and more specifically founded upon the capacity for heterosexual intercourse (*Corbett v Corbett*: 106–7). This suggests that at least some of the reluctance to recognise Ashley as female was based on a deep-seated fear of inadvertently allowing same-sex marriages. In fact Alex Sharpe goes so far as to describe the judgment in *Corbett* as "riddled with homophobic anxiety" (2001: para 3), an assessment that only becomes more damning when considering that *Corbett* remained valid precedent until the introduction of the GRA.

Building on this point of gender authenticity, a similar concern about a trans person pretending to be "normal" or heterosexual can be found in *J v ST (formerly J)(transsexual ancillary relief)* [1998] Fam 103. The judge specifically points out that S-T, who was the spouse of a trans man, had no previous sexual experience and generally describes her as sheltered and naive. According to him this allowed J to "pretend" to be male. The judgment is heavily based on concerns about maintaining marriage as an exclusively heterosexual union (*J v S-T*: 141) and again highlights the importance of "natural" heterosexual intercourse to marriage. Although *Corbett* and *J v ST* provide the most explicit judicial comments about a fear of trans people effectively committing fraud against either their spouse or the state, other pre-GRA cases also more generally highlight the idea that marriage should remain a purely heterosexual union. This implies that if a trans person married in a sex/gender other than the one that he or she was assigned at birth, that person would violate this principle and destabilise marriage as a heterosexual social institution (see Lord Nichols in *Bellinger v Bellinger* [2003] UKHL 21, [2003] 2 AC 467).

More specifically this line of cases also serves to give the impression that the cisgender spouses of trans people are always potentially vulnerable victims of deception who the law needs to protect. While this is made fairly explicit in the case law, there is no explicit statement about this in the GRA or the Marriage (Same Sex Couples) Act 2013. But the fact that applicants have to provide a tremendous amount of evidence of their gender identity[9] in addition to living in their desired gender for two years prior to their application, and then promise to stay in that gender for the rest of their lives, shows that there are clear, continuing concerns about the validity of trans people's gender identity (GRA, s.2). To that extent one reading of the GRA could suggest that it contains the potential for queer and non-binary forms of gender presentation, as it theoretically allows one to be recognised as a gender without possessing the physical characteristics normally associated with that gender. A closer look, however, shows that it is nevertheless a highly medicalised process that relies almost exclusively on medical concepts, terminology and evidence. This was made explicit in the parliamentary debates around the GRA, which ran parallel to the debates about the Civil Partnership Act 2004, in which even those in favour of granting trans people legal recognition highlighted the pressing need for legal tests and barriers so that trans people would prove their "commitment" to their gender: "It is a necessary part of ensuring that before a decision is taken by the panel, the person has demonstrated their fundamental commitment to the very major change that they want to undertake" (Lord Filkin, *Hansard*, HL Deb

(2003–4), vol 656, col 26, also HL Deb (2003–4), vol 657, col 375; Lord Chan, *Hansard*, HL Deb (2003–4), vol 655, col 1309). As a result the medical and legal experts on the Gender Recognition Panel become the gatekeepers tasked with checking the medical evidence and official documents provided by applicants to avoid the, entirely hypothetical, potential for "fraudulent" applications. And the queer or feminist potential of the Act is confined within the strict borderlines of normative sex/gender construction.

Obviously the law has moved on from the outright denial of trans people's existence and their right to marry that can be found in *Corbett v Corbett*. The GRA is clearly a positive development in transgender jurisprudence. It not only provides a method of obtaining legal recognition of their gender for trans people and as such brings English law in line with the decision made by the ECtHR in *Goodwin v UK*, but also proves to be a more progressive method of recognition than those currently available in many other countries as it does not make gender reassignment surgery an official requirement. In fact Alex Sharpe describes the GRA as one of the most progressive legal frameworks (in the European Union at that specific time) allowing for trans people's recognition (Sharpe, 2009: 242). However, until the introduction of same-sex marriage, a GRC was only available to unmarried trans people or those who were willing to convert their relationship from a marriage into a civil partnership, and vice versa, when applying for their certificate. This effectively amounted to a legally mandated divorce for applicants in a pre-existing recognised relationship and clearly highlights the difficulties inherent in relying on law to effect changes in wider social attitudes towards specific groups such as trans people (Spade, 2011).

Equal marriage rights for all?

The Marriage (Same Sex Couples) Act 2013 includes an amendment to the GRA which allows trans people who are married to legally remain in their relationship even if they transition. Once it comes into force it replaces the existing requirement contained in ss. 4–5 of the GRA. These sections together set out one of the key requirements for a successful GRC application, namely that applicants who are married had to dissolve their existing relationship, which they can if they so choose, change to the appropriate legal relationship to match their new gender. Stephen Whittle explains quite clearly that this requirement was introduced primarily to alleviate concerns by religious groups about the introduction of "inadvertent" same-sex marriages when one spouse changed their gender while remaining married (2006: 270).

This may also mirror the original medical requirements for the "treatment" of trans people, with many clinics originally demanding that patients divorce before undergoing treatment, again because of fears of "inadvertent" same-sex marriages; however, medical guidelines have since removed this requirement (Fausto-Sterling, 2000: 107). Trans individuals who want legal recognition of their gender identity have to conform with the dominant knowledge about the relationship between gender and sexuality; that is, if you become a man in the eyes of the law but continue to be in a relationship with another man you cannot be heterosexual and as such your relationship status must be changed. Those who fail to live up to these standards or reject them are excluded and denied legal rights. Considering the strongly worded and often homophobic statements made by judges in pre-GRA cases dealing with trans people, the idea that marriage needs to be maintained as a purely heterosexual union is clearly a key concern in this area.

The legalisation of same-sex marriage is obviously a positive development in so far as trans people will no longer be forced to choose between either the legal recognition of their relationship or the legal recognition of their gender identity. However, the amendment introduces a new requirement that states that the cisgender spouse will have to give written consent before his or her partner can obtain a full rather than an interim GRC and that the spouse will be officially notified once the application is made (Marriage (Same Sex Couples) Act 2013, sch. 5 s.2). The completed consent form needs to be submitted together with all other evidential documents and the application will then be processed as usual. However, if a relationship has broken down but still exists legally, without their spouse's consent trans people will only be able to apply for an interim GRC that expires after six months, at which point they have to re-start the entire recognition process (Marriage (Same Sex Couples) Act 2013, sch. 5 s.3). Apart from the emotional cost of this process, the financial cost of re-starting the legal process can be significant as there is a fee for each application. The creation of this amendment highlights that the debate around whether trans people are inauthentic or potentially trying to deceive someone is very much present in legal discourse, especially in the context of intimate relationships where a lingering fear of the transgression of the gender binary still seems to exist.

"Protecting" the non-trans spouse

This continuing transphobia is evidenced most clearly by some of the statements made during the debate stages of Marriage (Same Sex Couples) Bill. Until the final reading in the House of Lords there seemed to be some confusion, even on the part of law-makers, whether consent was meant to be to a spouse's transition or the continuation of the relationship itself (*Hansard*, HL Deb (2013–14), vol 747, col 296). The language used during the debates in both houses also clearly constructs the spouses of trans people as being in need of additional legal protection and remedies other than those available to couples already. For example, during the third reading in the House of Commons, Helen Grant MP specifically discussed that not disclosing the possession of a GRC makes a marriage voidable and argued that this could not be changed as it was crucial to protect cisgender spouses from not being aware of their partner's gender. She then carried on to explain that she had seen no evidence of cisgender spouses obstructing their partner's transition process out of spite, or to gain some material advantage, similar to some Jewish divorce cases, which was one of the key concerns mentioned by critics of the amendment (*Hansard*, HC Deb (2013–14), vol 563, col 1146). The obvious problem with Grant's reassurance is that until now spouses have never before been in a position to do so. It is very telling that in regards to the *get* concerns about undue influence on one of the spouses was exactly what triggered legal intervention, whereas in regards to married trans people such concerns are simply and erroneously dismissed. This seems to suggest that while Jewish women are seen as individuals who are deserving of state protection, quite the opposite applies to trans people with a cisgender spouse.

Julian Huppert MP actually highlighted some of the problematic assumptions about trans people made by many MPs in the context of this debate, which he argued seemed to suggest that legislators thought spouses actually were never fully or properly consenting when they married a trans person:

> I was worried by some of the language about not fully consenting to a marriage, although I am sure the Minister did not mean to imply that people need to be protected from transgender spouses or transgender people—I am sure that is not what was intended. (*Hansard*, HC Deb (2013–14), vol 563, cols 1146–47)

However other MPs seemed unwilling to engage with his argument, and the debate continued without acknowledging the problematic undertones of this new amendment, which was in general not covered in any detail by much of the media.

As a result of very vocal complaints by trans people about the new requirement for spousal consent, Baroness Barker in the House of Lords tabled an amendment that would have placed a time limit of six months on spouses' ability to withhold consent:

> The amendments would do two things. First, they would give a spouse the right to be notified. I understand that at the moment the first time a spouse may receive any notification that a partner is going through gender reassignment is when court papers are delivered seeking an annulment.
>
> (*Hansard*, HL Deb (2013–14), vol 746, col 1146)

Although this would have limited the damaging effect of the consent amendment somewhat, Barker nevertheless suggested that it was important that spouses would be notified when their partner applied for a GRC, based again on the unrealistic assumption that spouses are often not aware of their partner transitioning. This shows that at the very least law-makers have little awareness of how the legal recognition process actually works and at worst they seem to assume trans people are actively trying to deceive their partners.

Similarly, Baroness Butler-Sloss, who has generally been supportive of trans issues when sitting in the Court of Appeal described the spouses of trans people as "those who are left behind" and argued that they needed special legal protection. Even the language used here could be seen as parallel to the *get* issue where the *agunot* were left behind while their husband was free to move on to a new relationship without suffering any consequences. Clearly in regards to the GRA even those who are critical of this amendment seemed to assume that trans people's spouses need additional legal protection that goes beyond the legal remedies that are already available to couples when a relationship breaks down. This can only really be explained if we accept that there is a presumption that the spouses of trans people are somehow more at risk than everyone else:

> The Bill seeks to strike a fair balance between the Article 8 rights to respect for the private and family life of both spouses. The trans spouse has a right to be granted their gender recognition without unnecessary delay, but the non-trans spouse also has a right to have a say in the future of their marriage following their spouse gaining gender recognition.
>
> (Baroness Stowell of Beeston, *Hansard*, HL Deb (2013–14), vol 746, col 520)

As such it seems unsurprising that the amendment tabled by Baroness Barker failed with Baroness Stowell of Beeston arguing that it was more important to protect the right of trans people's spouses instead. She argued that while trans people could simply divorce a spouse who refused to give consent to their transition, the other spouse needed a remedy other than divorce, without ever articulating why exactly this was the case or what this would entail. The language used about balancing the rights of the two spouses here obscures the fact that the cisgender spouse seems to be treated by default as a victim.

Additionally, most peers in the debate seemed to assume that the cisgender spouse in need of legal protection would be female. This may be a coincidence but it also links back to cases such as *J v ST* where the female spouses of trans people were described as particularly vulnerable and as essentially victimised simply by the transgender status of their partner. This also gives support to Schilt's and Westbrook's (2009) argument that policy-makers generally make laws and regulations concerning trans people based on purely hypothetical examples with little or no regard for the day-to-day realities of living as a trans person in a specific society. In this case law-makers clearly imagined a married person who was assigned male at birth suddenly deciding to transition and being able to do so successfully in a matter of weeks with little regard for his spouse's feelings about this matter. The fact that this scenario is entirely unrealistic seems to have been of little importance to legislators.

Importantly, this amendment of the GRA also mirrors the governmental intervention on behalf of Jewish women. In both cases the female spouses seem to be perceived as being in an inherently disadvantaged position in their relationship which in turn justifies additional intervention to supposedly even the balance of power between spouses. This seems somewhat logical in Jewish divorces due to the gender discrimination inherent in the *get* rules, whereas in the case of GRA this can only be justified if being married to a trans person is treated as a disadvantage in and of itself.

Concluding thoughts

I would argue that trans people who want legal recognition of their gender identity clearly have to conform with existing dominant knowledge about what constitutes an acceptable expression of gender or sexuality. The GRA effectively encourages those who want or need legal recognition to adhere to traditional norms about gender and sexuality; whereas those who fail to live up to these standards are much less likely to meet the evidence threshold for a GRC application unless they modify their personal narratives to fit those norms. As a result a change of gender is always imagined to also lead to a change of sexuality, at least in the official imagination, which is why the introduction of same-sex marriage has brought some advantages to a specific group of trans people. Without it married trans people are not really able to escape the causal links made between gender and sexuality, which previously forced them to choose between the continuation of their marriage/civil partnership and the legal recognition of their gender identity.

There has clearly been a change from the way governmental technologies were employed in *Corbett v Corbett* to deal with the "problem" of trans people and the way the GRA provides a mechanism for legal recognition. However even in its most recent incarnation and with the legalisation of same-sex marriage, the GRA seems to be underpinned by fears about trans people potentially deceiving their partners. Following Freeman's argument, the new amendment clearly has a symbolic value. Just like the government's intervention in Jewish marriages designated Jewish women as a group in need of special protection due to their disadvantaged status; the new amendment to the GRA specifically designates cisgender spouses, who are again mainly imagined to be women, in need of similar protection. This means that while Jewish men are seen as potentially being tempted to hold their partners to ransom, all trans spouses are seen as disadvantaging or perhaps even harming their spouses by transitioning. Paradoxically, it is actually trans spouses who are now likely to be held to ransom by a vindictive spouse refusing to grant consent, thereby delaying the legal transition process until the marriage is dissolved. The fact that both measures seem to be primarily aimed at protecting cis women who are seen as particularly vulnerable may merely be a coincidence but nevertheless suggests some highly troublesome assumptions on behalf of law-makers about trans people, their gender identity, their motivations and their relationships and kinship.

One explanation could be that, following Helen Reece's argument, marriage is one of the key social mechanisms that shape an individual's identity (Reece, 2003: 111). Similarly, Sedgwick argues that erotic identity, in this case as expressed by marrying someone, is always relational and subject to transference (Sedgwick, 1990: 81). If we assume this to be true then a person's transition obviously does not just change their identity but also implicitly that of their spouse. Effectively, this suggests gender still seems to be so fundamental to marriage that just being married to a trans person is enough to make a person so vulnerable that extra legal "protection" is required. This seems to be based on a fear of trans people transitioning in secret thereby creating a need not just for written consent but also for an official notification process which in no way reflects the lived reality of most trans people. Despite the fact that same-sex marriage has now become a legal reality, the resulting amendments to the GRA suggest that gender and sexuality are still perceived as fundamental aspects of individual identity, as well as of marriage. That trans people cannot be granted equal access to marriage rights in line with cisgender people, as their very existence highlights how fragile the presumption is that sex, gender and sexuality are always fixed and causally linked. Logically, this means that while marriage is now available for homosexual as well as heterosexual couples this does not in fact make marriage blind to the respective gender of each party. The new amendment to the GRA clearly suggests that despite the legalisation of same-sex marriage sex/gender is far from becoming irrelevant to the concept of marriage itself.

Notes

1 Many thanks to Davina Cooper and Emily Grabham for their invaluable feedback and advice. Thanks also to P. S. Bouklis. I am grateful for funding and ongoing support from Kent Law School.
2 Following Dean Spade I am using the term "trans" throughout this chapter to "indicate people who identify as transgender, transsexual, or within the transgender spectrum" (Spade, 2003: 15–16).
3 For a detailed critique of this provision, see Sharpe (2012).
4 Similar to Schilt and Westbrook I am using "cis" or "cisgender" to replace "the terms "nontransgender" or "bio man/bio woman" to refer to individuals who have a match between the gender they were assigned at birth, their bodies and their personal identity" (Schilt and Westbrook, 2009). Although this term has generated some academic and non-academic debate, it nevertheless seems a useful shorthand term in this context and avoids stigmatising trans people as "others" in contrast to an otherwise "normally" gendered population.

5 See, for example, Press for Change's advice to applicants that suggests that even if applicants actually do not want surgery, their doctor should not mention this in the official medical statement (Press for Change, 'The Standard Track Gender Recognition Process").
6 By this I mean wide-reaching social practices and discourses that support the idea that sex and gender are both binary and causally linked to each other and that heterosexuality is, if not the only, then at least the most acceptable form of sexuality (for a more detailed discussion, see Rich 1980; Butler 1989; Kitzinger 2005).
7 Trans people who have obtained a GRC and want to enter into a civil partnership or marriage need to disclose the fact that they have obtained a GRC as otherwise their relationship will be voidable. This has not been changed with the introduction of same-sex marriage (for a detailed critique, see Sharpe, 2012).
8 The specific legal provisions dealing with the *get* as well as other forms of religious marriage/divorce can now be found in the Divorce (Religious Marriages) Act 2002.
9 Implementing GRA, s.3, this evidence generally includes at least two detailed medical reports and at least five other documents such as passports, driving licences and household bills.

References

AHRC Report "Social Cohesion and Civil Law: Marriage, Divorce and Religious Courts", 2011.

Butler, J. *Gender trouble: Feminism and the subversion of identity* (New York: Routledge, 1989).

Dean, M. *Governmentality: Power and Rule in Modern Society* (London: Sage, 2nd edn, 2010).

——"Foucault, government and the enfolding of authority" in Barry, A., Osborne, T. and Rose, N. (eds) *Foucault and Political Reason: Liberalism, Neo Liberalism and Nationalities of Government*, pp. 209–29 (London: UCL Press, 1996).

Fausto-Sterling, A. *Sexing the Body: Gender Politics and the Construction of Sexuality* (New York: Basic Books, 2000).

Freeman, M. "Divorce: 'The Dayanim Must Act'", *Jewish Chronicle* (17 December 1999).

Freeman, M. "Is the Jewish *Get* Any Business of the State?", in O'Dair, R. and Lewis, A. (eds), *Law and Religion: Current Legal Issues 4* (Oxford: Oxford University Press, 2001).

GOV.UK, 2014. "Passports: Change Your Name and Personal Details" [online] https://www.gov.uk/changing-passport-information/changing-your-gender [accessed 15 June 2014].

Grabham, E. "Governing Permanence: Trans Subjects, Time, and the Gender Recognition Act", *Social & Legal Studies* 19.1 (2010): 107–26.

Hansard, HL Deb (2003–4) 655.

——(2003–4) 656.

——(2003–4) 657.

——(2013–14) 563.

——(2013–14) 746.

Irving, D. "Normalized Transgressions: Legitimizing the Transsexual Body as Productive", *Radical History Review* 100 (2008): 38.

Katzenberg, S. and Rosenblatt, J. "Getting the '*Get*'", *Family Law* 29 (1999): 165–67.

Kitzinger, C. "Heteronormativity in Action: Reproducing the Heterosexual Nuclear Family in After-Hours Medical Calls", *Social Problems* 52.4 (2005): 477–98

Miller, J.D. "History of the Agunah in America: A Clash of Religious Law and Social Progress", 19 *Women's Rts. L. Rep.* 1 (1997–98): 1–16.

Miller, P. and Rose, N. *Governing the Present* (Cambridge: Polity, 2008).

Press for Change. "The Standard Track Gender Recognition Application Process" [online] http://www.pfc.org.uk/StandardTrackGRCS.html [accessed 18 May 2014].

Ratzlav-Katz, N. "Statistics Dispel Claims of 'Thousands of Israeli Agunot'", *Arutz Sheva*, 27.6 (2007) [online] http://www.israelnationalnews.com/News/News.aspx/122884#.U3ior_ldWSo last accessed 18.05.2014 [accessed 18 May 2014].

Reece, H. *Divorcing Responsibly* (Oxford: Hart Publishing, 2003).

Rich, A. "Compulsory Heterosexuality and Lesbian Existence", *Signs: Journal of Women in Culture and Society* 5.4 (1980): 631–60.

Schilt, K. and Westbrook, L. "Doing Gender, Doing Heteronormativity 'Gender Normals,' Transgender People, and the Social Maintenance of Heterosexuality", *Gender & Society* 23.4 (2009): 440–64.

Schilt, Kristen and Windsor, E. "The Sexual Habitus of Transgender Men: Negotiating Sexuality Through Gender", *Journal of Homosexuality* 61.5 (2014): 732–48.

Sedgwick, Eve Kosofsky. *Epistemology of the Closet* (Berkeley and Los Angeles: University of California Press, 1990, 2008 edn).

Sharpe, A. "From Functionality to Aesthetics: The Architecture of Transgender Jurisprudence", *Murdoch University Electronic Journal of Law*, 8.1 (2001) [online] http://www.murdoch.edu.au/elaw/issues/v8n1/sharpe81.html [accessed 2 December 2014].

——"English Transgender Law Reform and the Spectre of Corbett", *Feminist Legal Studies* 10.1 (2002): 65–89.

——"Gender Recognition in the UK: A Great Leap Forward", *Social and Legal Studies* 18.2 (2009): 241.

——"Transgender Marriage and the Legal Obligation to Disclose Gender History", *The Modern Law Review* 75.1 (2012): 33–53.

Spade, D. "Resisting Medicine, Re/modeling Gender", *Berkeley Women's LJ* 18 (2003): 15.

Spade, D. *Normal Life: Administrative Violence, Critical Trans Politics, and the Limits of Law* (Cambridge, MA: South End Press, 2011).

Valverde, Mariana. *Law's Dream of a Common Knowledge* (Princeton, NJ: Princeton University Press, 2009).

Westbrook, L. and Schilt, K. "Doing Gender, Determining Gender Transgender People, Gender Panics, and the Maintenance of the Sex/Gender/Sexuality System", *Gender & Society* 28.1 (2014): 32–57.

Whittle, S. "The Opposite of Sex is Politics – The UK Gender Recognition Act and Why it is Not Perfect, Just Like You and Me: FORUM", *Journal of Gender Studies* 15.3 (2006): 267–71.

Cases

Bellinger v Bellinger [2003] UKHL 21, [2003] 2 AC 467

Brett v Brett [1969] 1 All ER 1007

Corbett v Corbett [1971] P 83

Goodwin v United Kingdom (28957/95) [2002] Fam Law 738

J v ST (formerly J) (transsexual ancillary relief) [1998] Fam 103

Part II

Changing minds, changing practice?

After the wedding

Chapter 6

Social work and adoption

The impact of civil partnership and same-sex marriage

Christine Cocker

Introduction

Social attitudes towards lesbian and gay parents have changed markedly over the past 40 years. The last 10–15 years in particular have seen unprecedented legal changes across Britain in support of lesbian and gay equality regarding the age of consent, civil relationship recognition, marriage, and access to public goods and services. Many more lesbians and gay men are now choosing to have families of their own – some by birth, or a range of co-parenting arrangements, and others via adoption. Most will see these equality changes as something to be celebrated as signs of success, and indeed they are. Not because lesbian and gay families are now 'as good as' heterosexual families (weren't we always?), but because now it is possible for lesbian and gay partners to choose to have a family and for both parents to have parental responsibility for their children without the need to go to court umpteen times to secure this, which is not what most heterosexual couples have to do, apart from those who adopt. However, it is not quite as straightforward as that.

There is a great danger that in this new found 'equality' the diversity of ways in which lesbians and gay men understand 'family' and family structures will be ignored. This is because societal discourses about families are firmly entrenched within a heteronormative framework. Chambers states that the concept of heteronormativity 'reveals institutional, cultural and legal norms that reify and entrench that normativity of heterosexuality. In other words, "heteronormativity" tells us that heterosexual desire and identity are not merely assumed, they are expected' (Chambers, 2007: 664–65). Despite the interest by many councils and adoption agencies in assessing lesbians, gay men and transgendered individuals as prospective adopters, this discourse is also established within social work in terms of the kinds of families being approved by social workers. I want to explore why, within adoption, those lesbian, gay and other kinds of families that 'make the grade' are more likely to be those families that emulate heteronormative structures and patterns of behaviour.

Forty years of lesbian and gay parenting history

There are a small number of publications (Richardson, 1981; Hanscombe and Forster, 1982; Rights of Women Lesbian Custody Group, 1986) that offer important historical insights into the lives of lesbian parents, in particular across the UK in the 1970s and 1980s. Whilst some of the women in Hanscombe's and Forster's study had conceived children as single parents or within lesbian relationships, many of the women they had spoken to who had conceived children within marriages that had then ended had experienced custody battles as a result of their lesbianism. The Rights of Women Lesbian Custody Group reported that the negativity of the courts towards lesbian mothers at that time meant that many women lost custody of their children solely because of their sexuality, which stood in stark contrast to how courts treated heterosexual women, as they were almost always awarded custody. The attitude of the courts is exemplified by a House of Lords' judgment in 1976:

> Change in public attitudes should not entitle the courts to relax in any degree the vigilance and severity with which they should regard the risk of children at critical ages being exposed or introduced to ways of life which may lead to severance from normal society, to psychological stresses and unhappiness and possibly even to physical experiences which may scar them for life
>
> (Hanscombe and Forster, 1982: 67)

The effect of lesbian parenting on children has been investigated by a number of child psychologists in the UK and USA. Since 1983, Susan Golombok has published research investigating the sexual, educational, psychological and social outcomes of children raised by lesbians compared with children raised by single heterosexual mothers (Golombok et al., 1983; Golombok and Tasker, 1996; Golombok, 2000; Golombok et al., 2003). The majority of the sample of children in lesbian families included in the research were birth children. The overwhelming evidence from the UK, also supported by the US research (Patterson, 2005; Goldberg, 2010), suggests that the children of lesbians are just as likely as children growing up in heterosexual families to have good mental health, to have positive relationships with peers and to have good relationships with both male and female adults. There were no differences in gender-role behaviour or evidence of any gender identity confusion between the groups of children studied (Golombok, 2007). The clear message from the research, as Golombok notes, is that 'It is what happens within families, not the way families are composed, that seems to matter most' (2000: 101).

The research literature about gay men's parenting and outcomes for their children began being published 10–15 years after the research on lesbian parenting (Bailey et al.; 1995; Barrett and Tasker, 2001; Barrett and Tasker, 2002; Patterson, 2004), and the results are broadly similar to lesbian mothers in terms of the positive outcomes for the children parented by gay men.

The numbers of studies that have investigated the outcomes of children adopted by lesbians and gay men, and the experiences of lesbians and gay men of adoption is developing, but in the UK is still quite small (Hicks and McDermott, 1999; Hicks, 2006; Cocker, 2011; Mellish et al., 2013). In the USA there is a bigger research base with studies reporting satisfaction with adoption experiences (Ryan and Whitlock, 2009), the sexual orientation of the adopter not being significant for children achieving positive outcomes (Erich et al., 2009), that lesbian and gay families enjoy good levels of support from their networks (Erich, 2005; Kindle and Erich, 2005), that outcomes for older children placed with lesbian or gay adopters are particularly positive (Erich, 2005, Leung et al., 2005) and that children deemed 'high risk' at the point of placement show improved patterns of development over time in heterosexual and gay and lesbian adoptive households (Lavner et al., 2012). This growing evidence is welcome as hitherto there was an assumption that the outcomes for the birth children of lesbians and gay men would equally apply to the adopted children of lesbians and gay men (Brown and Cocker, 2011). There is now good evidence to show this (Erich et al., 2005; Averett et al., 2009, Mellish et al., 2013); however, there are some differences that are also worth exploring.

As with the literature commenting on lesbians' and gay men's skills as birth parents, much of the current research is based on reductionist methodological designs; that is, investigating whether lesbian' and gay adopters are comparable to heterosexual adopters. There is a place for this research; it has clearly shown that there are relatively few differences in outcomes for the children adopted by lesbian and gay families compared with heterosexual families and this has answered concerns raised by many critics about whether lesbians and gay men could effectively raise adopted children to be well-adjusted adults in the face of the adversity of their early lives. A few studies, whilst still for the most part using a comparative method, are also now able to comment on the strengths of adoptions with lesbian and gay carers compared with heterosexual adopters (Mellish et al., 2013), and the differences that are emerging are interesting. For lesbians and gay men, adoption is much more likely to be a first-choice option and is not in the main a decision made because of infertility; lesbians and gay men are prepared to adopt older children; lesbians and gay men are highly motivated parents and are more actively involved in the lives of their adopted children than heterosexual parents. This literature is particularly positive about the contribution of gay men as parents, where motivation is high:

> These gay fathers were the first to have gone through the adoption process to create their families; therefore, they were highly motivated and dedicated to being parents – something that, in many cases, they had never thought of as an option when they first came out as gay.
>
> (Mellish et al., 2013: 39)

Legal changes to lesbian and gay parenting

Before December 2005, in England and Wales, lesbians and gay men could not adopt jointly with their partners as a couple. Local authorities and the courts viewed lesbian and gay couple applications as a single-person adoption application. An application for a joint residence order (section 8 of the Children Act 1989) was usually applied for at the time of an adoption order to give the other partner 'parental responsibility' (PR) (section 3 of the Children Act 1989), but this ended once the child turned 18. For any biological children born to one partner, the other partner had to apply for a joint residence order in a bid to obtain PR. Again this ended at 18. The non-biological parent could not be entered on the birth certificate for a child born to the biological parent.

Three pieces of legislation fundamentally changed the landscape. First, the Adoption and Children Act 2002 enabled lesbians and gay men in partnerships (as distinct from civil partnerships which were introduced two years later) to jointly adopt, and for the partner of the birth parent of a child (or children) to apply to adopt in the same way as a heterosexual step-parent. Second, the Human Fertilisation and Embryology Act 2008 made it possible for the non-biological parent to be entered on the birth certificate of their child. Finally, the Equality Act (Sexual Orientation) Regulations 2007 prohibited discrimination on the grounds of sexual orientation in providing goods, facilities and services to the public. This was important because adoption agencies in England then had to assess lesbians and gay men who approached their agency. This is not the same thing as saying that all lesbians and gay men have the right to become adopters; rather, they now have the right to an assessment as a couple. They have always had the right to an assessment as a single adopter. This last piece of legislation had repercussions for some adoption agencies, most notably those with affiliations to the Catholic Church; those agencies have now either closed, merged with other voluntary sector organisations that allow lesbian and gay applicants to be assessed, or have cut their formal ties with the Catholic Church to enable them to meet these legal requirements (Brown and Cocker, 2011).

Is heteronormativity still the standard?

An adoption assessment is a complicated undertaking and this complexity is part of the everyday social work task when assessing who is suitable and not suitable to adopt. An often repeated phrase by the former Secretary of State for Education Michael Gove, was that children need a 'loving family', but what does a 'loving family' look like? Do lesbian and gay families have to act like heterosexual families in order to be assessed as capable?

In one of the first publications to address fostering and adoption practices, Skeates and Jabri (1988) highlighted many of the problems that lesbians and gay men experienced when being assessed by social services in the 1980s. Consequently, some lesbians and gay men chose not to 'come out' to their assessing social worker. Of those who completed the assessment, a high number were matched with disabled children, as children without disabilities were prioritised for heterosexual families, something that the film-maker Pratiba Parmar referred to as sending out messages of 'second class children for second class carers' (Parmar 1989, cited in Hicks, 2005: 44). There is no evidence to suggest that this practice continues, but lesbians and gay men still have many misconceptions about adoption and the adoption process because of previous social work practices.

Over ten years ago, Stephen Hicks suggested that the social workers assessing lesbian foster carers or adopters understood lesbianism through a heteronormative lens. He created three typologies of 'good' and 'bad' lesbians with associated characteristics, the 'man-hater', the 'militant' and the 'pedestal of virtue', and argued that this had a major impact on which applicants were seen as suitable. The lesbians that were most likely to be approved as foster carers or adopters were:

> able to deal with anti-lesbian prejudices of birth families, some children/young people and panel; were not threatening to gender norms; were integrated with heterosexuals;. … likely to know men, have male role models, present positive images of men; be integrated into the wider (heterosexual) community and family; … where child care abilities were emphasised as paramount, over issues of sexuality; were non-militant, non-radical, not political, not too feminist. …
>
> (Hicks, 2000: 164)

Since this time, there have been a small number of other studies investigating social workers' attitudes towards lesbian and gay fostering and adoption assessments (Dugmore and Cocker, 2008; Brown, 2011) as well as investigations of applicants' views about their assessment (Cocker, 2011; Mellish et al., 2013; Jennings et al., 2014; Ryan and Whitlock, 2009) which point to progress having been made in terms of the capability of social workers to undertake robust assessments. Most lesbians and gay men now think that their assessment was a fair process, which is a far cry from social work practices 15–20 years ago (Skeates and Jabri, 1988; Hicks and McDermott, 1999).

One of the interesting findings from current research is that what happens in lesbian and gay families is not very different from heterosexual families. Mellish et al. found that 'All parents assumed fairly traditional patterns of parenting responsibilities, with no difference between family types. Thus, it appears that family life is very similar for children, regardless of parents' sexual orientation.' (2013: 14). However, Golombok (2000) found in earlier research that the way in which lesbian and gay families divide up parenting tasks within their homes is not clustered in gender roles that are attributed to one partner or another. These findings raise questions about the kinds of lesbian and gay families coming forward to adopt. Examining the experiences of lesbian and gay adopters who did not find the process fair may provide us with critiques about what part of the process does not work well. For example, Monk discusses a case where two gay men in a civil partnership went from being seen as 'ideal' by the assessing local authority to 'untouchable', on the basis of their non-monogamous relationship being disclosed by the couple to the local authority (Monk, 2015). After successfully appealing against the local authority's decision not to approve them, and subsequently being approved, the couple concerned have not had children placed with them, which when considering the numbers of children waiting for adoption is surprising. During 2012–13, 2,943 children were referred to and 897 adopters were registered with the English Adoption Register (BAAF, 2013). Of this number, 7 per cent were same-sex couples, so numbers of lesbians and gay men in relationships being approved as prospective adopters are still small. Of the 3,980 children adopted in England during 2012–13, 77 per cent were adopted by married heterosexual couples, 7 per cent by unmarried heterosexual couples, 10 per cent by single adopters (this would include single lesbians and gay men), 4 per cent by lesbian and gay couples in civil partnerships and 2 per cent by lesbian and gay couples not in civil partnerships (Department for Education, 2013). This shows a slight percentage increase in lesbians and gay men who are in a civil partnership coming forward to adopt over the past five years, along with single adopters and heterosexual partners who are not married. The percentage of lesbian and gay couples who are not in a civil partnership who have adopted has stayed constant, whereas the percentage of heterosexual married couples adopting has fallen slightly.

In his more recent work, Hicks uses Michel Foucault's ideas about governmentality and subjectivity discourses, and the ideas of Mark Philp about social work knowledge (Philp, 1979) to explore the complexities of how social workers assess lesbians and gay men, and in so doing moves beyond the straightforward assertions of heteronormativity that can be made about social work decision-making. Social work does not take place outside a social and cultural context, or without reference to 'social conflicts and dominant interests' (Philp, 1979). Hicks suggests that this is critical:

> as social work has clearly been part of the creation of lesbian and gay foster care and adoption as possibilities in the first place. Social workers have had to create the image of particular lesbians or gay men as good carers, yet, at the same time, these subjectivities are constrained by institutional and dominant versions of sexual knowledge.
>
> (Hicks, 2011: 184)

I would add 'family context' to this list as well. An example of this is the male and female role-model question usually included in the assessment process. This has been well documented as an ongoing practice 'concern' that is not borne out by research results regarding the effect that gender has on parenting and the well-being of children (Golombok, 2000; Cocker, 2011). What is useful about Hicks's position is that he does not get caught up in an essentialist or didactic view of lesbian, gay, bisexual and transgender (LGBT) families as either heteronormative or assimilationist, on the one hand, compared with 'radical' families where difference is emphasised, on the other. As Fiona Tasker helpfully highlights: 'This is particularly in the case of state-controlled world of adoption and fostering where social work agencies both produce and reproduce societal conceptualisations to evaluate who is fit or unfit to parent in order to protect vulnerable children' (Tasker, 2013: 303).

Relationship recognition

If it is the case that societal conceptions about who is 'fit' or 'unfit' to parent affects how couples are treated by adoption agencies, it stands to reason that it may also have an impact on how applicants choose to present themselves to adoption agencies either as couples or as a single adopter. In particular, I am interested in whether lesbian and gay applicants think that they should have entered into a civil partnership in order to be successful in any adoption assessment. The statistics presented in Table 6.1 would suggest that this is the case as there are over twice as many civilly partnered lesbians and gay men coming forward to adopt than couples who are not in civil partnerships, and this pattern continues over a five-year period. Legally, it should not make a difference, but it would appear that almost as a form of self-selection, it does affect who applies and which applicants are successful. Couples may think that they will be taken more seriously if they are in a civil partnership, as if *their* legal commitment per se indicates a seriousness to their relationship that is not represented outside this legal framework. This pattern is more stark in the figures for adopters in heterosexual marriages compared with adopters in heterosexual partnerships outside marriage.

Table 6.1 Children looked after who were adopted during the years ending 31 March by number of adopters (1,2,-), legal status of adopters and by gender of adopters

Years ending 31 March 2009 to 2013
Coverage: England

	Numbers					*Percentages*				
	2009	*2010*	*2011*	*2012*	*2013*	*2009*	*2010*	*2011*	*2012*	*2013*
All children looked after who were adopted during the year ending 31 March	**3,330**	**3,200**	**3,090**	**3,470**	**3,980**	***100***	***100***	***100***	***100***	***100***
Number of adopters	**3,330**	**3,200**	**3,090**	**3,470**	**3,980**	***100***	***100***	***100***	***100***	***100***
1 person	270	280	300	290	420	*8*	*9*	*10*	*8*	*10*
2 persons	3,050	2,920	2,800	3,180	3,560	*92*	*91*	*90*	*92*	*90*
Legal status and gender of adopters	**3,330**	**3,200**	**3,090**	**3,470**	**3,980**	***100***	***100***	***100***	***100***	***100***
Single adopter	**270**	**280**	**300**	**290**	**420**	***8***	***9***	***10***	***8***	***10***
Single male adopter	10	20	20	10	20	-	*1*	*1*	-	-
Single female adopter	260	260	280	280	400	*8*	*8*	*9*	*8*	*10*
Same sex couple not in civil partnership	**50**	**60**	**40**	**50**	**80**	***1***	***2***	***1***	***1***	***2***
Adopting couple are both male	20	30	20	20	50	*1*	*1*	*1*	-	*1*
Adopting couple are both female	30	30	20	30	30	*1*	*1*	*1*	*1*	*1*
Different sex unmarried couple	**190**	**180**	**230**	**260**	**290**	***6***	***5***	***7***	***7***	***7***
Civil partnership couple	**70**	**60**	**60**	**110**	**150**	***2***	***2***	***2***	***3***	***4***
Adopting couple are both male	40	30	30	50	80	*1*	*1*	*1*	*2*	*2*
Adopting couple are both female	40	30	30	60	70	*1*	*1*	*1*	*2*	*2*
Married couple	**2,740**	**2,620**	**2,460**	**2,760**	**3,050**	***82***	***82***	***80***	***80***	*77*

Source: SSDA 903 https://www.nationalarchives.gov.uk/doc/open-government-licence/version/3/

1. Numbers have been rounded to the nearest 10. Percentages have been rounded to the nearest whole number.
2. Historical data may differ from older publications. This is mainly due to the implementation of amendments and corrections sent by some local authorities after the publication date of previous materials.

- Negligible. Percentage below 0.5%.

For single gay men and lesbians, the issues are different again. In 2013, 10 per cent of adoptions were single adopters (mostly female), which is the largest category of adopters after married heterosexual adopters. We do not know how many single adopters are lesbian or gay. This remains hidden.

How do social workers assess lesbians and gay men?

The adoption assessment process is an in-depth assessment that examines many aspects of people's lives. There are debates about whether all applicants should be treated exactly the same in assessments regardless of circumstance or whether the assessment should be flexible enough to be able to respond to people's individual situations. Cocker and Hafford-Letchfield argue that:

> There are occasions when certain types of assessments do need to cover different areas, because some experiences are particular to the lives of lesbians and gay men, for example of coming out or homophobia. The question is whether existing frameworks should be flexible enough to adapt to people's individuality, and incorporate differences in a reflexive manner rather than as an 'add on', or not address them at all.
>
> (2010: 2002)

There are two known examples of practice guidance (Mallon, 2005; Hicks, 2007) that comment on the issues for the assessing social worker when undertaking home study reports with lesbians and gay prospective applicants. There is, however, some debate about whether the production of such practice guides and frameworks detailing best practice when working with lesbians and gay men and their families, or specialist books for lesbian or gay prospective adoption applicants (Hill, 2009) are useful (see Hicks, 2008) or whether they are in themselves reductionist because of the normative position they unconsciously or consciously adopt (Cocker and Brown, 2010; Cocker and Hafford-Letchfield, 2010; Brown and Cocker, 2011; Hicks, 2014).

But these differences do need to be acknowledged. Brown (1991) identified five[1] areas that she suggested should be covered within an assessment of lesbian and gay prospective adopters (Brown, 1991). Cocker and Brown (2010) developed the SPRIINT[2] model, which built on Brown's earlier work and addressed issues of sexuality for all, including for heterosexual couples and single adopters, which is also an area overlooked in the literature and in practice. The 'untouchable' gay couple referred to earlier (Monk, 2015) provides an example of why this is important to cover. The assessing local authority appears to have responded to their non-monogamous relationship as problematic, as it does not 'fit' within mainstream expectations about how intimate relationships should be conducted within a civil partnership or marriage. This then clouded judgements and recommendations made by the assessing local authority about the suitability of the applicants to become parents, until the prospective adopters formally complained to the local authority and, formally at least, won. The issue here is not about monogamy or non-monogamy at all. It is about exploring how this couple's choices regarding their sexual practices impact on their ability to be parents. What does this non-monogamy mean for the couple concerned and how might this impact on the child or children living in the household? In raising this issue, there is an honesty in this couple's approach towards their assessment process that should be welcomed, as many couples are involved in extra-marital affairs in secret, which often have disastrous consequences for relationships when unearthed. With regard to exploring many of the different ways lesbians and gay men create their own rules in terms of how they live their lives, Harding discusses the interplay between the law, sexuality and parenthood, and highlights not only the complexity of the process but the drive, commitment and acts of resistance from the lesbians and gay men who go through the assessment process.

> This type of resistance is not one which could be described as working 'against' the system, as adoptive/foster parents have no choice but to work within the framework of rules set down by governmental actors such as social services, social workers and adoption panels … all these parents have had to battle against discriminatory provision, and have succeeded in their desire to become parents (Harding 2011: 100).
>
> Adoption, like everything else, takes place in a social, cultural, political and economic context, and although many positive legal changes have brought about legal equality within adoption for lesbian and gay prospective adopters alongside their heterosexual counterparts, these, 'have not (yet) sufficiently disrupted the heteronormative assumptions that underpin the ideological force of "the family"' (Harding, 2011: 106).

Some of the more obvious differences for lesbian and gay prospective adopters are their coming out experiences and the effect this may have on extended family support and their different family gender constructs and what this might mean regarding the family's particular experiences living within their particular local community. This may or may not be significant. Hitherto, for some lesbians and gay men, having the state in their sitting room as a part of the assessment process meant different things, as for many years their home was one of a very few private spaces where societal and institutional discrimination did not occur. However, practice is now changing, but it may well be that it is the current legal framework that is changing social work practice in this area, rather than social work advocating for fairness and equity because of injustice. Brown (2011) showed that social workers in statutory and voluntary sector organisations are becoming more confident and competent in their skills in conducting assessments of lesbians and gay men as prospective foster carers and adopters.

After adoption

As difficult as the adoption assessment is, it is just the beginning of a much longer process. In looking at the experiences that lesbian and gay adopters have post-adoption, it is clear that there are different hurdles for these adopters than their heterosexual counterparts. One example of this is the constant coming out process for the parents, and to a certain extent the child, within the school environment. Lesbian and gay parents constantly have to explain their family structure to school teachers, other parents and a variety of agencies in a way that heterosexual parents do not have to. There are also differences in the narrative that is told with regard to how children came to be in lesbian and gay families. This differs from the majority of heterosexual families, except possibly those heterosexual families who have adopted, because the assumption is that the children of heterosexual parents are birth children, unless people are told otherwise, whereas that is not the assumption made about the children of lesbian and gay parents. As one gay adopter commented:

> Where the gay thing plays out differently is that every single person who comes to our house, asks about it, where you got them, where they came from, particularly children, as the parents are slightly embarrassed about it. The adoption group at school, adoptive parents worry about whether they should tell someone or not. It's a bit like coming out. We are the opposite, there is no way you can pretend, as gay men, it has to be explained and I am endlessly telling people the story of how we came together. It's never an unpleasant thing. Both of you share that relationship with the school.
>
> (Gay adopter A, Cocker et al, 2013: 11)

There are also some things that lesbians and gay men are good at, having (unfortunately) experienced decades of homophobia: 'LGBT are very accustomed to dealing with and negotiating difficulties' (gay adopter B, Cocker et al, 2013: 14). Cocker et al, 2013 also show that sometimes the challenge for the adopted children of lesbians and gay men is not about their parents' sexuality at all. For lesbian and gay adopters, their experiences in schools shows that for their children it is far more difficult coping with the long-term effects of adversity that led to the need for the children's adoption in the first place. Two gay adopted fathers commented that, for their children, having gay dads is not the biggest issue at school – the reasons for the children's adoption is more pertinent in terms of the effect this has on the children's ability to learn in the classroom. This has been discussed previously in relation to the specific needs of adopted children and the ongoing support often required from education and Child and Adolescent Mental Health Services (Brown and Cocker, 2011; Cocker, 2011; Cocker and Allain, 2013). There is concern that agencies may have a negative view of lesbian and gay parents, and see their help seeking as indicative of problematic parenting rather than an act of strength (Brown and Cocker, 2008).

The role of class and other inequalities

According to Dana Berkowitz, much of the research about lesbian and gay kinship and families has not sufficiently addressed issues of race and social class, and the intersectionality of heterosexism, and class dynamics within LGBT families is complex (Berkowitz, 2011). I have also found this in my own research, where lesbian and gay adopters have commented about the nature of class as a significant but unspoken issue in adoption. As one gay adopter commented:

> Class is totally the issue, for the children coming into a posh family where nothing about their previous lives that would make any sense. There is a sense of wanting to wipe the slate clean, for example, the whole thing about coming to London, having to reframe their lives, all of which fits the dream of being adopted. Definitely, that was the thing, the changes that they have made, have been totally about that and not about gay parenting.
>
> (Gay adopter A, Cocker et al, 2013: 7)

Hicks (2011) also concurs that class is not often talked about in relation to lesbian and gay parenting. The mobility of adopted children across class boundaries should be discussed, as class is an important determinant of identity and kinship. In some quarters, adoption is seen as the last in a long line of efforts by the state at 'social engineering', with a number of conservative figures, such as Christopher Booker writing in the *Daily Telegraph* (2010) and the MP John Hemming (BBC, 2011) commenting that much adoption practice in the UK is a human rights issue – a way of forcibly removing working-class children from poor families into middle-class families, without giving working-class families the opportunities to defend themselves. This is referred to as 'forced adoption' (see http://www.childprotectionresource.org.uk/forced-adoption). Paradoxically perhaps, this view is shared by Spade and Willse (2013) who write from a queer left perspective – and locate increased adoption as a part of a neo-liberal economic policy. Although this is a rather crude analysis, it shows the powerful interplay of issues and emotions present in adoption from all sides of the political spectrum. The reason why class is important in debates about adoption is that by far the majority of children who are adopted now have had early experiences of abuse or neglect and are predominantly from poor families, whereas the majority of adopters are middle class.

The majority of adopters are also white. Official statistics show that children from minority ethnic communities are over-represented in care

(Department for Education 2013) and there has been concern that many children from these communities wait longer for adoptive placements than do their white counterparts. This is one reason for the coalition government's push for change in policy regarding ethnicity not being the primary factor used to match a child with prospective adopters, but it never was the only factor. This remains a controversial area of practice in the UK (Frazer and Selwyn, 2005; Wood, 2009), driven by government policy and legislation (Selwyn and Wijedasa, 2009; Cocker and Anderson, 2011: 167–70). There is not enough known about the ethnicity of lesbian and gay prospective adopters to know whether there is more variation in ethnicity in the partnerships of lesbians and gay men and the communities from which they come, which would support trans-racial placements.

Conclusion

Some queer activists critique the rise of same-sex marriage and adoptions within lesbian and gay families as a step towards assimilation and respectability. Spade and Willse from the USA argue that marriage does nothing for the status of the majority of lesbians and gay men and is instead a tool of gendered social control, material distribution and protection of material wealth (2013). Marriage equality then creates a barrier between LGBT partnerships and family forms, which are seen as 'state sanctioned', and those lesbians and gay men who choose to live their lives outside this legal structure. For many lesbians and gay men, to have legal equality by way of 'parental responsibility' in their parenting roles is an important step in the state legitimising their family choices regarding adoption, and they see this as a positive development. However, civil partnership or same-sex marriage is not necessary for lesbians and gay men to adopt. Parenting status and civil partnership/same-sex marriage are separate issues. The reason for this is because successful parenting has nothing to do with the emotional attachment that may come with a public endorsement of a partnership between two people, but having parental responsibility affects the way in which public services then relate to the adults within the family, for example at school and accessing health services, in the everyday actions involved for adults being parents to their children. Having equal legal status as parents is very helpful but civil partnership/marriage is not necessary for this to be given to the adults when they adopt. Homophobia is still experienced by adopters in many different ways during the process of adoption, so civil partnership and marriage will not help this. Those lesbians and gay men who are civilly partnered or married are more likely to fit the bill of 'pedestal of virtue' (Hicks 2000) and more likely to make 'the grade' and one could argue that they are emulating heteronormative structures and patterns of behaviour by their choices. But I worry about who this leaves out from the process. No one has the right to be an adopter, but if we continue to rely on current societal conceptions of what makes a family, it means we are fishing in a pretty shallow pool.

We need more families and single adults to adopt children. New policy and guidance expects councils to approve more people in quicker time-scales. So do we need to think differently about what defines a family? It is unfortunate that social work practice continues to reinforce this 'othering' of alternative family structures. Whilst the legislative changes may have, in turn, transformed the current context for social work practice with lesbians and gay men, challenges for practice remain. Dugmore and Cocker suggest that 'the legislative framework will only be as effective as the practitioners and managers responsible for its implementation' (2008: 166). Discussions about lesbian and gay issues in social work remain marginalised, and continue to be neglected by social work researchers, teachers and practitioners in conversations around equality and diversity within social work. Given that social work is a profession committed to working with excluded communities, this is shameful.

Legislation does not force people who think homosexuality is immoral and wrong to change their views; however, it does require them to be more tolerant and treat people alike (Brown and Kershaw, 2008: 129). Mellish et al. believe that:

> with increased experience of working with same-sex prospective adopters in the future, and with increased training, gay and lesbian parents entering the adoption system should not face the same explicit or implicit homophobia as did the 'pioneers' of lesbian and gay adoption.
> (2013: 38)

Let us hope so. However, the discussion now needs to move on from one of 'equality' to appreciating and seeing as positive the complex family forms and structures that lesbians and gay men create in their lives.

Notes

1 The five areas were: 1. The individual's experience of their homosexuality (their own and their families' response historically); 2. How confident they feel in relation to their sexuality and how comfortable they are as lesbians and gay men; 3. How homophobia and heterosexism has impinged on their lives and how they feel they dealt with this and what coping devices they use; 4. Their present relationships – sexual, emotional, supportive, family, etc – and how they negotiate homophobia within close relationships (eg with siblings); 5. Transition to parenthood – making links with the local community regarding child care resources and contact arrangements with birth family members of fostered/adopted children.

2 SPRIINT is an acronym that stands for: Sexual orientation; Previous sexual relationship histories; Relationships (current); Intimacy (the expression of this with each other); Integration into the community; Not so nice bits: digging below the surface; exploring the long term nature of relationships; coping with

difficulties, stress, disagreements etc; Think: about the patterns and the gaps within the stories being told.

References

Averett, P., Nalavany, B. and Ryan, S. 2009. An evaluation of gay/lesbian and heterosexual adoption. *Adoption Quarterly*, 12, 129–51.

BBC. 2011. MP claims 1,000 children 'wrongly' adopted every year. Available at: http://www.bbc.co.uk/news/uk-politics-16157124 [accessed 28 April 2014].

Bailey, J. M., Bobrow, D., Wolfe, M. and Mikach, S. 1995. Sexual orientation of adult sons of gay fathers. *Developmental Psychology*, 31, 124–29.

Barrett, H. and Tasker, F. 2001. Growing up with a gay parent: views of 101 gay fathers on their sons' and daughters' experiences. *Educational and Child Psychology*, 18, 62–77.

——2002. Gay fathers and their children: what we know and what we need to know. *Lesbian and Gay Psychology Review*, 3, 3–10.

Berkowitz, D. 2011. 'It was the Cadillac of adoption agencies': intersections of social class, race, and sexuality in gay men's adoption narratives. *Journal of GLBT Family Studies*, 7, 109–31.

Booker, C. (2010) Forced adoption is a truly dreadful scandal. *Telegraph*, 3 July. Available at: http://www.telegraph.co.uk/comment/columnists/christopherbooker/7870342/Forced-adoption-is-a-truly-dreadful-scandal.html [accessed 28 April 2014].

British Agency for Adoption and Fostering (BAAF) (2013) *Adoption Register Annual Report 2013*. Available at: http://www.adoptionregister.org.uk/sites/default/files/basic_page_file_uploads/Adoption_Register_Annual_Report_2013.pdf [accessed 28 April 2014].

Brown, H. C. 1991. Competent child-focused practice: working with lesbian and gay carers. *Adoption and Fostering*, 15, 11–17.

——2011. The assessment of lesbian and gay prospective foster carers: twenty years of practice and what has changed? In Dunk-West, P. and Hafford-Letchfield, T. (eds) *Sexual Identities and Sexuality in Social Work: Research and Reflections from Women in the Field*. Farnham: Ashgate.

Brown, H. C. and Cocker, C. 2008. Lesbian and gay fostering and adoption: out of the closet into the mainstream? (Report). *Adoption & Fostering*, 32, 19.

——2011. *Social Work with Lesbians and Gay Men*. London: Sage.

Brown, H. C. and Kershaw, S. 2008. The legal context of working with lesbians and gay men. *Social Work Education*, 27, 122–30.

Chambers, S. A. 2007. 'An incalculable effect': subversions of heternormativity. *Political Studies*, 55, 656–79.

Cocker, C. 2011. Sexuality before ability? The assessment of lesbians as adopters. In Dunk-West, P. and Hafford-Letchfield, T. (eds) *Sexual Identities and Sexuality in Social Work: Research and Reflections from Women in the Field*. Farnham: Ashgate.

Cocker, C. and Allain, L. 2013. *Social Work with Looked After Children*. London: Learning Matters/Sage.

Cocker, C. and Anderson, J. 2011. Adoption. In Cocker, C. and Allain, L. (eds) *Advanced Social Work Practice with Children and Families*. Exeter: Learning Matters.

Cocker, C. and Brown, H. C. 2010. Sex, sexuality and relationships: developing confidence and discernment when assessing lesbian and gay prospective adopters. *Adoption & Fostering*, 34, 20–32.

Cocker, C. and Hafford-Letchfield, T. 2010. Out and proud? Social work's relationship with lesbian and gay equality. *British Journal of Social Work*, 40, 1996–2008.

Cocker, C. Hafford Letchfield, P. and Barran, C. 2013. Case studies of LGBT Families. Middlesex University/RAINBOW HAS. Available at: http:www.rainbowhas.eu/docs/Great_Britain/4%20Case%20Studies%20families%20GB.pdf.

Daily Telegraph 2010, http://www.telegraph.co.uk/comment/columnists/christopherbooker/8148987/Forced-adoption-another-win-for-the-child-snatchers.html. Accessed 3 March 2015

Department for Education. 2013. *Statistical First Release 2013 38 – National Tables Children Looked After 1*. London: Crown Copyright.

Dugmore, P. and Cocker, C. 2008. Legal, social and attitudinal changes: an exploration of lesbian and gay issues in a training programme for social workers in fostering and adoption. *The International Journal*, 27, 159–68.

Erich, S. 2005. Gay and lesbian adoptive families: an exploratory study of family functioning, adoptive child's behaviour and familial support networks. *Journal of Family Social Work*, 9, 17–32.

Erich, S., Hall, S. K., Kanenberg, H. and Case, K. 2009. Early and late stage adolescence: adopted adolescents' attachment to their heterosexual and lesbian/gay parents. *Adoption Quarterly*, 12, 152–70.

Erich, S., Leung, P. and Kindle, P. 2005. A comparative analysis of adoptive family functioning with gay, lesbian and heterosexual parents and their children. *Journal of GLBT Family Studies*, 1, 43–60.

Frazer, L. and Selwyn, J. 2005. Why are we waiting? The demography of adoption for children of black Asian and black mixed parentage in England. *Child and Family Social Work*, 10, 135–47.

Goldberg, A. E. 2010. *Lesbian and Gay Parents and their Children: Research on the Family Life Cycle.* Washington: American Psychological Association.

Golding, J. 2003. Children with lesbian parents: a community study. *Developmental Psychology*, 39, 20–33.

Golombok, S. 2000. *Parenting: What Really Counts?* London, Routledge.

——2007. Foreword: research on gay and lesbian parenting: an historical perspective across 30 years. *Journal of GLBT Family Studies*, 3, xxi–xxvii.

Golombok, S., Perry, B., Burston, A., Murray, C., Mooney-Somers, J., Stevens, M., Golombok, S., Spencer, A. and Rutter, M. 1983. Children in lesbian and single parent households: psychosexual and psychiatric appraisal. *Journal of Child Psychology and Psychiatry*, 24, 551–72.

Golombok, S., Perry, B., Burston, A., Murray, C., Mooney-Somers, J., Stevens, M., and Golding, J. 2003. Children with lesbian parents: A community study. *Developmental Psychology*, 39, No. 1, 20–33.

Golombok, S. and Tasker, F. 1996. Do parents influence the sexual orientation of their children? Findings from a longitudinal study of lesbian families. *Developmental Psychology*, 32, 3–11.

Hanscombe, G. and Forster, J. 1982. *Rocking the Cradle: Lesbian Mothers, a Challenge in Family Living*. London: Sheba Feminist Publishers.

Harding, R. 2011. *Regulating Sexuality: Legal Consciousness in Lesbian and Gay Lives.* Abingdon: Routledge.
Hicks, S. 2000. Good lesbian, bad lesbian … regulating heterosexuality in fostering and adoption assessments. *Child and Family Social Work*, 5, 157–68.
——2005. Lesbian and gay foster care and adoption: a brief UK history. *Adoption and Fostering*, 29, 42–56.
——2006. Genealogy's desire: practices of kinship amongst lesbian and gay foster-carers and adopters. *British Journal of Social Work*, 36, 761–76.
——2008. Thinking through sexuality. *Journal of Social Work*, 8, 65–82.
——2011. *Lesbian, Gay and Queer Parenting: Families, Intimacies, Genealogies.* Basingstoke: Palgrave.
——2014. Deconstructing the family. In Cocker, C. and Hafford-Letchfield, T. (eds) *Rethinking Anti-Discriminatory and Anti-Oppressive Theories for Social Work Practice.* Basingstoke: Palgrave.
Hicks, S. with Greaves, D. 2007. *Practice Guidance on Assessing Gay and Lesbian Foster Care and Adoption Applicants.* Manchester: Manchester City Council.
Hicks, S. and McDermott, J. 1999. *Lesbian and Gay Fostering and Adoption: Extraordinary yet ordinary.* London: Jessica Kingsley Publishers.
Hill, N. 2009. *The Pink Guide to Adoption for Lesbians and Gay Men.* London: British Association for Adoption and Fostering.
Jennings, S., Mellish, L., Tasker, F., Lamb, M. and Golombok, S. 2014. Why adoption? Gay, lesbian, and heterosexual adoptive parents' reproductive experiences and reasons for adoption. *Adoption Quarterly*, 17(3), 205–26.
Kindle, P. A. and Erich, S. 2005. Perceptions of social support among heterosexual and homosexual adopters. *Families in Society*, 86, 541–46.
Lavner, J. A., Waterman, J. and Peplau, L. A. 2012. Can gay and lesbian parents promote healthy development in high-risk children adopted from foster care? *American Journal of Orthopsychiatry*, 82, 465–72.
Leung, P., Erich, S. and Kanenberg, H. 2005. A comparison of family functioning in gay/lesbian, heterosexual and special needs adoptions. *Children and Youth Services Review*, 27, 1031–44.
Mallon, G. A. B. 2005. *Recruiting, Assessing and Supporting Lesbian and Gay Carers and Adopters.* London: British Association for Adoption and Fostering.
Mellish, L., Jennings, S., Tasker, F., Lamb, M. and Golombok, S. 2013. *Gay, lesbian and heterosexual adoptive families: family relationships, child adjustment and adopters' experiences.* London: British Association for Adoption and Fostering.
Monk, D. 2015. Sexuality and children post equality. In Leckey, R. (ed.) *After Legal Equality: Family, Sex, Kinship.* London: Routledge.
Patterson, C. J. 2004. Gay fathers. In Lamb, M. (ed.) *The Role of the Father in Child Development.* 4th edn. New York: John Wiley.
——2005. *Lesbian and Gay Parenting.* Washington: American Psychological Association.
Philp, M. 1979. Notes on the form of knowledge in social work. *Sociological Review*, 27, 83–111.
Richardson, D. 1981. Lesbian mothers. In Hart, J. and Richardson, D. (eds) *The Theory and Practice of Homosexuality.* London: Routledge & Kegan Paul.
Rights of Women Lesbian Custody Group 1986. *Lesbian Mothers' Legal Handbook.* London: The Women's Press.

Ryan, S. and Whitlock, C. 2009. Becoming parents: lesbian mothers' adoption experience. In Mercier, L. R. and Harold, R. D. (eds) *Social Work with Lesbian Parent Families: Ecological Perspectives.* New York: Routledge.

Selwyn, J. and Wijedasa, D. 2009. The placement of looked after minority ethnic children. In Schofield, G. and Simmonds, J. (eds) *The Child Placement Handbook: Research Policy and Practice.* London: British Agency for Adoption and Fostering.

Skeates, J. and Jabri, D. 1988. *Fostering and adoption by lesbians and gay men.* London: London Strategic Policy Unit.

Spade, D. and Willse, C. 2013. Marriage will never set us free [Online]. Organizing Upgrade. http://www.organizingupgrade.com/index.php/modules-menu/beyond-capitalism/item/1002-marriage-will-never-set-us-free [accessed 28 April 2014].

Tasker, F. 2013. Book review: Hicks S. (2011) *Lesbian, gay and queer parenting: Families, intimacies, genealogies. Journal of GLBT Family Studies*, 9, 302–4.

Wood, M. 2009. Mixed ethnicity, identity and adoption: research, policy and practice. *Child and Family Social Work*, 14, 431–39.

Chapter 7

Civil partnership and ordinary marriages

Brian Heaphy

Introduction

In the UK and elsewhere, civil unions and same-sex marriage signal the extent to which the everyday possibilities for same-sex relationships have altered radically in recent decades. Here, I consider how such possibilities were engaged with by 'younger' generations of same-sex civil partners prior to legalisation of same-sex marriage, and highlight a shift that is occurring in culturally dominant constructions of same-sex relational life. Until relatively recently, personal and broader cultural narratives of same-sex relationships were framed in terms of 'otherness'. Nowadays, such narratives are as – if not more – likely to be framed in terms of 'ordinariness'. Generational dynamics, as they are linked to social and legal developments, are key to understanding this shift, and I argue here that a generational sub-sector of relatively 'young' same-sex partners, who model their relationships on 'the ordinary', are poised to become the hegemonic – or culturally dominant – narrators of the new realities of same-sex relationships.

The chapter begins by briefly outlining developments in the 'privatisation' of marriage and the 'intimate turn' in same-sex relational cultures that are the backdrop to shifting personal claims about the distinctive or ordinary qualities of same-sex relationships. It then draws on a study based on joint and individual interviews with 50 couples, where both partners were aged up to 35 when they entered into in civil partnership, to consider how the majority interpreted and constructed civil partnership as a form of marriage. Following this it considers how couples compared their own formalised relationships to the heterosexual marriages they grew up with and lived alongside, and how they sought to achieve 'good' marriages by adopting ordinary – or conventional – marriage practices. In conclusion, I draw out how younger generational stories of ordinary same-sex marriages fit especially well with the claim that sexual minority battles for citizenship have been 'won', and also with mainstream claims about the continuing salience of marriage. By virtue of this fit, and the introduction of 'full' same-sex marriage in mainland UK in 2014, the story of same-sex relational ordinariness is poised to become a hegemonic one – even if it limits as much as it expands everyday understandings of relational 'rights', equality and citizenship.

The privatisation of marriage and the turn to intimacy

For over a decade now, same-sex couples in the UK have had access to civil partnership, which, some commentators suggest, is marriage only under a different name (Weeks, 2010: 130). As of 2014, same-sex couples in Britain also have legal access to marriage. So, it seems, the battle for the legal recognition of same-sex relationships in the UK is almost won, and this combined with the host of equalities legislation introduced in the 2000s shores up the idea that in legislative terms lesbian and gay citizenship has been achieved in the UK (Heaphy et al., 2013: 16–17). However, now that same-sex couple formalisation has become embedded in the UK, it is timely to consider the everyday implications of the terms on which same-sex relationship recognition and citizenship has been claimed and achieved.

In terms of everyday practices, by the time civil partnerships were introduced in the UK in 2004, marriage had long been the focus of contingent commitments, where partners cohabited, married, may or not have had children, divorced, and could then cohabit with or marry another partner or, indeed, a series of partners. By then, marriage sat alongside myriad other possibilities for organising adult heterosexual relationships (for example, cohabitation, serial and more ad hoc partnering, 'living apart together'). In the 1980s, cohabitation was already well established as precursor or an alternative to marriage, and Mansfield and Collard (1988: 4) noted the definition of marriage itself was changing and in practice being extended to encompass a broad range of relationships. They linked this to changes in the public image of marriage where there was a shift 'in emphasis from the external structure of married life to the private meaning of marital relationships: the public institution of marriage has become privatized' (1988: 4).

Indeed, the definition of marriage had become so extended by the 1980s that the term 'informal marriage' was sometimes used in policy debates to include cohabiting and committed couples. Well before civil partnership came into law, 'marriage' could, notionally at least, refer to all manner of committed couple relationships, so it was only a matter of time before same-sex couples should be included within the definition of informal marriage and then seek formal recognition of the status – not least because cohabitation did not (and still does not) afford legal recognition for relationships. Despite this, and the claims made to relational citizenship by critical sexual communities from the 1980s onwards, there is some research evidence of a high degree of ambivalence about marriage amongst sexual minorities themselves (Mitchell et al., 2009; Weeks et al., 2001).

The intimate turn

In terms of lesbian and gay politics, it has been argued that the 1980s saw a shift from an emphasis on identity to a concern with relationships and intimacy. Claims to citizenship by sexual minorities were framed in relational terms at a time when same-sex relationships and 'queer' families were denigrated in law and policy (symbolised most vividly in the UK by Section 28 of the Local Government Act 1988, which prevented local authorities from promoting homosexuality as 'pretended family relationships'). Such denigration was the result of anxieties that were linked to sexual 'liberation', lesbian and gay parenting and AIDS, that were inflamed by the New Right. At the heart of these claims were demands for respect and recognition of lesbians' and gay men's significant relationships at a time when their personal decisions about (co-)parenting, 'chosen' next-of-kin, end-of-life care and inheritance could be, and often were, contested. Such claims gathered further momentum throughout the 1990s and into the 2000s as a politically confident generational sub-sector of lesbians and gay men, who had forged their identities through their engagements with feminist and critical sexual communities of the 1960s and 1970s, were reaching a chronological age when issues of next-of-kin, inheritance, pension benefits, care, bereavement and support were especially pertinent.

Combined with the 'privatisation of marriage', the 'intimate turn' in lesbian and gay politics might be interpreted as providing the initial impetus for claims to same-sex marriage. However, a study of same-sex intimacies and chosen families that my colleagues and I conducted eight years before the introduction of civil partnership suggested that, amongst lesbians and gay men, the idea that marriage was the preferred way of recognising intimate and relational 'rights' was far from universally accepted. Commenting on this finding, we stated:

> [The] tension between wanting to be treated equally, yet not really desiring the heterosexual option of marriage, was a common theme we encountered […]. While most non-heterosexuals in this study think that they should have the choice to get married, and a small minority would like to get married, there are also those who feel that […] their relationships are – or have the potential to be – radically different from heterosexual relationships. And thus, marriage is perceived to be a restrictive institution of the state, epitomizing the worst aspects of heterosexuality with its prescribed gendered roles and unequal power balance.
>
> (Weeks et al., 2001: 192–93)

As noted in the above quotation, participants in that mid- to late 1990s study (most of whom would now be aged over 50) emphasised *the difference* between their relationships and heterosexual married ones. They saw their own relationships as more conducive to working towards 'equality' on the basis of gender sameness. They drew on examples from their own previous heterosexual relationships and marriages, as well as those of their parents and heterosexual friends and associates, to underline the distinctiveness of their relationships in terms of creative constructions of family that did not necessarily prioritise legal or 'blood' ties over friendship bonds (except in the case of children). Such constructions did not usually prioritise 'the couple' as the exclusive focus of sexual and emotional intimacy and commitment, and were underpinned by a critical aspiration to co-independence as opposed to the 'interdependence' that was the hallmark of constraining and unequal heterosexual relationships. In terms of legal recognition, the dominant desire was for the recognition and protection of their relationships as they were – be they cohabiting, co-parenting, friendship or couple based, multi-partnered, polyamorous, sexually and emotionally monogamous or not – and not through the 'imposition' of marriage.

In light of the range of relationships that critical sexual communities sought recognition for, and their ambivalence about couple-centred families and marriage, where did the political push for recognition in the form of same-sex *couple* and *marriage* 'rights' come from? Some have argued that this push reflected the economic and social interests of global lesbian and gay political elites, while others argue that it represented the grassroots desires of 'ordinary' lesbians and gay men (Weeks, 2010). These are not incompatible arguments. Rather, it is likely that by the 2000s, the public and behind-the scenes activities of lesbian and gay political elites converged with the desires of cross-generational sub-sectors of lesbians and gay men whose aspirations to 'ordinariness' made couple and marriage 'rights' seem like the obvious focus of claims to intimate and relational citizenship (even if there were alternatives; see Donovan et al., 1999). While the ordinary marriage desires of older and mid-life same-sex partners were often dismissed by critical sexual communities as reactionary attempts to 'ape' heterosexuality, those of younger generational sub-sectors have been less easy to dismiss because of the prevailing sense that nowadays heterosexual and same-sex relationships are very much alike in that neither blindly follow a script and that marriage is a 'lifestyle' choice that should be open to consenting adults. Younger civil partners certainly shared this view, as we shall see after a brief description of the study that generated younger partners' personal narratives of formalised relationships.

'Younger' civil partnerships

The reminder of this chapter draws on personal narratives of relating that were generated through joint and individual interviews with 50 couples, where partners were aged up to 35 when they entered civil partnership. The study that generated the interviews was funded by the Economic and Social Research Council (ESRC reference: RES-062-23-1308) and was carried out in 2009–11, before the current government's plan to introduce same-sex marriage was announced. It was undertaken by Brian Heaphy, Carol Smart and Anna Einarsdottir. Equal numbers of male and female civil partners were recruited with the help of registrar offices in urban and rural settings in England and Wales, and through the General Registrar Office of Scotland. Fifty partners were aged between 25 and 30 when they entered into civil partnership, 43 partners were aged between 30 and 35, and the remaining number were aged under 25. Ages at the time of interview ranged from the early 20s to the late 30s. The sample was mainly white (91 participants), but was mixed in terms of the indicators of social class, rural/urban location and religion. Eight female couples had children in their care, but none of the men did. Relationship length ranged from less than six months to over ten years, and civil partnership length from one month to five years. Couples were first interviewed together and then separately. Joint interviews were focused on the 'couple story' of the relationship, and individual interviews were focused on personal relational histories and socio-biographically shaped orientations to relating.

The cohorts included in the study are those that were born between the mid-1970s and the late 1990s. They had entered into their teens between the mid- to late 1980s and the early 2000s, and entered into their 20s between the mid-1990s and the late 2000s. If one of the defining experiences of earlier cohorts was that of a more or less absolute heterosexual landscape (where the public visibility of homosexuality was highly policed and enforced), one of the differentiating aspects of younger cohorts' experience is the increasing visibility of sexual minorities. By the mid-1980s homosexuality had entered the public consciousness through AIDS, but also through battles against negative representations of lesbian and gay relationships. By the late 1980s, public debates about lesbian and gay families were in full swing and Denmark had legalised same-sex unions. By the mid-1990s (when the oldest of the younger cohorts were aged in their mid-twenties and the youngest were still young children) same-sex relationships were being represented in the media and television programmes such as *Friends, Ellen, Brookside, Queer as Folk* and the such as. By the mid-2000s civil partnership was culturally constructed as akin to marriage in the UK. Thus, these cohorts have to a greater or lesser degree grown up with the cultural visibility of lesbian and gay identities and same-sex relationships, and will have legal recognition for their identities and relationships (in variety of ways) for most of their adult lives. Many had grown up with a sense of the relative ordinariness of lesbian and gay identities and same-sex relationships or developed this fairly early on in their lives. I now turn to the narratives tha the majority of study participants told of civil partnership as a form of marriage.

Just like marriage

> It's nice that a same-sex relationship has the potential to be able to view each other as husbands and married, and it's been quite wonderful […] the support of friends and people that have said to us, 'Wow, I really admire the commitment' it's so great, you know sign of the times that we are the first sort of revolutionary era in terms of same sex relationships that this is possible
>
> (OJ, 225b)

OJ's comments above point to three striking themes that emerged in younger civil partners' narratives, which were linked to the distinction between their and previous generations' same-sex relational experience. First, was the extent to which younger partners were confident and comfortable with using the terminology of marriage to describe their relationships. Of the 100 partners, 74 described and presented themselves as married, and it is mostly these partners' narratives that I focus on here. It is these kinds of sub-generational narratives, I suggest, that are poised to become culturally dominant in representing the new realities of same-sex relationships. While civil partnership has often been termed 'gay marriage' in the mainstream culture, civil partners deployed marriage terminology partly to underscore that civil partnership was a legitimated form of commitment – that was just like marriage, despite the fact that civil partnership and marriage were legally distinct. In line with the privatisation of the meaning of marriage as discussed earlier on, couples emphasised that personal meanings mattered as much, if not more than, the legal distinctions. As Sara put it: 'I just think that we were both raised with parents who were married and we've been around people who are married and we consider we have a marriage' (Sara, 121b). Many partners believed that while marriage and civil partnership were technically different, the 'rights' were the same. As Jorge (205b) put it: 'we've never really ever felt discriminated against in that it [is] a civil partnership and not full marriage, the rights are the same, only the name'. As civil partnership was a legally formalised relationship, it could make sense to see it as not merely 'like' marriage, but as being a form of marriage, especially because the everyday practices involved in 'doing' heterosexual and same-sex relationships were perceived to be the same – a point that Kathryn (105a) and Louise (105b) make in the following exchange:

KATHRYN: I probably view it in the same way as a marriage

LOUISE: Yep, don't see it any differently […] you get on my nerves sometimes, I get on yours, other times we don't

KATHRYN: You've got decisions to make about your family

LOUISE: Decisions to make, yeah, you're knackered at the end of the day, […] running around doing a hundred and one things

KATHRYN: Yeah, and as we've said before, the majority of our friends are married and heterosexual and we just

LOUISE: Don't see any difference.

Second, while OJ refers to the support and admiration of 'friends and people', most younger partners talked about the support and validation for their marriage that they received from family of origin, friends and other associates (for example, work colleagues). In contrast to previous generations, the majority of younger civil partners were not estranged from family of origin because of their sexuality. While participants' parents could initially be unsettled by the idea that their child was lesbian, gay or in a same-sex relationship, this was mostly resolved in a relatively short period of time. Also, in contrast to older cohorts, younger partners did not recount encountering hostility from their lesbian and gay peers for 'selling out' by entering a heterosexual institution (Smart et al., 2006). In most cases, family, friends and close associates seemed to acknowledge that civil partnership was 'the same' as marriage, and were willing to actively participate in supporting the couple in their entry into 'marriage':

> I think in my experience of […] entering into civil partnership, I think most of my friends, the people that I'd discussed it with, were also referring to it […] as getting married.
>
> (Otto, 212a)

> [My] sister really wanted us to get married while she was still alive […] Tammy's mama paid for the food, my mam paid for the hall and the disco.
>
> (Hanna)

Younger couples mostly described their civil partnership ceremonies and celebrations as 'weddings'. These were often critical moments where partners, families, friends and other associates confirmed the authenticity of the marriage, and marked the couple's achievement of a mature relational status. Overall, most (but not all) partners' immediate and extended family members were willing, if invited, to participate in the ceremonialism surrounding the entry into civil partnership. Tim recounted how older members of his extended family were initially nervous about attending their first same-sex wedding. However, according to his partner Fredrick, 'to this day, [they] say, "Oh, it's the best wedding I've ever been to […] it was so lovely […] It was so romantic." In light of such responses it is understandable that the "marriage" and the wedding made the commitment "more complete"' (Tim, 209b).

Like heterosexual couples, same-sex couples were faced with a range of 'conventional' and 'alternative' options for their ceremonies and celebrations, and couples could model, borrow from or wholly reject 'traditional' ceremonies and weddings (with the exception of religious elements). Overall, decisions were made in accordance with their lifestyles, tastes and aspirations. However, one common element of approaches to the 'wedding' was the seriousness with which partners and their personal networks treated the occasion. Some partners explicitly rejected what they termed a 'gay wedding' style, on the basis that it could become a 'circus' or would seem 'ridiculous' to the guests. OJ (225b) and his partner, for example, did not want to obstruct the 'real' message of becoming family, so opted for 'an austere wedding […] it was about becoming family […] it was a serious event and I think both of us were very keen that the way the event was organised would show that to us'. Developing Berger's and Kellner's (1964) classic point about the ceremonialism of marriage, civil partnership ceremonies, celebrations and weddings could *confirm* the couple's 'reality' with respect to civil partnership being an authentic form of marriage. As Berger and Kellner suggest, the ceremonialism surrounding marriage is indicative of the ways in which 'the groups with which the couple associates are called upon to assist in co-defining [the couple's] reality' (1964: 9). In this respect, family, friends and personal associates were not called upon to simply witness the couples' expression of their commitment, but to be actively involved in co-defining the reality of their 'marriage' and in co-constructing the 'little world' that, Berger and Kellner contend, married life becomes.

Third, like OJ, many younger partners viewed the introduction of civil partnership as indicative of a revolutionary era as far as same-sex relationships were concerned. Despite growing up with the relative social acceptance of same-sex relationships, few had expected that they would be able to marry. As Cori put it: 'I don't even think that was something that even occurred to me as an option [it] is completely different […] a million miles away from when I was a kid.' In this respect partners often presented themselves as at the cutting edge of social change. However, while previously dominant (or hegemonic) generational sub-sectors saw their *novel* and *distinctive* relational forms as 'revolutionary', the dominant story that younger civil partners tell is of the ground-breaking opportunities they have to *embrace* social norms and conventions, and to have 'ordinary' marriages. As Tim and Fredrick put it:

TIM: It's almost like a process you go through [*laughs*] of kind of getting to know someone, going out with them, and kind of the next complete step of that is kind of marriage […] I think that's where we got to, wasn't it?

FREDRIK: It's kind of the way that society does things […] [you] expect that your life process is to meet someone, you marry them, you grow old together

As Fredrik's comments make clear, younger same-sex partners were not always naïve about how their desires to marry were socially shaped. Rather, they often reflexively – or knowingly – *chose* ordinary or mainstream conventions with respect to couple commitment, marriage and family.

'Good' marriages and ordinary marriage practices

Previously dominant narratives of lesbian and gay life have emphasised the implications of non-heterosexual identity for social relocation from families and communities of origin to 'chosen' families and affective communities. Such narratives tended to be centred on two claims: that estrangement from 'given' families and communities could have high personal costs, but that they also enabled a degree of freedom from the norms and practices associated with heteronormativity (see Plummer, 1995). Building on this latter claim, it has been argued that because of their gender sameness, non-heterosexual relationships are guided by an ethos of creativity, egalitarianism and co-independence (as opposed to an ethic of interdependence that defines heterosexual coupledom) (Blasius, 1994; Weeks et al., 2001). In these constructions, because heterosexual coupledom, marriages and family forms were viewed as foundation stones of the heteronormative order, they were rejected as models for same-sex relating.

Younger civil partners could be critical of what they termed 'traditional' models of coupledom, marriage and family form on the basis of the (gendered) roles and constraints they implied. However, because of their aspirations to ordinariness they did not wholly reject 'given' or conventional models of relating and marriage. Rather, in reflecting on the marriages they had grown up with – those of their parents' generations – they identified marriages that were 'unhappy' and 'ambivalent', but also those that were 'good' which they aspired to. Also, in terms of the everyday practices in which their marriages were grounded, they adopted conventions that they believed were common to the 'good' marriages they lived alongside: those of their heterosexual generational peers.

'Good' marriages

In reflecting on the marriages that they were most familiar with – their parents' – partners tended to 'fix' them in accordance with three kinds of marriage: the 'unhappy' marriage, the 'ambivalent' marriage and the 'good' one. The unhappy parental marriage was one that was not entered into for love but for the 'wrong reasons'. In practice, it involved little mutual respect, communication and limited sharing between partners who had not 'fully' given themselves to the relationship. Partners in unhappy parental marriages were thought to have had little choice but to follow 'traditional' expectations that one *should* marry, and to engage in 'traditional' male and female 'roles' and family practices. Such marriages were deemed to be inherently unstable and volatile because of the resentments, arguments and separations that could ensue over time. As Louise (105b) put it, her father was often 'in a temper' because 'he was married to someone he didn't love, but I guess it's a different generation isn't it'. Partners in such relationships, and especially women, were often cast as victims of tradition, as Theresa noted: 'it was quite traditional […] my Dad made the decisions' (Theresa, 216b).

The ambivalent marriage contained many characteristics of the unhappy marriage. Its foundation may have once been love, but had transformed into duty. It was distinct from the unhappy marriage in that couples tried to make the best of their lot and do the best they could. Above all it was stable, but short on communication. As Todd (214b) put it:

> I haven't tried to emulate their relationship [*laughs*] any way, shape or form and nor will I ever want to. I think my mother and father have struggled on and you know duty bound […] tried to work things out […] so that duty, that sense of duty [keeps them together].

In contrast to the unhappy and ambivalent marriage, the 'good' parental marriage did provide a model to aspire to, and was the one that most closely approximated the relationships that younger same-sex partners claimed to have. It was based on love, and involved working together on potential problems, being in it for the long run and standing by each other through thick and thin. Above all, it entailed mutual respect and communication and a high degree of stability. As Ellen (114a) recounted:

> What I think I have inherited or brought from seeing them is a big thing about respect and communication. And that they're both very important in the sense that my parents had a great deal of respect for each other, and that means that you take the time to understand the other person's opinion […] my parents' relationship was largely very stable.

In describing their parents' marriages, younger partners articulated the marriage ideals that they worked towards in their relationships: an enduring commitment that was based on love and grounded in practices of *mutual* decision-making, commitment, sharing, communication, respect and equality. In discussing their parents' marriages as they did, they also articulated the belief that it was not the gender make-up of the relationship per se that made for a 'good' contemporary marriages or otherwise, but the everyday practices through which partners chose to construct their marriages. Good marriages, they believed, were nowadays equally open to same-sex *and* heterosexual couples. While they reflexively – or knowingly – identified 'traditional' demands, expectations, norms and sanctions as underpinning unhappy or ambivalent marriages amongst their parents' generation, they believed that 'tradition' no longer held the sway it once did, leaving the door open for heterosexual couples to choose or negotiate an egalitarian marriage. In these respects, contemporary heterosexual and same-sex 'marriages' were very much the same. Kevin (205a) and Jorge (205b), for example, saw such similarities as linked to the interpersonal challenges that *all* partnerships involved. As Kevin remarked:

> I think the key thing is that […] being in a partnership is you're a team and you kind of, deal with the good and bad stuff as a team and it's kind of what it's about really. And generally there's more, you know you hope for more good than bad, but you know life's a bit full of surprises, so […] the partnership thing is about working through stuff together and being a team really.

The benefits of formalising the couple commitment went far beyond a narrow conception of legal 'rights'. Rather, civil partnership as a kind of marriage formalised the commitment to working towards an enduring relationship as a team, and this in turn could provide a sense of enhanced security and stability in the relationship itself, and in day-to-day living. As the following participants put it:

VICTOR (216B): I think it feels more secure to me […] it's given a sense, a feeling of stability. You know, because it's more formal.
OLIVER (210B): […] having done that then it does feel more
BEN (210A): Secure
OLIVER: And serious.

Because younger same-sex partners associated unhappy, ambivalent and unequal marriages with 'tradition' and the constraints faced by previous generations, and not with institutionalised heterosexuality itself, in a post-traditional era it could make sense to see heterosexual and same-sex marriages as much the same. However, their definitions of 'good' and 'ordinary' marriages were as conventional as they were 'post-traditional'. Indeed, there are striking similarities between the ideals and practices that younger same-sex couples describe, and those of their parents' generations as outlined in Mansfield's and Collard's 1980s study of newly wed heterosexual couples (who would have included the generational peers of our interviewees' parents). Mansfield and Collard found that when asked to reflect on their parents' marriages, newly-weds considered such marriages to be '"good" because they had been secure and stable' (1988: 15). Also, their participants who could articulate specific aspects of marriage that they viewed as a model referred to 'sharing and companionship and their fathers having shown respect for their wives' (1988: 16). In short, there are notable continuities in what was defined as 'good' marriage by younger heterosexuals in the early 1980s and younger same-sex partners in the late 2000s: security, stability, sharing, companionship and respect. Mansfield and Collard also found a considerable degree of naivety with respect to marriage expectations amongst newly-wed women especially, but also men. Newly-weds had expected their relationships to continue along the lines of mutuality in which they were formed, but in reality they soon became entrapped in conventional practices of (unequal) relational labour. This could undermine the sense that marriage was a joint or 'team' project and a primary source of stability and security, and lead to the kind of ambivalent marriages that were discussed earlier on. This raises the question about the extent to which younger same-sex couples knowingly engaged with – or chose – conventional marriage practices and the consequences for the 'ordinary' marriages they claimed to have.

Ordinary marriage practices

Compared with the couples studied by Mansfield and Collard, younger same-sex couples seemed more reflexive or less naive about the marriage conventions they embraced. As noted earlier, it was not unusual for couples to acknowledge that desires to marry were socially shaped, or to be critical of 'traditional' marriages on the basis of the constraints and inequalities they supported. However, by constructing past generations' marriages as 'traditional' they cast their own marriages – and those of their heterosexual generational peers – as 'post-traditional' ones. Thus, it could make sense to claim, as they did, that contemporary same-sex and heterosexual marriages were free of the entrapments of tradition. In post-traditional circumstances, this logic implied, partners and couples were free to adopt and discard conventions as they choose. Yet, the limits of their reflexivity and knowingness with respect to marriage conventions was evident in their subscription to a key 'truth' that guided their commitment practices: that the couple is, or should be, the 'natural' and 'inevitable' focus of adult relationships, families and a secure and contented life. As Neil (218b) put it: 'It's nice to come home to somebody. I certainly wouldn't want to be single, certainly wouldn't want to be gay and single ... because I don't see it as being really much of a life, do you?'

A committed couple relationship was often framed as a driving desire or even an essential need, rather than a choice, and entry into civil partnership or 'marriage', along with the wearing of wedding rings, adopting the same surnames and the use of spousal terminology were practices that could testify to a sense of pride in having achieved this 'natural' aspiration. In addition, amongst those couples that wanted to parent children, civil partnership or 'marriage' could also be seen as a natural desire to provide a legitimate and stable family environment. To reduce such aspirations and desires to the ideology of the couple risks trivialising personal life as it is experienced on the ground. At the same time it is the case that younger partners' accounts displayed little evidence of an engagement with cultural critiques of the primacy of the couple. Rather, there was a tendency to frame personal 'quests' to meet and commit to 'someone' as part of an ordinary and natural need for love. 'To be alone, it's not our, […] Human beings, they need to be, feel that they are loved at some point in their life. And they need to give love to someone' (Radinka, 103a).

Committing to 'someone' was also commonly framed as a mature and responsible practice. Younger partners emphasised that they entered into civil partnership for themselves, to confirm already existing commitments. In practice, however, civil partnerships made these commitments publically visible and intelligible as mature and responsible ones, and could also prompt the couple to review or change their relating practices. For example, while most couples were already engaged in mutual care prior to the civil partnership, the formalisation of the relationship was viewed as an explicit commitment to the ongoing nature of such practices in the long run, but could also be the basis for securing joint responsibility for broader family care. This was highlighted in Hanna's (108a) and Tammy's (108b) narratives, where Tammy, reflecting on recent family events including the illness and death of Hanna's sister, a family member's disability and another member's bankruptcy, commented that 'all the sort of caring responsibilities [for both their families] always seem to end up on us', and Hanna recounted:

> I'd like to think that if anything happened to Tammy […] that I'd stand by her through thick and thin […] like me Dad stood next to me Mam […]. When [Mam's disability] started coming on […] their friendships started to disappear […] they've just got each other and obviously like me and me brother […] they're quite happy and I think sometimes that's all you need if you've got like the love of your family.

Hanna's comments about the family (including partners) as being the most reliable source of love and care raise the issue of the links between friendship and 'family' practices. While friends were clearly significant to many younger partners, only in 28 out of one 100 cases did they seem to be as centrally significant as suggested by studies of previous generations of lesbians and gay men (Weston, 1995; Weeks et al. 2001). This seems in large part due to the convention that ordinary married couples rely first and foremost on their partners and families of origin for material, financial and emotional support and physical care, while friends are for socialising and additional emotional support. In terms of their socialising practices, many partners claimed to have moved beyond commercial and sexual minority scene-based activities, and now socialised with other couples. In doing so, they implied their now formalised couple commitments had marked a transition to mature adult status. Eric (220a) recounted how, besides a couple of gay friends, 'all of our other friends are just normal heterosexual couples'. By emphasising their friendships with 'just normal … couples' young partners often underscored how aspirations to relational ordinariness could influence, and be influenced by, the couple-centred 'little worlds' they constructed.

Claims to maturity, responsibility and ordinariness also emerged as significant in partners' accounts of their emotional and sexual commitments. The majority of young partners assumed the well-established convention of emotional and sexual monogamy, which they often equated with a 'mature' and 'responsible' commitment. However, the fact that a total of 26 out of 100 interviewees had explicitly agreed the nature of their emotional and sexual commitment illustrates that young same-sex partners do not always follow convention in an unthinking way. At the same time, the fact that only five couples in total agreed to sexual non-monogamy underlines the continuing salience of the conventional links between sexual exclusivity and commitment, even if couples were aware of the alternative possibilities. Also, in their individual accounts several partners indicated that the conventional association between sexually monogamous and stable relationships meant that they or their partners were unwilling to address the possibility of sexual non-monogamy – even where sex was a rare or non-existent feature of the relationship. Sex itself, especially where it concerned one partner's declining sexual 'drive', was not always openly discussed in the relationship, often out of fear that revealing different or declining sexual desires could destabilise the relationship. This could cause a considerable degree of anxiety, as Natalie (117b) recounted in discussing her experience of her declining sex drive within relationships:

> It's kind of happened in this relationship as well but […] it's to do with me [not my partner …] it's happened before in a previous relationship because I just did not want to. I didn't feel attracted to the person anymore. And, also wasn't great, [I] was on medication etc. and just, it wasn't happening and I just … I don't know I've just got issues with it […] I just seem to lose my sex drive really. And then it'll come back. But it's, it's a bit of a problem really, I'm not happy about it.

Finally, younger civil partners approaches to finances were not 'traditional', in that they commonly held joint accounts to pay for household bills, mortgages, rent and joint purchases, and held separate accounts for personal items and savings. However, this approach also seems to be emerging as a mainstream convention, with 50 per cent of heterosexual couples in the UK adopting it (see Vogler and Pahl, 1994), particularly younger heterosexual couples (Vogler et al., 2006). Nevertheless, the conventional idea that marriage was a springboard for the mature and responsible organisation of the couple's finances could still be a powerful one, especially when it came to practices with respect to debt. Over a third of civil partners had accumulated debts prior to civil partnership, and this could cause a considerable degree of tension where one partner was in debt and the other debt-free, or where partners' biographically habituated approaches to accumulating or avoiding debt were very different. Debt and different practices with respect to it could, like different or declining sexual desires, also introduce a degree of instability into the relationship. Thus, well-established marriage conventions (such as those linked to practices of family care and sexual monogamy) and emerging conventions (such as those linked to practices of financial management and debt) could not guarantee the 'good' relationships and stable and secure 'little worlds' that younger partners sought to achieve.

Conclusion

The same-sex partners whose personal narratives were considered here do not represent the diversity of relationships that it is possible for younger generations of sexual minorities to construct. They do, however, represent the realities of a generational sub-sector whose accounts of their relational desires, ideals and practices are likely to become the hegemonic – or dominant – in broader cultural constructions of 'good' same-sex relationships and marriages. This is largely because their stories do not *fundamentally* challenge, but shore up, already existing mainstream (or conventional) understandings of 'good' relationships and marriages. While they challenge the idea that heterosexuality is an essential element of a 'naturally' and socially good marriage, they leave intact core relational norms that underpin the idea that marriage is a 'natural', social and legal institution that is the 'right' choice for a stable and secure way of living, and for broader social order. They do not trouble existing norms about 'good' marriages, but underscore the value of both long-established as well as emerging marriage conventions. In these respects they are distinct from the stories of relational experimentation told by previously hegemonic – or dominant – generational sub-sectors that sought to more thoroughly deconstruct such norms.

As Mansfield's and Collard's work in the 1980s suggested, the public institution of marriage has become privatised. However, as they show with respect to gendered practices, it is mistaken to suggest that privatisation means that marriage is free-floating from its histories or conventions. Rather, whatever its make-up (heterosexual or same-sex) or its form (self-defined, civil partnership or 'full' marriage), 'marriage' continues to provide cultural guidelines, social supports and state-sponsored benefits for *specific* ways of organising relational life. In theory and in practice people may choose not to follow these models. However, as was illustrated by the younger same-sex couples discussed here, numerous incentives still exist that encourage people to 'choose' marriage, and to model their relationships on the ordinary: not least the links that are made in mainstream culture between couple commitments and the 'natural' couple-centred family, love, mutual care, mature social status, financial responsibility, family and community connectedness, emotional and sexual monogamy, and enhanced security and stability. Not only did the couples discussed here subscribe to the belief that couple-centred commitments should be the focus of their ordinary 'little worlds', they also worked hard at constructing ordinary marriages around which their little worlds were centred.

Now that 'full' same-sex marriage has been legalised in Britain, the stories of ordinary marriages told by younger generational sub-sectors of same-sex partners seem poised to become incorporated into more mainstream cultural narratives of the continuing salience of marriage – for a sense of social, familial and personal security and order. At the same time, more radical relational experiments in alternatives *to* marriage and couple-centred ways of doing relationships and families (for example, friendship-based families, elective parenting networks, polyamorous and non-monogamous relationships and communal living) seem likely to become less visible and more marginalised in terms of social and legal supports. While the social and legal recognition of same-sex marriage is a battle that has been won for future generations in mainland Britain, battles for recognition and support of radically diverse same-sex *and* heterosexual relational lives (including the non-couple centred lives of the ever increasing numbers of unmarried cohabitees and those who live alone) seem to be lost for the immediate future at least. In summary, while it may be timely to celebrate same-sex couples' rights to be ordinary, it is also timely to reflect on the ways in which adults in non-couple-centred relationships continue to be socially and legally cast – or ignored – as 'other'.

References

Berger and Kellner (1964) 'Marriage and the social construction of reality', *Diogenes*, 12(46): 1–24.

Blasius, M. (1994) *Gay and Lesbian Politics: Sexuality and the Emergence of a New Ethic*. Philadelphia, PA: Philadelphia University Press.

Donovan, C., Heaphy, B. and Weeks, J. (1999) 'Citizenship and same sex relationships', *Journal of Social Policy*, 28(4): 689–709.

Heaphy, B., Smart, C. and Einarsdottir, A. (2013) *Same Sex Marriages: New Relationships, New Experiences*. Basingstoke: Palgrave Macmillan.

Mansfield, P. and Collard, J. (1988) *The Beginning of the Rest of your Life?* Basingstoke: Macmillan.

Mitchell, M., Dickens, S. and O'Connor, W. (2009) *Same-Sex Couples and the Impact of Legislative Changes*. London: NatCen.

Plummer, K. (1995) *Telling Sexual Stories*. London: Routledge

Smart, C., Mason, J. and Shipman, B. (2006) 'Gay and lesbian 'marriage': an exploration of the meanings and significance of legitimating same-sex relationships'.

http://www.socialsciences.manchester.ac.uk/medialibrary/morgancentre/ research/gay-marriage/gay-marriage-findings.pdf [Last accessed 3 March 2015].

Vogler, C. and Pahl, J. (1994) 'Money, power and inequality within marriage', *The Sociological Review*, 42(2): 263–88.

Vogler, C., Brockmann, M. and Wiggins, R. (2006) 'Intimate relationships and changing patterns of money management at the beginning of the twenty first century', *British Journal of Sociology*, 57(3): 455–82.

Weeks, J. (2010) *Sexuality*. London: Routledge.

Weeks, J., Heaphy, B. and Donovan, C. (2001) *Same Sex Intimacies: Families of Choice and other Life Experiments*. London: Routledge.

Weston, K. (1991) *Families We Choose: Lesbians, Gays and Kinship*. New York: Columbia University Press.

——(1995) 'Get thee to a big city: Sexual Imaginary and the great gay migration', *GLQ*, 2(3): 253–77.

Chapter 8

The Church of England and gay marriage

What went wrong?

Giles Goddard

On 12 April 2014, the first same-sex marriage in a church was held at the Metropolitan Community Church in Bournemouth. On the same day, Rev. Jeremy Pemberton became the first Anglican clergyman to marry his same-sex partner. The *Mail on Sunday* headline read: 'First gay clergyman to wed plunges Church into crisis: Archbishop under pressure to sack canon who flouted ban on same sex marriage' (Petre, *Mail Online*, 12 April 2014). But the Bishop of Lincoln, Rev. Pemberton's superior, simply commented: 'The priest concerned wrote to me in advance to explain his intention and we had a subsequent meeting in which I explained the guidelines of the House of Bishops' (ibid.). At the time of writing, there is inconsistency in the Church of England's (C of E) response to Rev. Pemberton's marriage. In one diocese in which he acts as a priest, his licence to practise has been withdrawn, but in Lincoln Diocese no serious sanctions have been taken. A second priest, Rev. Andrew Cain, married his partner on 21 June 2014. It is likely that there will be many more same-sex marriages by clergy, and that the blessing of same-sex marriages will be carried out in many parishes in the C of E.

The C of E's official response to the introduction of civil partnerships, and then of equal marriage, has been consistently negative. The House of Bishops resisted the civil partnerships proposals and offered only half-hearted acceptance once they had been introduced. The C of E's statements and actions during the legislative process for same-sex marriage were also consistently oppositional. As a result, the C of E is now out of step with public opinion and with the legislature, and has lost an opportunity to engage with a large proportion of English society.

What went wrong? How did the Church manage to put itself so completely on the traditionalist side of the arguments over lesbian, gay, bisexual and transgender (LGBT) inclusion, despite the diversity of opinion within its own ranks, and despite strong public encouragement to take a more positive line?

I am a parish priest in central London. I have been working for greater inclusion since my ordination in 1996; I was for five years chair of the lobbying organisation Inclusive Church, and am now a member of the General Synod. I have been very closely involved in debates and conversations at all levels of the church on questions of human sexuality. This chapter seeks to give a personal view of how and why the C of E has found itself in its current position. It considers how the church's structures and polity tend to work against innovation. It reflects on how three factors have together created a resistance to change within the Church – first, the complexity and unaccountable nature of Church structures, second its strong sense of tradition, and third its role as the C of E established by statute. But it also identifies areas of hope, and ends with an assessment of the potential for progress.

Complexity, tradition, establishment

By any standard, the C of E is a complex institution. Power is dispersed among several bodies, and relationships between them are in some cases structural and in others rely on consent. The Archbishop of Canterbury has no structural authority over his colleagues in the House of Bishops. He is *primus inter pares*, first among equals. The Archbishops' Council, chaired by the Archbishops of Canterbury and York, has a limited remit including financial oversight of the activities of the Church House bureaucracy. The General Synod is the only body other than Parliament entitled to make laws for England. However, individual parishes are technically independent, and individual clergy usually have tenure, which trumps the rights of the diocesan Bishop, although he or she is understood to have moral authority over the clergy.

The closest equivalent the C of E has to a board of directors is the House of Bishops – made up of the bishops of the 44 dioceses along with seven elected suffragans. The House of Bishops is one of the three Houses of the General Synod – the other two are the House of Clergy and the House of Laity – and is understood to have a leadership role. The C of E is said to be 'episcopally led, synodically governed'. But statements issued by the House of Bishops have only moral authority; canon law can only be introduced or amended by General Synod, and any canon law passed by Synod must then be authorised by Parliament and signed by the Queen.

The C of E is like a convoy of different sized boats, and there is little to stop the boats going in different directions. The voices of those who are conservative on questions of human sexuality have been disproportionately dominant in recent decades; conservative evangelical Christians have, for example, been effective in elections to the General Synod, resulting in a stronger presence there that would be expected from their representation within the church at large.

In addition, the C of E is part of the Anglican Communion, which consists of 42 independent provinces, across the world – mainly defined by nationality and in most cases a legacy of the British Empire. The Anglican

Communion includes churches that are predominantly liberal and inclusive – such as the Episcopal Church of the United States, the Anglican Church of Canada and the Anglican Church in New Zealand – and churches which are mainly conservative on questions of sexuality and gender – for example, the Anglican Church of Uganda and the Anglican Church of Nigeria. The Archbishop of Canterbury's role is both senior bishop of the Province of Canterbury and 'focus of unity' for the Anglican Communion; as such, both the previous and the present incumbents have resisted moves towards liberalisation in the C of E for fear of alienating other provinces.

The C of E is an institution with a strong sense of tradition. It was originally created as a result of King Henry VIII's desire to divorce Catherine of Aragon – evidence that marriage as a fault line within the church is not new. Initially, it retained the structure and hierarchy of the Roman Catholic Church, simply replacing the Pope with the King. But Henry's daughter Elizabeth I pursued a policy that developed the C of E as a 'broad church'. Trying to bring an end to the murderous conflicts between Catholic and Protestant, she encouraged the C of E to define itself through practice rather than doctrine – she is said to have asserted that 'I do not wish to make windows into men's souls'. Her permissive policy is indicated by the fact that two of her court composers, Thomas Tallis and William Byrd, retained their Catholic faith until their death. England at the time, as now, contained a very wide range of interpretations of Christian faith, from stern Puritanism to ritualist Catholicism: Elizabeth and her advisers tried with some success to create one church that included all, and this breadth has continued to the present day.

The C of E's status as the established church of England has a part to play. The church's state-supported role diminished greatly during the twentieth century, particularly after the 1945 post-war settlement established universal state education and health care. It retains a role in education – over 5,000 schools in England are identified as C of E – but numbers of church weddings, baptisms and funerals carried out by the C of E are in steady decline. However, the role of parish clergy as registrars for marriages is one of the very few remaining functions where the church acts as an arm of the state.

As a result of all these factors, the C of E has become fiercely protective of the traditional role of marriage in society. Debates in the General Synod on any subject related to marriage are well attended and attract speakers determined to defend both the traditional understanding of marriage, and the church's role as registrar.

The openness and complexity of C of E structures means that its internal disagreements tend to be very public, and difficult to resolve. Much of the church's energy has been taken up, over the past 20 years, with argument over ordination of women as priests and then as bishops.

Meanwhile, the church has taken retrograde steps in relation to LGBT Christians. As society has become more affirming, the official stance has becoming less accepting. For many years – probably for centuries – the C of E has offered a place of safety for gay men; there have been disproportionate numbers of gay men in the ranks of the clergy (the first women were ordained in 1992) but an atmosphere of 'don't ask, don't tell' has been replaced by an atmosphere of fear and anxiety in direct contradistinction to the increasing welcome within secular society of LGBT people. The House of Bishops has struggled to find a satisfactory line that acknowledges not only the reality of same-sex relationships but also the concerns of conservative Anglicans. Its first official statement on the subject – *Issues in Human Sexuality* – was issued in 1991. It offered grudging acceptance to lay people who were lesbian or gay (or 'homophile', in its odd use of language), but included the now notorious paragraph 5.17: 'We have, therefore, to say that in our judgement the clergy cannot claim the liberty to enter into sexually active homophile relationships' (House of Bishops, 1991: para 5.17).

Since then, a series of statements either by the House of Bishops or by Church House, some of which are discussed below, have hardened the official line that lesbian or gay clergy are expected to refrain from sexual activity. But these statements conceal a much more nuanced situation. Dr Geoffrey Fisher, the Archbishop of Canterbury at the time of the Wolfenden Report, supported decriminalisation, saying in 1957 that: 'There is a sacred realm of privacy … into which the law, generally speaking, must not intrude. This is a principle of the utmost importance for the preservation of human freedom, self-respect, and responsibility' (quoted in Jeffery-Poulter, 1991: 33).

In 1979, the C of E's Board for Social Responsibility produced a report 'Homosexual Relationships; a contribution to the discussion'. But this was considered too liberal by many, and the House of Bishops requested the current Dean of Salisbury, June Osborne, to produce a further report. That report was produced in 1989: it was also considered too liberal, and suppressed. It was finally published, illicitly, in January 2012.

In 1994, Jeffrey John, then Canon Theologian of Southwark Cathedral, published a monograph, *Permanent, Faithful, Stable* (John, 1994), which called for the recognition of same-sex relationships. Individual clergy have been offering blessings for same-sex relationships since at least the 1970s, and many clergy – it is difficult to know precise numbers but there are reliable estimates suggesting 500 couples – have entered into civil partnerships, often with the tacit or explicit support of their bishops.

Within the ranks of the C of E there has always been a great diversity of practice and belief. This diversity has been reflected within the ranks of the House of Bishops; I have spoken with many bishops who are frustrated by the current situation; but, collectively, the House has been increasingly determined to resist change.

Bishops are expected to be the 'focus of unity' for their dioceses; for most, this means taking the line of least resistance. In large part this is a response to the traditional nature of the church, and the mistrust of modernity among many of its members. Same-sex relationships are seen as a radical departure from the witness of scripture, reason and tradition for which the present age does not have authority. Archbishop Rowan Williams said in the Archbishop of Canterbury's Advent Letter for 2007:

> We recognise each other in one fellowship when we see one another 'standing under' the word of Scripture ... Understanding the Bible is not a private process or something to be undertaken in isolation by one part of the family. Radical change in the way we read cannot be determined by one group alone.
>
> (Archbishop of Canterbury's Advent Letter, 2007)

Most opposition to equal marriage within the C of E comes from those who are more in the Protestant tradition – that is those who identify with the strand of Christianity that seeks inspiration from theologians such as Martin Luther and John Calvin. This strand – often known as evangelical Christianity – maintains that the Bible contains all knowledge necessary for salvation and holiness. *Sola Scriptura*, scripture alone, holds the truth, and scripture is self-authenticating.

The sociologist of religion Linda Woodhead (2013) recently carried out a survey which demonstrated that:

> The section of religious people most opposed to same-sex marriage is made up of those who both (a) believe in God with certainty and (b) make decisions primarily on the basis of explicit religious sources – God, scriptures, teachings and religious leaders.

Amongst this group, closely allied to the Christian Right in the USA, homosexuality has been turned into a line in the sand (Herman, 1997). In October 1994, a broad cross-section of Religious Right groups met at a secret summit in Colorado to discuss a co-ordinated effort to combat the 'gay agenda'. Representatives from more than 40 groups attended, including Focus on the Family, Concerned Women for America, the Christian Coalition, the Family Research Council, the Traditional Values Coalition, the Eagle Forum and the American Family Association. Many of these groups are not part of the Episcopalian Church (the Anglican church in the USA); but their influence is strong within American Christianity. Opposition to LGBT inclusion and equal marriage is often allied to opposition to women in leadership, and to a traditionally patriarchal approach to family life. (See, for example, Held Evans, 2014.) Explicit connections are regularly made by the leaders of conservative provinces – notably but not exclusively those in sub-Saharan Africa – between the decline of moral standards in the West and the acceptance of same-sex marriage. The issue has crossed continental boundaries; there are well-documented connections between the Religious Right in the USA and the repressive laws that have recently been passed in Uganda and Nigeria (Rawls, 2012).

The status of the C of E as the established church has also contributed to its championing of heterosexual marriage; it has come to see itself as the guardian of tradition. The Archbishops' Council resisted the proposals for civil partnerships in these terms: 'As they stand these proposals risk being seen as introducing a form of same-sex marriage with almost all of the same rights as marriage.'[1] During the parliamentary debates on civil partnerships a significant number of the House of Bishops supported a wrecking amendment that would have extended civil partnership rights to members of the same family living together. Six bishops voted in favour of the wrecking amendment, one against. But when the amendment was introduced a second time, only two bishops voted in favour and eight against.

When the Marriage (Same Sex Couples) Bill was under consideration, the Bishops were subject to the most extensive lobbying campaign they had ever experienced. Those who wrote in were preaching to the choir. The Church of England's response to the proposals said:

> Such a move would alter the intrinsic nature of marriage as the union of a man and a woman, as enshrined in human institutions throughout history. Marriage benefits society in many ways, not only by promoting mutuality and fidelity, but also by acknowledging an underlying biological complementarity which, for many, includes the possibility of procreation.[2]

In the main debate in the House of Lords, on 3 June 2013, the Archbishop of Canterbury said:

> The result [of the proposed legislation] is confusion. Marriage is abolished, redefined and recreated, being different and unequal for different categories. The new marriage of the Bill is an awkward shape, with same-gender and different-gender categories scrunched into it, neither fitting well. The concept of marriage as a normative place for procreation is lost. The idea of marriage as a covenant is diminished. The family in its normal sense, predating the state and as our base community of society, as we have already heard, is weakened.[3]

The polity of the C of E, then, has created a climate of resistance to same-sex marriage, despite the range of opinion among its members. As indicated earlier, those who continue to take a traditional line claim theological and biblical support for their views; they refer to the witness of scripture and of tradition. But so do those who support liberalisation. A brief look at the biblical roots of the disagreement follows.

'It's not biblical!'

There have always been controversies in Christianity. The first Council of Jerusalem was called in around 50 CE by the early followers of Christ, including St Peter and St Paul, to try to reach agreement on whether or not Gentile Christians should be required to follow Jewish law. There have been numberless disagreements since – some leading to religious wars and others resulting in a new understanding of an aspect of Christianity, for example regarding slavery or the ordination of women.

The controversy over the equal treatment of LGBT people contains a particularly toxic combination of factors that, shaken together and stirred, has become explosive. These include: power and patriarchy, authority and freedom, identity, institutional integrity, scriptural interpretation and the place of the Bible, and ritual purity.

Opponents of same-sex marriage regularly cite scripture as the foundation for their opposition. 'Bible-believing' is often code for traditionalist views on these matters, and those who want change are accused of betraying or ignoring the Word of God. Evangelicals and liberals have different understandings of the nature of the Biblical witness. Liberals tend to understand the Bible as having an overall emphasis on the love of God, but recognise that it was written in a particular time for particular people. The moral codes and prohibitions cannot, therefore, be simply read off the page and applied to twenty-first-century society. Evangelicals tend to hold that the codes and prohibitions retain their force, although in practice some prohibitions have more force than others.

Given the heat of the debate, there is surprisingly little material in scripture on the subject of same-gender sexual relationships. The Bible contains only seven references: the story of Sodom and Gomorrah in Genesis 19, the prohibitions of male-to-male relations in Leviticus 18.22 and 20.13, Romans 1.27, I Cor 6.9–10, I Timothy 1.10 and Jude 7 (referring to Genesis 19).

All of these are open to different interpretations. There is now general acceptance that the story of Sodom does not help the traditionalist view; when the residents of Sodom ask Lot to send out his two visitors 'that we may know them', he refuses, and offers to send out his virgin daughters instead. The mob then attack the house to destroy it, at which point the mob are blinded, and then the city is destroyed. The sin of Sodom is generally taken to be radical inhospitality; the residents of the city refused to offer hospitality to visitors. The destruction of the city is the result.

The Levitical references to same-gender sexual relationships are also of limited usefulness; there is too much in Leviticus that is now ignored (including the wearing of mixed fibres, the consumption of pork and the nailing of slaves' ears to doorposts for insolence) to enable a strong case for the observation of these two verses to be made.

The Greek words that are used in I Cor 6.10 (*arsenokoitai*) and I Timothy 1.10 (*malakoi*) are of too unclear a meaning to be applicable to twenty-first-century situations – *arsenokoitai* appears to be closely related to Temple prostitution and *malakoi* to a form of effeminacy among men. Certainly neither mean 'lesbian' or 'gay' in the way in which these terms are understood in English.

Referring to Romans 1.27, Rowan Williams (2007) points out that the text:

> is not very helpful to the conservative cause ... because Paul insists on shifting the focus away from the objects of moral disapprobation in chapter 1 to the reading/hearing subject who has at this point been happily identifying with Paul's castigation of someone else ... Paul is making a primary point not about homosexuality but about the delusions of the supposedly law-abiding.

Others consider that the Romans verse is not relevant because it refers to people acting against their own nature; and if same-gender attraction is innate, then this does not pertain.

Christians working for greater inclusion often cite the story of David and Jonathan in the first book of Samuel, and of the 'disciple whom Jesus loved' in the Gospel of John. They often place the two 'Great Commandments' to love God and to love your neighbour as yourself as the overriding biblical principles; the rest of scripture is to be read through the lens of the love of God and neighbour, so that, in the words of the letter to Galatians 3.28, 'There is no longer Jew or Greek, there is no longer slave or free, there is no longer male and female; for all of you are one in Christ Jesus'.

In this controversy, there are also deep issues of purity and impurity. Just as, in former centuries, women menstruating were considered 'unclean' or marriages between people of different ethnic groups were illegal in many countries, so, now, lesbian and gay people have become the scapegoats in the desire for purity which is often linked with religious conviction. The Laws in the Hebrew Scriptures were created with the very specific aim of enabling the people of Israel to keep themselves pure, and untouched by the ways of the peoples around them – the Canaanites, the Jebuzites, the Hittites, the worshippers of Baal. Much of the Holiness Code in Leviticus is to do with ensuring that the Israelites remain separate and remain identifiable:

> You shall keep all my statutes and my ordinances, and observe them, so that the land to which I bring you to settle in may not vomit you out. You shall not follow the practices of the nation that I am driving out before you.
>
> (Lev, 20:22).

For many on the conservative wing of the church, the 'other' is the 'homosexual'.

There are similarly diverse views on the meaning and significance of marriage. For some, the heart of the matter is the sanctity of the sacrament of marriage; marriage is seen as the fullest human expression of the relationship between Christ and his Church, and is also understood, on the basis of Genesis 2.24, to be exclusively heterosexual: 'Therefore a man leaves his father and his mother and clings to his wife, and they become one flesh.' Others respond that the essential characteristics of marriage are love, fidelity, commitment; that gender is a secondary characteristic, and that in any case the Bible is not a good sourcebook for examples of ideal marriage – they cite, for example, Abraham's begetting of children by Hagar his slave girl and Sarah his wife, and Solomon's 700 wives and 300 concubines (1 Kings 11.3).

Within the C of E, arguments over the interpretation of scripture and arguments from tradition quickly reach stalemate. The church's revision of its understanding of slavery and the role of women are often cited by progressives in support of change; conservatives assert that same-sex relationships are in a different category.

My own experience of discussions on these matters bears this out. I initiated a public email correspondence with Andrew Goddard, a leading conservative evangelical, 'Goddard 2 Goddard', in 2006/7, which ran for over a year and was published on the websites of Inclusive Church and Fulcrum.[4] I have also met privately with members of Anglican Mainstream, a group that works closely with the Anglican churches of sub-Saharan Africa and conservative groups in the USA, as well as with members of the Evangelical Group on General Synod and many others. These meetings have been characterised by an expressed desire on the part of the conservatives to get to know and indeed to become friends with me as a gay person in a relationship. But every time the question of the acknowledgement in church of a same-sex relationship has emerged, or the appointment of a lesbian or gay bishop, we have reached impasse. There is no killer blow to close off the discussion.

Chipping away

In seeking to oppose same-sex marriage, therefore, the House of Bishops has been faced with a particularly difficult challenge. The theological arguments are inconclusive. And the subtlety of the staged approach to its introduction has caused the House additional difficulties. The Bishops half-heartedly acknowledged the legitimacy of civil partnerships in their Pastoral Statement published on 25 July 2005. The statement reiterated the traditional view that marriage is exclusively heterosexual:

> The new legislation makes no change to the law of the land in relation to marriage. It remains the case that in law, as in the eyes of the Church, marriage can be entered into only by a man and a woman. The Government has stated that it has no intention of introducing 'same-sex marriage'. Civil partnerships are not a form of marriage … The

> legislation does, however, leave entirely open the nature of the commitment that members of a couple choose to make to each other when forming a civil partnership. In particular, it is not predicated on the intention to engage in a sexual relationship.
>
> (House of Bishops, 2005: para 5)

On these grounds, albeit reluctantly, the House of Bishops opened the possibility of prayerful response to civil partnerships:

> It will be important, however, to bear in mind that registered partnerships do allow for a range of different situations – including those where the relationship is simply one of friendship. Hence, clergy need to have regard to the teaching of the church on sexual morality, celibacy, and the positive value of committed friendships in the Christian tradition. Where clergy are approached by people asking for prayer in relation to entering into a civil partnership they should respond pastorally and sensitively in the light of the circumstances of each case.
>
> (House of Bishops, 2005: para 18)

It went on to recognise the likelihood of clergy entering into civil partnerships:

> Partnerships will be widely seen as being predominantly between gay and lesbian people in sexually active relationships. Members of the clergy and candidates for ordination who decide to enter into partnerships must therefore expect to be asked for assurances that their relationship will be consistent with the teaching set out in Issues in Human Sexuality [i.e. that the relationship is celibate].
>
> (House of Bishops, 2005: para 21)

Although the House of Bishops could hardly have been less enthusiastic about the existence of civil partnerships, this statement recognised the reality of legally registered same-sex relationships, and acknowledged the church's responsibility to respond appropriately:

> What needs to be recognised is that the Church's teaching on sexual ethics remains unchanged. For Christians, marriage – that is the lifelong union between a man and a woman – remains the proper context for sexual activity. In its approach to civil partnerships the Church will continue to uphold that standard, to affirm the value of committed, sexually abstinent friendships between people of the same sex and to minister sensitively and pastorally to those Christians who conscientiously decide to order their lives differently.
>
> (House of Bishops, 2005: para 27)

The door was thus opened to the recognition of legally constituted same-sex partnerships. By the time equal marriage legislation was introduced by the coalition government, significant numbers of clergy had already entered into civil partnerships and many services of thanksgiving or blessing had been held in church.[5] The grounds for opposing equal marriage were therefore weakened. Bishops and others in authority had worked out forms of words that enabled them to satisfy the letter of the Pastoral Statement if not its spirit; one Diocesan bishop told me that his approach was to say: 'I am required to ask whether your relationship is celibate, but you are not required to answer.'

Civil partnerships were widely understood in society and within the church to be a good thing, encouraging mutual fidelity and support; so how could the House of Bishops oppose the rectification of what was perceived by many, including the prime minister, to be an obvious anomaly in the law?

The undated 'Response to the Government Equalities Office Consultation – "Equal Civil Marriage" – from the Church of England' recognises this difficulty. Paragraph 9 reads:

> We are conscious that within both Church and society there are men and women seeking to live faithfully in covenanted same sex relationships. As we said in our response to the consultation prior to the same sex marriage legislation, the proposition that same sex relationships can embody crucial social virtues is not in dispute. "Same sex relationships often embody genuine mutuality and fidelity, two of the virtues which the Book of Common Prayer uses to commend marriage. The Church of England seeks to see those virtues maximised in society".
>
> (Church of England, 2013: para 5)

The C of E could not, therefore, object on the basis that same-sex relationships are intrinsically undesirable or immoral, or that the virtues of fidelity and constancy implicit in civil partnerships are not worthy of respect. Indeed, the unnamed writer of this response wants them to be 'maximised'. In this legal context, theological arguments would carry no weight.

The response identified a number of grounds for its opposition – the illicit distinction between civil and religious marriages, the inadequacy of the consultation process, the difficulties over defining non-consummation – but the primary objection was regarding the complementarity of the genders in opposite-sex marriage.

Immediately following the paragraph quoted above, the Report asserts that the complementarity of the sexes is intrinsic to marriage:

> However, the uniqueness of marriage – and a further aspect of its virtuous nature – is that it embodies the underlying, objective, distinctiveness of men and women. This distinctiveness and complementarity are

> seen most explicitly in the biological union of man and woman which potentially brings to the relationship the fruitfulness of procreation. And, even where, for reasons of age, biology or simply choice, a marriage does not have issue, the distinctiveness of male and female is part of what gives marriage its unique social meaning.
>
> Marriage has from the beginning of history been the way in which societies have worked out and handled issues of sexual difference. To remove from the definition of marriage this essential complementarity is to lose any social institution in which sexual difference is explicitly acknowledged.
>
> (Church of England, 2013: para 11)

The argument for complementarity reads uncomfortably in twenty-first-century England, where the equality of men and women is paramount and traditional gender roles, whether in terms of parenting, the workplace or leisure, are being replaced by much greater diversity. But the slender grounds for a coherent argument of opposition appear to have left those responding with little choice. Not all of the House of Bishops agreed with this position: the Bishop of Salisbury, Nicholas Holtam, wrote to Lord Alli on 30 May 2013 supporting same-sex marriage (Bishop of Salisbury, 2013), and his support was frequently referred to in the subsequent debate.

The Bishop of Salisbury was in a minority of one. Of the 14 who were present for the vote on Lord Dear's wrecking amendment to deny the Bill a Second Reading, nine voted in favour and five abstained. But the amendment was rejected by 390 votes to 148, after which the House of Bishops gave up the fight.

When the Marriage (Same Sex Couples) Bill was published, it included what has become known as the 'quadruple lock' (see Barker and Monk in this volume), which was designed to protect the C of E, and the Church in Wales (the C of E's equivalent in Wales) from being forced to carry out same-sex marriages against its will. Primary legislation, carried through the General Synod of the C of E and then approved by Parliament, will be required to permit same-sex marriage in the C of E; the Church in Wales will require secondary legislation, which could be introduced if it makes a request to the Lord Chancellor.

This provision also has the effect of protecting the C of E and the government against the possibility of cases being brought against it under the European Convention on Human Rights by transferring the responsibility for agreeing same-sex marriage in church to the C of E. It is highly unlikely that the General Synod would, with its current membership, agree to amend the marriage provisions in this way, so the C of E is unlikely in the foreseeable future to permit same-sex marriage.

International considerations

This situation arises from the combination of complexity and tradition that characterises the C of E and the Anglican Communion more widely. It is certainly the case that both the former and the current Archbishops of Canterbury have tried not to alienate conservative Christians at home or abroad. The previous Archbishop of Canterbury joined with all the other Primates of the Anglican Communion in condemning homophobia in 2005:

> The victimisation or diminishment of human beings whose affections happen to be ordered towards people of the same sex is anathema to us. We assure homosexual people that they are children of God, loved and valued by him, and deserving of the best we can give of pastoral care and friendship.
>
> (Dromantine Declaration, 2005)

But as *primus inter pares* internationally as well as in England, he was unable to take a leadership role in moving matters forward. Over one hundred bishops out of a total of over 880 stayed away from the 2008 Lambeth Conference in protest at the actions of the Episcopal Church of the USA, including the consecration of Bishop Gene Robinson, a partnered gay man, as Bishop of New Hampshire.

The most vocal resistance within the Anglican Communion to including LGBT people and to same-sex marriage has come from provinces in sub-Saharan Africa. On 1 April 2014, the Archbishop of Kenya said:

> From outside, we are being pressed by the West, and even parts of the Anglican Communion, into treating homosexuality as a human right, but this is to cheapen rights so that they become a demand that we tolerate individual preferences that are destructive of our moral fabric. The homosexual movement has become an ideology that attacks our human identity as male and female created in the image of God, and same sex marriage, which became legal yesterday in England, is therefore a profound rejection of the law of God.
>
> (Archbishop of Kenya's Statement, 2014)

The present Archbishop of Canterbury, Justin Welby, located the C of E very graphically in an international context in a radio interview on 4 April 2014:

> It's [the church's resistance to rapid change] about the fact that I've stood by a graveside in Africa of a group of Christians who'd been attacked because of something that had happened far far away in America, and they were attacked by other people because of that and a lot of them had been killed. And, I was in the South Sudan a few weeks ago, and the church leaders there were saying, please don't change what you're doing because then we couldn't accept your help, and we need your help desperately.
>
> (LBC phone-in, 4 April 2014)

No Archbishop of Canterbury wishes to be the one who presides over a tear in the fabric of the Anglican Communion; both recent incumbents have been very clear that their job is to maintain unity, as far as possible. Over the past 15 years there have been steady moves towards the creation of an independent, conservative grouping of Anglican provinces and churches. The Fellowship of Confessing Anglicans, of which the Anglican Church in Kenya is a member, has created its own subsidiary federations, the Anglican Mission in America and the Anglican Mission in England. The Anglican Mission in England has, so far, had only marginal influence, but it, and other membership bodies in the C of E, notably Reform and Anglican Mainstream, are influential in General Synod and strongly opposed to same-sex marriage.

There is, however, evidence of increasing openness to equal marriage within the evangelical wing of the church. A leading UK pastor, Steve Chalke, came out in favour of equal marriage in January 2013. He told me that of the 70,000 emails his church, Oasis, had received as a result, less than 10 per cent were fundamentally opposed; most said, 'we need to discuss this more'.

The winds of change

What, then, of the future? At present, the senior hierarchy is continuing to resist any accommodation of same-sex marriage. The C of E's website 'Your Church Marriage' reads as if the Marriage (Same Sex Couples) Act 2013 has not been passed. The internal conversations continue: Anglican Mainstream, a leading conservative organisation, issued a 'Position Statement' on April 14 2014, which said, 'In short, we have no intention of changing our views simply because Parliament has passed a new law or because public opinion is against us' (Anglican Mainstream, 2014). On the other hand, on 28 March 2014 the Bishop of Salisbury said:

> Tomorrow, the first same-sex civil marriages will take place in this country. This is a new reality being undertaken by people who wish their relationships to have a formal status which embodies a commitment to them being faithful, loving and lifelong … I therefore congratulate those who are getting married, assure them of my prayers, and wish them well in all that lies ahead.

Which of these views will prevail? The C of E's response to the Equal Marriage consultation ended by expressing concern about the consequences if the proposals become law: 'The Church of England's unique place in the current marriage law of England means that the proposals will potentially have a very significant impact on our ability to serve the people of the nation as we have always done' (Church of England, 2013). However, an intriguing debate arose following the publication of the House of Bishops' Pastoral Statement in February 2014, which included this paragraph:

> There will, for the first time, be a divergence between the general understanding and definition of marriage in England as enshrined in law and the doctrine of marriage held by the Church of England and reflected in the Canons and the Book of Common Prayer.
>
> (House of Bishops, 2014: Appendix, para 9)

The sociologist of religion, Linda Woodhead, responded to this paragraph by quoting the then Archbishop of Canterbury, Randall Davidson, speaking in the House of Lords in 1907:

> For the first time in the history of the Church of England has the law of the State been brought on one specific point into direct, open, overt contrast with and contradiction of the specific and defined law laid down in the authoritative regulations of the National Church.[6]

She went on to say:

> The fact that many in the Church of England contested the recension of the Deceased Wife's Sister Act (1835) until defeated in 1907 sounds ridiculous to us. And that's the point. What to contemporary generations seems an unsupportable divergence between the law of the land and the Church's teaching on marriage (the BCP's Table of Kindred and Affinity in this case) seems a storm in a teacup for later generations for whom it is established social fact … The fact that the House of Bishops' statement above is in error matters a great deal … because it reveals a wider mindset amongst the bishops and their advisors which is forgetful of the church's own history and therefore proverbially condemned to repeat it. The bishops are in a false position because they believe that the scale of the challenge which gay marriage presents to the Church is much greater than it really is.
>
> (Woodhead, 2014)

The C of E is a complex and traditional institution, but it has reinvented itself many times. This issue is one that bears particularly heavy freight, and as such it has presented significant challenges. But there are straws in the wind. Clergy have already entered into same-sex marriages. Churches have already celebrated them. Bishops have supported them. If the C of E is to retain the breadth, diversity and relationship with English society that it has had for so long, it will be unable for much longer to resist change.

Notes

1 Archbishops' Council response to the Civil partnership proposals, 30 September 2003.
2 The undated 'Response to the Government Equalities Office Consultation – "Equal Civil Marriage" – from the Church of England, 2013.

3 *Hansard*, 3 June 2013.
4 No longer available online.
5 There are no accurate statistics available on the numbers of clergy in Civil partnerships and the numbers of services of blessing.
6 Archbishop Randall Davidson, on the passage of the deceased wife's sister legislation, *Hansard*, 1907; quoted in Woodhead, 2014.

References

Brown, Terry (ed.), *Other Voices, Other Worlds*, London, DLT, 2006.
Dormor, Duncan, and Jeremy Morris (eds), *An Acceptable Sacrifice?*, London, SPCK, 2006.
Goddard, Giles, *Space for Grace, Creating Inclusive Churches*, London, Canterbury Press, 2008.
Held Evans, Rachel, *A Year of Biblical Womanhood: How a Liberated Woman Found Herself Sitting on Her Roof, Covering Her Head, and Calling Her Husband 'Master'*, Nashville, Thomas Nelson, 2014.
Herman, Didi, *The Antigay Agenda: Orthodox Vision and the Christian Right*, Chicago, University of Chicago Press, 1997.
Jeffery-Poulter, S., *Peers, Queers and Commons; The Struggle for Gay Law Reform from 1950 to the Present*, London, Routledge, 1991.
John, Jeffrey, *Permanent, Faithful, Stable: Christian Same-Sex Partnerships*, London, Darton, Longman & Todd Ltd, 1994.
Rawls, K., 'How deep is the Republican Christian Right's connection to the anti-gay bills sweeping sub-Saharan Africa?', 6 February 2012: http://www.alternet.org/story/153723/how_deep_is_the_republican_christian_right's_connection_to_the_anti-gay_bills_sweeping_sub-saharan_africa.
Woodhead, Linda, 'Do Christians really oppose gay marriage?', Westminster Faith Debates, 2013: http://faithdebates.org.uk/debates/2013-debates/religion-and-personal-life/do-christians-oppose-gay-marriage/.

Reports, lectures, articles and public letters (chronological order)

House of Bishops, *Issues in Human Sexuality*, Church House Publishing, 1991,
Archbishops' Council response to the CP proposals, 30 September 2003.
Anglican Communion Primates' Meeting; Dromantine Declaration, February 2005: http://www.anglicancommunion.org/communion/primates/resources/downloads/comm unique%20_english.pdf.
House of Bishops Pastoral Statement on Civil Partnerships, 25 July 2005: http://www.churchofengland.org/media-centre/news/2005/07/pr5605.aspx.
Williams, Rowan, 'The Bible Today, Reading and Hearing', 16 April 2007: http://rowanwilliams.archbishopofcanterbury.org/articles.php/2112/the-bible-today-reading-hearing-the-larkin-stuart-lecture.
Archbishop of Canterbury's Advent Letter 2007: http://www.anglicannews.org/news/2007/12/archbishop-of-canterburys-advent-letter.aspx.
Church of England The undated 'Response to the Government Equalities Office Consultation – "Equal Civil Marriage" – from the Church of England, 2013.

A response to the Government Equalities Office Consultation: http://www.churchofengland.org/media/1475149/s-s%20marriage.pdf.

Bishop of Salisbury: Letter to Lord Alli, 29 May 2013: http://www.salisbury.anglican.org/news/bishop-restates.

House of Bishops Pastoral Guidance on same-sex marriage, 15 February 2014: http://www.churchofengland.org/media-centre/news/2014/02/house-of-bishops-pastoral-guidance-on-same-sex-marriage.aspx.

Woodhead, Linda; An Error in the House of Bishops Guidance on Same-Sex Marriage, 19 February 2014: http://www.thinkinganglicans.org.uk/archives/006460.html.

Pastoral Letter, 28 March 2014: http://www.salisbury.anglican.org/whos-who/bishops/the-bishop-of-salisbury/sermons-articles-and-media/bishop-congratulates-and-prays-for-same-sex-couples-getting-married.

Archbishop of Kenya's Statement on Marriage, 30 March 2014: http://gafcon.org/news/statement-on-marriage-archbishop-of-kenya.

Anglican Mainstream Position Statement, 4 April 2014: http://www.anglican-mainstream.net/2014/04/14/the-ministry-continues-a-position-statement-from-the-trustees-of-anglican-mainstream/.

Petre, Jonathan, 'First gay clergyman to wed plunges Church into crisis: Archbishop under pressure to sack canon who flouted ban on same sex marriage', *Mail Online*, 12 April 2014: http://www.dailymail.co.uk/news/article-2603295/First-gay-clergyman-wed-plunges-Church-crisis-Archbishop-pressure-sack-canon-flouted-ban-sex-marriage.html#ixzz3KOaYZQa4.

Archbishop of Canterbury's phone-in, LBC, 14 April 2014: http://lordsspiritual.wordpress.com/2014/04/05/archbishops-radio-phone-in-on-lbc-radio-transcript/.

Chapter 9

Even sociologists get civilly partnered?

Loving same-sex marriage and other contradictions

Yvette Taylor

In 'Even Sociologists Fall in Love', Stevi Jackson (1993) highlights the neglect of the cultural meaning of love as an emotion, as against long-standing attention to the institutionalisation of love in (heterosexual) marriage. In making, and querying, a distinction between being 'in love' and love as a longer-term feeling, questions around the shaping of emotions and subjectivity are raised: as culturally specific, varied and constructed in time and place. Here I ask what does it mean to be 'in love' in a time of UK – and indeed international – equalities legislation, seemingly heralding the arrival of a 'world we have won' (Weeks, 2007; McDermott, 2011), which uneasily exist alongside heightened inequality, gendered austerity and a post-welfare climate. I include my own research reflections and analysis, based on interviews with 46 lesbian mothers and 14 gay dads across a range of localities in the UK: I love doing my research but I do not always love what I find out ...

Much research on gay parenting is based upon samples with white, middle-class, educated professional women (Dunne, 1997), where 'middle classness' is left fairly un-interrogated and frequently unnamed. In my research interviewees were asked to self-identify in class terms, with about half defining as 'middle class' or 'lower middle class' and half identifying as 'working class'.[1] While not refuting the difficulties of class measure and (dis)identifications, the overwhelming ability to define in class terms, as well as describe classed terrains and experiences (such as schooling, leisure, employment, etc.), is evidence to its continued relevance and indeed its intersectional complexity, where class is discussed as operating on and beyond the economic level, including distinctions of worth, decency and 'ordinariness' (Taylor, 2007). In exploring the relevance of class and sexuality, I highlight who may still be tenuously qualified, or even be disqualified, in inclusive moments: what classed resources are required to engage and be recognised as 'legal and above board'? I argue that working-class and middle-class interviewees express varied tensions and ambivalences rather than a straightforward capitalisation. Nonetheless, the 'costs' of civic acceptance work to disadvantage working-class parents, while the advantages of middle-class parents often become re-embedded in new legal contexts. These new-old moments, and (un)comfortable positions, are also felt up close in 'watching weddings'.

'Love', as a long-term and laboured effort may be enduringly familiar to many same-sex couples who may, in contrast, not feel 'in love' with legitimated loving, through civil partnerships/same-sex marriages. I want to consider the contractions of being in – and out of – love in a particular time. These 'loving contradictions', places the feminist sociologist in a somewhat paradoxical place. I have felt this as I recently came to a stop in my tracks. I stood and stared as I began to watch a wedding; a deliberately public event announcing itself, lakeside on a bright – but still cold – winter day (in Canberra). I did not know the guests, the bride or the groom. But I still stopped. Maybe weddings were different in Australia, where same-sex marriage debates had intensified during my visiting fellowship at the Australian National University? Maybe I was about to witness something different (Taylor, 2012)?

I gauged presence as certain guests were ushered forward, shown to selected seats, or made to wait; others stood on the grassy public periphery and heads turned back to await the main arrival (of the bride). I guessed who-belonged-to-who, as the groom stood and waited too, gazing out into his own audience and his own future. There seemed a rehearsed pattern to these presentations. Pausing to take in the format and rules (where to sit and stand, how long to wait, when to get fed-up, frustrated and perhaps even change your mind), I realised that *of course* this event was rehearsed (over and over again). Compellingly, it still pulled me in despite the rules, rehearsals and reproductions. I sat, like a patient guest, in someone else's day.

I sat getting colder, watching cold guests wait for a (likely cold) bride. Shivering bridesmaids in a matched array of satin sleeveless dresses were also part of the waiting. Despite the chills I persisted, the guests did similarly, and more and more people filled the lakeside front to watch and take part in someone else's public–private commitment. Pictures were taken and I wondered how the event could fill a general public 'memory' of what-happened-today (as everyday): we are all called upon to participate in weddings, marriages, civil ceremonies and to celebrate relationships that are already recognisable in normative, legitimate ways. Sometimes this stops us in our tracks and pulls us in unexpectedly.

To mark the place, chairs were dressed-up and covered, flower petals were distributed and expectations were raised. I was waiting, the guests were waiting, but for what? I found myself pausing and questioning as I still stood smiling: Why was this sight so appealingly anticipated, and where was my usual sociological cynicism? I did not imagine or fantasise this event as mine – but it seemed a shame not too wait for *the moment* since I had already invested time in the gaze.

When does the wedding event 'arrive'? Why does the anticipated appearance of the bride and groom (in whatever combination) signal a new arrival, a private–public 'moment' – in something we know is often problematically repeated even as it is celebrated? Does the display of affection, familiarity and consumption provide a seductive gloss over what and whose 'private' lives might be made public? What public returns are (re)made in following a set-track towards legitimised, visible relationships? The bride can appear in the moment, and claim the day as hers, but we know that inequities in marriage may mean new invisibilities and un-viabilities (her care, his career).

I found myself asking, why have a wedding in public? Why have a wedding at all? In *Lesbian and Gay Parenting: Securing Social and Educational Capital* (Stacey and Biblarz 2009), I came across lesbian and gay couples desperately wanting to marry, to present publically as 'all legal and above board'; I also came across women and men who refused this kind of public recognition, as well as others who felt somewhat in-between, critically observing an institution from which they had been excluded while intrigued by new possibilities now available. As I argued in the research generally, the celebration of civil partnerships as *one-off* special days reinforces the moment of celebration/acceptance, against everyday, ongoing struggles (and the significance of class in this both subjectively and materially). One interviewee, Kathy, spoke of the draw of big parties, where roles can be played with if not defined, and potential gift lists imagined if not received:

> Every now and again I'll say, 'Well, if we did, we could get the house tidied … Think of all the gifts we could get, we could actually get a toaster that pops up on both sides at the same time. But no, it's a bit of a joke and we're not thinking about it. But they [her children] have been to a few civil ceremonies and so they're quite like, 'Oh.' Both of them, they've been to a fancy dress one, so it's not a good example of people taking things very seriously. They know about it and they ask about it, Harry's very much, 'Well you could do, you know, you really, really could', and they've chosen what role they want to play. Celia doesn't want to do bridesmaid because she doesn't want to wear a dress but she'll happily show people to their seats and throw petals … no doubt it will be on and off the agenda for many years, but I can't see it happening, unless we have to, for the kids. If it was a case we had to, we might do it, but it's not something either of us either seriously mentioned or contemplated at all. But we're looking at the colour co-ordinated kitchen stuff at Fenwick's and we're thinking, 'Just think, if we could tie in the new house with a civil ceremony and get things!'
>
> (Kathy, 42, working-class background)

Kathy's evaluation moves from the humorous to the serious (including her kids' (dis)investments), bringing in a sense of solidarity and refusal in considering what her closest friends are doing – against that which others want and expect to see, negotiating points of sameness and difference. This is as a classed continuation and constancy that pulls value into certain presences while pulling away from others who are positioned as lacking, failing and falling behind – as un-loveable others. This distinction works at institutional and interpersonal levels, shaping intimate and material dis-investments, where legal consolidation may be seen as actively materialising family. Arguably, the strong focus on same-sex marriage as the epitome of citizenship inclusion, has eclipsed other concerns and exclusions, as well the interconnectedness of status categories with different levels and degrees of (sexual) citizenship. For some this represents a new 'conditionality', a 'new homonormativity', enabling recognition of lesbians and gay men as 'ordinary' responsible and valued members of society, rather than challenging the re-production of *de*valued categories of behaviour and identity (Meeks and Stein, 2006; Kandaswamy, 2008).

Many interviewees experienced this shifting terrain ambivalently. Despite shared ambivalence amongst interviewees, classed divisions emerge in the erosion or consolidation of 'worth', 'normality' and 'entitlement', through which claims are made, families (un)done and citizens materialised. While parenting is distinct from issues of partnering they are related, not least in the ways that such policies themselves categorise and produce families, offering new possibilities for societal recognition, legal recourse and access to welfare services. Both working-class and middle-class interviewees expressed varied uncertainties but the material and subjective 'costs', rather than benefits, of civic acceptance work to disadvantage working-class parents, while the advantages of middle-class parents are often re-constituted and re-embedded in changing legal and welfare contexts (such as benefits cut-backs and the bedroom tax, which are returned to in closing this chapter).

Context

Much has been written about the costs of same-sex marriages and civil partnerships, focussing on material and symbolic gains – and losses – where the fight for 'equal rights' can itself uphold normative frameworks for inclusion (Richardson, 2004; Taylor, 2009). This is not to entirely dismiss the extension of gains but rather to question the scope and effect of these, where hoped for and achieved benefits are animated by existing inequalities. Despite the appeal of inclusion, Kath Weston's expectation highlights the continuation of class and sexual inequalities, rather than a sidestepping of these in new times:

> If gay people begin to pursue marriage, joint adoptions, and custody rights to the exclusion of seeking kinship status for some categories of

> friendship, it seems likely that gay families will develop in ways largely congruent with socio-economic and power relations in larger society.
>
> (1991: 209)

Practical benefits are accorded much importance in, for example, accessing welfare provision and services, where such practicalities frequently merge with what should 'ordinarily' be expected, provided and welcomed. Jeffrey Weeks sums up the appeal and importance of 'ordinariness', set against a queer critic of assimilation into heteronormativity as an affront to 'different' ways of being:

> at a deeper level surely, what we see here is the wish for recognition for what you are and want to be, for validation, not absorption, a voting with our feet for the ordinary virtues of care, love, mutual responsibility. We should never underestimate the importance of being ordinary. It has helped transform the LGBT [lesbian, gay, bisexual and transgender] and the wider world.
>
> (2008: 792)

Parental negotiations are always subject to structural framings and 'wider world' constraints, yet where 'ordinariness' and 'stability' is apparently welcomed, there are frequent hints at something less welcoming, where 'stable' becomes standardised, reproducing new partnership and parenting hierarchies (Meeks and Stein, 2006). 'Ordinariness' seemingly appeals to 'basic' desires and obvious 'normality', while 'failed' capacities and (ir)responsibilities are frequently coupled with this. This prompts the question of whether the dominance of (hetero)normative values and practices is consolidated as much by this reimagining of lesbians and gay men as 'ordinarily' included – as it was in the past through their location as 'excluded other'.

'Ordinariness' is specifically constructed through classed positionings. This has the effect of re-creating new normativities or 'but for' lesbian and gay citizens – those who are just like their idealised heterosexual counterparts *but for* sexual status (Agigian, 2004). Set against a wholesale 'homonormativity', lesbian and gay movements may be seen to simultaneously involve both assimilation and transformation, oscillating between a 'moment of transgression' and a 'moment of citizenship' (Weeks et al., 2001). Fraught negotiation may involve striving to become part of mainstream *and* self-positioning as different: but the resources, limitations and classing within are significant. Within complex citizenship claims, there are justifiable and pragmatic reasons why lesbians and gay men invoke 'ordinariness', as 'the family next door', but there are also limitations to and exclusions from this, where 'ordinariness' cannot be established or socially endorsed, and 'just like you' models of inclusion (white, middle-class heterosexuals) may do little for unemployed, working-class parents.

In my research, both working-class and middle-class interviewees express varied ambivalences but the material and subjective 'costs', rather than benefits, of civic acceptance work to disadvantage working-class parents, simultaneously questioning and re-inscribing constructions of 'respectable' 'ordinary' middle-classness, where sexual status did not necessarily erode classed claims and capitals. Such processes are suggestive of the need to consider class in discussions of lesbian and gay parents' citizenship struggles, over-loaded with expectations of 'success' or condemned to 'failure', both of which gloss over the tensions in inhabiting classed and sexual positioning.

All legal and above board

Interviewees spoke of how the legislation showed their children that 'everything's normal' and that 'we are almost equal', also providing emotional validation in now being able to 'make the feeling official'. The comparison with heterosexual 'normality' was frequently invoked in comparing the now equally 'firm and solid' commitments that lesbians and gay men can now demonstrate, as their heterosexual counterparts always could. Civil partnerships were welcomed if 'you're so much in love with each other and you know that your relationship is firm and solid as solid as a heterosexual marriage could be then I'm really, really happy with it' (Stephen, 48, middle class).

Edward (63, middle class) spoke of his friends becoming civilly partnered, explaining that this makes good sense given that they were 'living together already and have bought a house together and they have two sets of kids, echoed by Peter (43, middle class) in the rationalisation of civil partnerships as simply a sign of 'civilised society', which endorses multiple versions of family and partnership. Potential endorsement of 'multiplicity' is perhaps undercut by the sentiments of 'good sense' and 'civility' which, in pointing to stability, commitment and love, within secure households, reinscribe ideas of who and what is seen as sensible and fitting. The repetition and apparent endorsement of 'neatness' constructed through monogamous coupledom, stable family units, resources (e.g. housing) gives weight to the desirability of 'ordinariness'.

Other interviewees were more forthright in their rejection of civil partnerships, fearing these to be 'just like bad marriages' producing a certain 'squeamishness' in being witness to them. Legislation was also viewed critically, based on 'straight society', with a troublesome 'misogynistic history', illustrating the gendered nature of legal framings. For example, notably Kevin claims that the financial concerns, familial desires and a personal sense of 'difference' are probably 'a middle-class thing'. The linkage and securing of middle-classness through property and ownership is at once endorsed and disputed where the ability to 'protect' involves the securing of assets, even as the feeling of 'love' beyond (if not outwith) such dynamics, is also emphasised:

> a lot of my friends see it as a very middle-class thing, it's about property and all the usual middle-class notions. On the other hand, for me, it's about protection of some of the people I love. I think we're at the stage where it's starting to plan a civil partnership and it just seems to me a great opportunity to have a wild party and a really good time with the people who are important to you … The kids are really into it, they like the idea and think it'll be fantastic. So it feels a bit more like a celebration than a civil partnership. But I do have this very different sense of what it means and should we be doing it.
>
> (Kevin, 36, middle class)

Kevin's commentary is suggestive of some ambivalences in celebratory times – scepticism is displaced by the necessity of protecting loved ones and opportunities are grasped even as these are named as constituting and continuing usual 'middle-class notions'. Such a classed critique (and continuation) is also powerfully evoked by pointing to the entrenchment of a 'two-tiered world' where some faced being placed firmly in the margins, as others are rescued and redeemed as now in the mainstream. Once again the good homosexual is placed in opposition to the bad one and sides must be chosen, or allocated. The option of civil partnership can been seen as making this differentiation more concrete:

> I think the danger of it is that I think it's fantastic for people that want to do it, I've been to lots. But I think the danger of it is that it's creating a sort of two-tiered world where you are kind of jolly and out and no problems and equal to straight people and then the kind of slightly grotty ones who decide not to. You know, like an underclass, and I'm in that! (laughter). I'm in that underclass … again! Back in the margins. And I think, I mean, that's one way of looking at it and also, because I've done that, I've been married and I spent most of my adult life married … you're not really going to start wandering back into that world and, you know, I don't care about the legal and the financial links really.
>
> (Katerina, 54, working class)

Katerina's assessment of a 'two-tiered' division emerging, based on implicit and explicit classed markers (financial, aesthetic, behavioural) that intersect with sexuality, is seen to place some 'back in the margins' as against a mainstreaming (Duggan, 2002; Kandaswamy, 2008).

Such distinctions press at whether citizenship struggles inevitably constitute an impossible bid for respectability or a realistic claim on being and becoming 'normal', working within the system, while others are rendered 'outside' and 'a bit grotty'. The ability to enact changes and choices is shaped by the weight of expectations, as outlined by Sophie (45, working class), who is pleased that there is a choice, even as she is sick of people asking her 'if' and 'when' she will be civilly partnered, seemingly weighed down by the expectation that now she can, she actually should.

Tensions between possibilities and practicalities were ever present in interviewees' accounts, as desires were enabled – and constrained – by what was on offer, simultaneously viewed as a benefit and a limitation. Vicky (42, working-class background) and Beth's (35, working class) experience is one of being caught between varied personal and legal camps, where having the 'bit of paper' is invested and fraught. Such 'bits of paper' (or the lack thereof) have material consequences, where the Civil Partnership Act 2004's 'real importance' can be grounded in the mediation of parenting by social, medical and welfare services:

> I mean I can see, immediately, the difference in how seriously lesbian and gay couples are being taken as, potentially, adoptive parents, just because it has been legitimised, like the state is saying, 'These are okay'. So the questioning that used to go on, you know, the real bottom-line question about, 'Is this an okay thing to do?' It's like, well, 'It is, and it's legal'. So anything that questions it immediately falls into ranks of discrimination.
>
> (Angie, 46, middle class)

Angie's account asserts 'serious', 'bottom line' legal entitlements, as well as the new, enforced, social approval; this contrasts with Katerina's (54, working class) depiction of a 'two-tiered' systems where being 'recognised' was subject to doubt and financial benefits were dismissed, due to the lack of applicability ('I don't care about the legal and the financial links really'). The pull of being 'normal', of receiving state validation, was repeated in respondents' celebration of the Civil Partnership Act 2004 as 'neat' and corresponding with familial longevity, commitment and 'obvious' ordinariness (home ownership, assets and 'protective' capacities). But it was overwhelmingly middle-class respondents who spoke of realising such linkages through same-sex partnership recognition, even as critical comments were made, including the explicit, if embarrassed, naming of such linkages as 'middle class'.

For richer, for poorer

The potential negative impact on resources and entitlements were considered in relation to new legal responsibilities, whether or not civil partnerships were undertaken. While the benefits could be perceived and realised as a 'great step forward' (Elizabeth, 52, middle class), securing 'the practical things' (Carol, 53, middle class), the complexities and tensions within this can increase disadvantage, experienced most by those who were the least well off: the material worth and legal responsibilities contained within a piece of paper have effects beyond recounted lived experiences and ambivalences, reproducing material (dis)advantages more broadly.

One of the ways that middle-class positioning and subject-hood is arguably (re)produced is in aligning with and actualising sentiments that seemingly 'just make good sense', effacing the classing of resource accumulation and transference (Adkins and Skeggs, 2004). The ability to make legal claims on, for example, residences and pensions constitutes a very significant change where the claiming of such could be expressed as a political fulfilment as well as a protective buffer (Taylor, 2009). Many middle-class interviewees told of the financial benefits as significant in her decision, of the practicalities of everyday life simply becoming much easier, even if some were also critical about the implied economic dependence in 'being seen as one entity'. Economic benefits outweighed these feelings, echoed in Harriet's (38, middle class) rationalisation of a now secure 'safety net', enabling her to make claims on shared resources, such as pensions. Others mentioned the avoidance of inheritance tax, where prior disadvantages could be reconciled through new legislative benefits. There were many dilemmas to be puzzled and maybe solved, some new, some ongoing. But in a changing legal context some subjects may be recognised as exercising a new agency, where the classed investment in and ability to capitalise upon changes perhaps suggest continuity, rather than transformation, of citizenship inclusions and exclusions.

Others spoke of losing out and facing greater financial risk. Both Elizabeth (52, middle class) and Beth (35, working class) were reluctant to consider legally 'coming out', as it were, in enacting a civil partnership, given that they had financial ties to ex-partners and would lose out in terms of pensions if they effectively re-married. Such ties and endurances represent another neglected aspect of partnership recognition, where couples are often positioned as emerging 'from nowhere' and coming into being just in that moment, a positioning that erases 'past' and continued classed resources in 'getting there'. For example, many working-class parents' routes into pregnancy were achieved in the context of ex-heterosexual relationships, rather than through alterative reproductive technologies and strategies. At times, these different parental routes were differently affirmed within – and beyond – the LGBT community, with non-heterosexual routes often favoured as more 'authentic, 'creative' and 'chosen', positioned against an un-choosing narrative of 'falling pregnant', represented by the supposedly unfortunate figure of the generalised working-class women/single-parent.

Beth also articulates another tension, where the loss of benefits confuses the gains to be made 'I'm a bit confused about this really but nowadays if you start, say if I started living with a woman, I would no longer be able to claim my benefit'. The change in benefit law, while, on one hand, signifying a recognition of gay and lesbian relationships has, on the other hand, been detrimental to the very people who can least afford to lose, so sometimes acknowledgement is not that welcome.

For Jacqui, the opposition to civil partnerships was not just theoretical or principled but rather thoroughly practical, where once 'dis-counted' partners are assessed for benefits purposes, even if there has been no civil partnership. Jacqui details the gendered dimensions of this and the risks around income and housing where she positions (all) lesbians as 'worse off':

> because when we were together, because it was a long time ago, because the law didn't accept that lesbians could have relationships, if one of us was working and the other one was on benefit, neither of the two were connected, even though we wrote on all the forms. So, in terms of financial, lesbians are now worse off financially, because of the Civil Partnership, because now, if you are two lesbians living together and one of you is working, they would be expected to support the other one. Unfortunately, women's wages aren't as good as the majority of men's so we're not in a position maybe to support our partner financially. I'm not saying all men are. There are men that, you know, will struggle with that as well, but it wasn't the same for women. So, in terms of financially, I think we're worse off. But in terms of more equality, and obviously you can make that commitment to your partner, there's all the issues about if one of you dies and, you know, you've got a joint tenancy or a joint mortgage or whatever, it clears up a lot of those kinds of issues … like with most change, there's good and there's bad (laughter).
>
> (Jacqui, 43, middle class)

Jacqui's account points to gender inequalities as structuring new 'inclusions' – her sentiments of lesbian 'sameness', in being disadvantaged compared to their higher earning male counterparts, is widely recognised (Dunne, 1997), yet there are classed differences within lesbians' – and gay men's – experience as benefit claimants, home owners and 'normal' taxpayers (Taylor, 2007). The connections and disruptions between class and sexuality, highlight who may still be tenuously qualified, or even be disqualified, in inclusive moments, where classed resources are required to engage and be recognised as 'legal and above board'; this may be rather circular, where those with such resources are able to gain more. Both working-class and middle-class interviewees express varied tensions and ambivalences, rather than a straightforward capitalisation. Acknowledging this complexity does not dissolve classed positions as the advantages of middle-class parents are re-constituted and often re-embedded in changing legal contexts, where the consolidation (or erosion) of 'worth', 'normality' and 'entitlement', differentially materialise sexual citizens (Binnie, 2004; Kandaswamy, 2008).

Measuring the costs of civic acceptance is no easy matter, where these may constitute a rightful entitlement for some, while acting as a severe impediment to others. The intersections between class and sexuality are evident in the materialisation and potential negation of respondents' families, negotiated and celebrated in claiming an 'ordinary' success into 'neat' legal terrain, alongside practical gains and financial security. Such successes compare to those who, to paraphrase one interviewee, exist on the margins of approval in their inhabitation of particular classed and sexual positions, where some respondents' fears and actual material setbacks, sit uneasily alongside declarations of savings, property, investment and propriety. The issue of class and economics is significant, resourcing – or denying – various possibilities; as was witnessed, class and sexuality also intersect in the construction of 'normal', 'ordinary' citizens (Duggan, 2002). New presences are based around profoundly classed notions of exchange, transference and inheritance (Skeggs, 2004): on setting-up intimacy as attractiveness and loyalty to certain relations, feelings and futures.

Polarised academic debates on sexual citizenship, framed as a positive step towards equality or, alternatively, as an accommodation to heterosexual standards and the loss of distinctive differences, ways of being and relational practices, frequently sideline the classed tensions with 'inclusive' moments. In between such positions more complex lived realities exist, where the difference of class can be seen as relevant to practical and symbolic gains and losses. The symbolic sense of inclusion achieved through recognition and affirmation is classed, where those with recognised social, economic and cultural capitals can often achieve standing as legitimate subjects. Attention to the ways that class and sexuality intersect in the (non)achievement of symbolic and practical inclusions suggests the need to account for class both theoretically and empirically in debates on sexual citizenship, where public policies materialise parenting, spatially situating and legally producing costs and benefits – we witness the cultural (as well as policy) continued and intensified vilification of working classes in programmes such as *Benefits Street*, meaning that certain groups are particularly unlovable, irredeemable and out of place.

Recently, Jamieson (2013) asked 'just how "spare" are bedrooms?', differently unpacking post-welfare citizen realities, claims and distinctions. Spare bedrooms are now taxed under the changes to housing benefit, meaning 'unoccupied' bedrooms incur penalties, as the coalition government declares appropriate, supposedly made-to-measure occupancy (without the bespoke provision). This 'bedroom tax' sits within a wider austerity climate of cutting back, as the most vulnerable are regularly asked to carry the burden and blame with no room to move – literally. The problem with this tax, as is pointed out, is that our lives exceed such measures of 'spare', 'unoccupied', 'vacant' – and, importantly, diminished housing stock means a profound lack of fit between governmental, familial and individual desires and possibilities (as with fitting in to 'same-sex marriage').

To call into question the (in)appropriateness of the bedroom(s) is to evoke an intimacy that is both visible and invisible in such debates; images and ideas of hyper-sexualised feral council dwellers, as surplus population taking up too much room, sit alongside a rather silenced and stifled notion of (hetero)sexuality, represented, for example, in the familiar invocation of children's needs and rights. Like equalities legislation – now awkwardly sitting in a post-welfare climate – the 'fit to size' seems ever-present though, as once 'invisible' same-sex partners, under the radar of recognition, are now made official and, potentially, sized-up and penalised (as we have seen in empirical quotes).

While such accounts have been made, sociologists have arguably not provided a 'close up' or close enough version of these stretched and stifled intimacies, with a tendency to talk about the lives of others 'out there' (perhaps from our home offices/spare bedrooms). To speak personally, and to risk professional, public 'outing', is an enduring feminist concern. In following such concerns, I want to end on my own occupation of my friend's 'spare bedroom' (as a sociological concern, in getting close, as Stevi Jackson's invokes in 'Even Sociologists Fall in Love'). Our relationships move and change: these 'pasts' often affect the present, rather than becoming closed doors. So, to end on a personal–public note:

I have a key to my (ex-partner) friend's house; this is a space in common, even as our lives are separated, as we live and work in different cities. We did not have children, but we did have a cat; I am sure my 'claim' and cares would not be recognised as urgent or viable and as I try to articulate these I am aware of overstating my case ('just a cat!'), of making a broader social problem mine. But such connections are signalled in Jamieson's (2013) account of 'what if?' (as with commentaries on same-sex marriage) and the possibilities that are afforded by having a 'spare bedroom' (such as having a friend stay over and having that friend care for the cat), and the lives and leisure that are enabled in such space. Only in a very dismal social world would we seek to restrict these possibilities, as beyond that which our lives and housing can accommodate. This intimate restriction and regulation is not, however, felt as penalty to me: I have that key and can open doors, connecting my pasts and present; I can consider – and even practise – what collective living might be. Others are told to move on or, more realistically, to move out, representing a continued pathologisation of some intimate ties and community, as unloving and unlovable others, which continues and even heightens in a moment of 'coming forward', of loving same-sex marriage, while cutting back.

Note

1 Including parents with partners, parents in variously combined households, 'step-families', and single mums and dads, ranging from 18 to 63-year-olds. Interviewees' routes to parenting also varied, with most participants having children through previous heterosexual relationships; those who had pursued other 'alternative' routes to parenting, such as adoption or assisted inseminination, were mostly from middle-class backgrounds.

References

Adkins, L. and Skeggs, B. (eds) (2004) *Feminism After Bourdieu*. London: Wiley.

Agigian, A. (2004) *Baby Steps: How Lesbian Alternative Insemination is Changing the World*. Middletown, CT: Wesleyan University Press.

Ahmed, S. (2004) *The Cultural Politics of Emotion*. Edinburgh: Edinburgh University Press.

Allen, K. and Taylor, Y. (2013) 'Failed femininities and troubled mothers: gender and the riots', *Studies in the Maternal Special Issue on Austerity Parenting*, 4(2): http://www.mamsie.bbk.ac.uk/documents/AllenTaylor_SiM_4(2)_2012.pdf [accessed 25 June 2014].

Armstrong, J. (2010) 'Class and gender and the intersection: working-class women's dispositions towards employment and motherhood', in Y. Taylor (ed.) *Classed Intersections: Spaces, Selves, Knowledges*. Farnham: Ashgate, pp 235–54.

Back, L. (2007) *The Art of Listening*. Oxford and New York: Berg.

Beck, U. and E. Beck-Gernsheim (1995) *The Normal Chaos of Love*. Cambridge: Polity Press/Blackwell.

——(2002) *Individualization: Institutionalized Individualism and Its Social and Political Consequences*. London: Sage.

Beck-Gernsheim, E. (1998) 'On the way to a post-familiar family: from a community of need to elective affinities', *Theory, Culture and Society*, 15 (3–4): 53–70.

——(2002) *Reinventing the Family: In Search of New Lifestyles*. Cambridge: Polity Press.

Binnie, J. (2004) *The Globalization of Sexuality*. London: Sage.

——(2011) 'Class, sexuality and space: a comment' in Y. Taylor (ed.) Special Issue 'Sexuality and Class', *Sexualities*, 14(1): 21–26.

Browne, K. (2011) '"By partner we mean ... ": alternative geographies of "gay marriage"', in Y. Taylor (ed.) Special Issue 'Sexuality and Class', *Sexualities*, 14(1): 100–22.

Dixon, C. (2011) 'Working-class lesbian parents' emotional engagement with their children's education: intersections of class and sexuality', in Y. Taylor (ed.) Special Issue 'Sexuality and Class', *Sexualities*, 14(1): 79–99.

Duggan, L. (2002) 'The new homonormativity: the sexual politics of neoliberalism', in R. Castonovo and D. Nelson (eds) *Materializing Democracy: Towards a Revitalized Cultural Politics*. Durham, NC: Duke University Press.

Dunne, G. A. (1997) *Lesbian Lifestyles. Women's Work and the Politics of Sexuality*. London: Macmillan.

Giddens, A. (1992) *The Transformation of Intimacy: Sexuality, Love and Eroticism in Modern Societies*. Cambridge: Polity Press.

Gillies, V. (2006) 'Working class mothers and school life: exploring the role of emotional capital', *Gender and Education*, 18(3): 281–93.

Hennessy, R. (2000) *Profit and Pleasure. Sexual Identities in Late Capitalism.* London: Taylor & Francis

Hines, S. and Taylor, Y. (eds) (2012) *Sexualities: Reflections and Futures.* Palgrave Macmillan.

Hull, K. (2006) *Same-Sex Marriage. The Cultural Politics of Love and Law.* Cambridge: Cambridge University Press.

Jackson, S. (1993) 'Even sociologists fall in love', *Sociology*, May, 27(2): 201–20.

Jamieson, L. (1998) *Intimacy: Personal Relationships in Modern Societies.* Cambridge: Polity Press.

——(2013) 'How spare are bedroom-tax rooms?': http://www.discoversociety.org /2013/11/05/how-spare-are-bedroom-tax-rooms/ [accessed 25 June 2014].

Kandaswamy, P. (2008) 'State austerity and the racial politics of same-sex marriage in the US', *Sexualities*, 11(6): 706–25.

McDermott, E. (2010) '"I wanted to be totally true to myself": class and the making of the sexual Self', in Y. Taylor (ed.) *Classed Intersections: Spaces, Selves, Knowledges.* Farnham: Ashgate, pp 199–216.

McDermott, L. (2011) 'The world some have won: sexuality, class and inequality', *Sexualities*, February, 14: 63–78.

Meeks, C. and Stein, A. (2006) 'Refiguring the family: towards a postqueer politics of gay and lesbian marriage', in D. Richardson, M. Casey and J. McLaughlin (eds), *Intersections Between Feminist and Queer Theory.* Basingstoke: Palgrave, pp 136–55.

Parker, S. (2010) 'Working capital: ownership and (some) means of production', in Y. Taylor (ed.) *Classed Intersections: Spaces, Selves, Knowledges.* Farnham: Ashgate, pp 13–34.

Peel, E. and Harding, R. (2008) 'Editorial introduction: recognizing and celebrating same-sex relationships: beyond the normative debate', *Sexualities*, 11(6): 659–66.

Richardson, D., McLaughlin J. and Casey, M. (2006) (eds) *Intersections Between Feminist and Queer Theory.* Basingstoke: Palgrave.

Richardson, D., (2004) 'Locating Sexualities: From Here to Normality' 7(4) *Sexualities* 391–411.

Ryan-Flood, R. (2005) 'Contested heteronormativities: discourses of fatherhood among lesbian parents in Sweden and Ireland', *Sexualities*, 8(2): 239–54.

Ryan-Flood, R. (2005) 'Contested heteronormativities: discourses of fatherhood among lesbian parents in Sweden and Ireland', *Sexualities*, 8(2): 239–54.

Santos, C. (2012) *Social Movements and Sexual Citizenship in Southern Europe.* Basingstoke: Palgrave Macmillan.

Seidman, S. (2011) 'Class matters … but how much? Class, nation, and queer life', in Y. Taylor (ed.) Special Issue 'Sexuality and Class', *Sexualities*, 14(1): 36–41.

Shipman, B. and Smart, C. (2007) '"It's made a huge difference": recognition, rights and the personal significance of civil partnership', *Sociological Research Online* 12(1): http://www.socresonline.org.uk [accessed 2 January 2013].

Skeggs, B. (1997) *Formations of Class and Gender.* London: Sage.

Skeggs, B. (2004) *Class, Self, Culture.* London: Routledge.

Stacey, J. and Biblarz, T. J. (2001) '(How) does the sexual orientation of parents matter?', *American Sociological Review*, 66(2): 159–83.

Taylor, Y. (2005) 'Real politik or real politics? Working-class lesbians' political "awareness" and activism', *Women's Studies International Forum*, 28(6): 484–94.

——(2007) *Working-Class Lesbian Life: Classed Outsiders.* Basingstoke: Palgrave Macmillan.

——(2008) '"That's not really my scene": working-class lesbians in (and out of) place', *Sexualities*, 11(5): 523–46.

——(2009) *Lesbian and Gay Parenting: Securing Social and Educational Capital.* Basingstoke: Palgrave Macmillan.

——(2011) 'Queer Presences and Absences: Citizenship, Community, Diversity – or Death', *Feminist Theory*, 12(3): 335–41.

——(2011) 'Lesbian and gay parents' sexual citizenship: costs of civic acceptance', *Gender, Place and Culture*, 18(5): 583–601.

——(2012) 'Watching a wedding: private-publics': http://www.genderandeducation.com/issues/watchingawedding/ [accessed 25 June 2014].

Taylor, Y. and Addison, M. (eds) (2012) *Queer Presences and Absences.* Basingsoke: Palgrave Macmillan.

Taylor, Y., Hines, S. and Casey, M. (eds) (2010) *Theorizing Intersectionality and Sexuality.* Basingstoke: Palgrave Macmillan.

Weeks, J. (2007) *The World We've Won.* London: Routledge.

——(2008) 'Regulation, resistance, recognition', *Sexualities*, 11(6): 787–792.

Weeks, J., Heaphy, B. and Donovan, C. (2001) *Same Sex Intimacies: Families of Choice and Other Life Experiments.* London and New York: Routledge.

Weston, K. (1991) *Families We Choose.* Boston: Beacon Press.

Part III

The end of (the) marriage

Dissolutions, disputes and the future

Chapter 10

'Square peg, round hole'?

The legal regulation of plus-two-parent families

Chris Dietz and Julie Wallbank

Introduction

For many years donor insemination has been used by lesbians in order to create their own families. In the UK, choices will be made on whether or not to use known heterosexual or gay donors and what level of input, if any, the donor/father will have. Though the terminology is loaded, this chapter will engage with debates about the role of the gay father in lesbian families when relationships break down, particularly where there is evidence that he was intended pre-conception to play some sort of role in the child's life, and has assumed actual responsibilities post-birth. It will reflect upon the assimilationist strategies of the UK Human Fertilisation and Embryology Act 2008 (hereafter the 2008 Act), which positions different lesbian families on a hetero-normative continuum of acceptability. Questions will also be raised about how courts to date have approached what might be called 'plus-two-parent' (PTP) families[1] and in particular how gay fathers find themselves positioned therein.

The 2008 Act homogenises lesbian families through an equality-based approach, treating them in much the same way as heterosexual ones while failing to engage with the possibilities and challenges they pose for the law. A steadily growing body of case law indicates that PTP projects can prove difficult. It may be that the 2008 Act will reduce the numbers of known donors approached by lesbians as the available legal frameworks of civil partnership and licensed treatment and growing social acceptance make reproduction easier. However, empirical research indicates that prospective lesbian parents choose known donors for broadly political reasons, including challenging the traditional two-parent model and choosing to co-parent with one or more gay men and their extended family.

This chapter argues that future courts could attend to the wider social imperative of recognising diversity in families by considering these political motivations as part of the individual welfare test. When exercising this test – which requires courts to place children's welfare as paramount in their decisions – lesbian couples have to date been construed as 'vulnerable' and in need of protection from the 'threat' of the gay father. These fathers and their partners have been regarded as playing a subsidiary role to the nuclear family – although the appropriateness of the distinction between principal and secondary parenting has been disputed by judges.[2] Attempts to equate the position of the gay father with that of the heterosexual father have been thwarted by courts, with pre-conception intention and the patterns of relationships and responsibilities assumed post-birth deemed more apposite concerns.

We will interrogate these recurring themes by viewing the 2008 Act as part of an assimilationist and hetero-normative strategy, drawing upon empirical research on lesbian parents' choice of conception partners and on the relative position of gay fathers in respect of sexuality, gender and power. If disputes arise early on in the child's life, the father will face difficulties in establishing family life and he may find himself positioned firmly outside the family.[3] Questions are raised about how gay fathers are responded to by law and what sort of experience they enjoy in their attempt to establish family relationships. The chapter will suggest that it is important to avoid creating new forms of discrimination for gay fathers by being overly restrictive in respect of their and their children's mutual relationships of care.

We begin by outlining the parenting provisions of the 2008 Act through a framework that is sensitive to the problems shored up by an assimilationist hetero-normative strategy that *allows* lesbian families to be treated by law as equivalent to heterosexual two-parent families. Although the continued promotion of the two-parent model by the 2008 Act has been discussed (Lind and Hewitt 2009; McCandless and Sheldon 2010; Smith 2010; Wallbank 2010) our aim is to expand upon that thesis by developing the idea of a hetero-normative continuum; with the dyadic parental paradigm at one end and the PTP family at the other and as sliding along, or perhaps being pushed off, the line. This new legislative strategy, which encompasses the Civil Partnership Act 2004 and the Marriage (Same Sex Couples) Act 2013, conveys the impression that all that is needed is more permissive legal provisions permitting lesbian parents to join the hetero-normative parenting club on the same terms as heterosexuals.

The hetero-normative continuum

Our discussion of law's assimilationist tendencies demands engagement with the question of 'heteronormativity'. Coined over two decades ago (Warner 1993), this analytical concept addresses the privileging of patterns of behaviour that conform in some way to hetero-norms. More specifically, do Mar Castro Varela et al. (2011a: 11) define heteronormativity as:

> a regime that organizes sex, gender and sexuality in order to match heterosexual norms. It denotes a rigid sexual binary of bodily

> morphology that is supported by gender and sexual identities. […] It demands a coherence of idealized morphologies, presumptive heterosexual desire and a thoroughly constructed gender binary.

The implication is that heteronormativity should not be discussed without some reference to heterosexual intimate practices. Yet while heteronormativity may presume heterosexual desire, it would be reductive to suggest that it is reliant on the mechanics of hetero-sex for its prevalence; that such an argument is premised upon a rigid gender binary suggests its own logic is marked by heteronormativity. Questions arise as to whether homosexual intimate practices are themselves capable of undoing heteronormativity. Queer theorists have long doubted the transformative potential supposedly inherent in 'being' homosexual or 'doing' homosexuality. For Butler (1990), all gendered identities – including 'gay' and 'lesbian' – are an 'effect' of a 'heterosexual power formation' (151). To cite homosexual identities as a site of political struggle arguably reiterates the hetero-norm it supposedly seeks to undermine (Ludwig 2011: 43).

Campaigns for LGBT (lesbian, gay, bisexual and transgender) inclusion have succeeded in having the 'continuum of "normality"' extended in some instances, yet the importance of heteronormativity 'for the constitution of intelligible subjects and the social order' has remained effective (Ludwig 2011: 48). The suspicion that the latter could not have come without the former informs a critical perspective. Even as originally conceived, Warner's (1993) critique of heteronormativity was defined 'against the normal rather than the heterosexual' (xxvi). Jackson (2006) agrees that 'heteronormativity needs to be thought of as defining normative ways of life as well as normative sexuality' to ensure its critical utility (117). Only this conceptualisation holds the key to unpacking the extent to which all subjects, regardless of their sexual identity, are expected to consent to hetero-norms (do Mar Castro Varela et al. 2011b). Hence we identify a 'hetero-' rather than a 'homo-normative' (Duggan 2003) continuum.

While constructing this continuum we acknowledge that identifying a hetero-norm is no simple proposition. Ryan-Flood (2005) considers it 'more precise to discuss a plurality or multiplicity of *heteronomativities*, rather than invoke a notion of heteronormativity as a homogenous concept' (200–201). Given the fluidity of these norms, the line between imitation and subversion will never be easily drawn – and what might appear to an observer to be 'imitation' may be experienced as 'subversion' by those involved. Smith (2013: 378) identifies this paradox at the crux of the current debate:

> Excluding known donors from legal recognition through a system which recognises only two parents validates and protects lesbian families but also reinforces the dyadic parenting norm based on heterosexual reproduction. Conversely, giving legal recognition to multiple parents

> undermines the dyadic norm but reasserts heteronormativity by elevating the importance of genetic parentage and fathers.

Like Smith (2013), we suspect that this double-bind will only be broken by creating legal space for the 'reflexive transformation' of families (358). The 2008 Act resolutely fails in this respect, privileging certain family types while excluding the legal possibility of others.

The 2008 Act

The provisions that determine who will be treated as the legal parents of a child conceived by donor insemination and the new section 14(2)(b) need for supportive parenting both regulate parentage within prescribed parameters. Under sections 42–43 the non-carrying lesbian civil partner may be recognised as the child's legal parent provided the biological mother conceives by artificial insemination. This insistence on artificial insemination – as opposed to (hetero-)sexual intercourse – maps onto same-sex relationships the moral concerns about potentially adulterous conduct that remain central to the divorce law relating to heterosexual couples. The lasting emphasis of sexual intercourse in the status-based provisions of marriage – and civil partnership as the equivalent – means that a donor/co-parent may seek to claim or avoid parental responsibility on the basis that pregnancy resulted from sexual intercourse rather than insemination (or *vice versa*), in which case the method of conception could become important.[4]

The significance of this provision is that it permits civil partners to use a known donor without that donor being legally recognised as the parent. Civil partnership thus confers legal parental responsibility on the social parent in much the same way that marriage does for heterosexual couples.[5] The provisions of the 2008 Act retain a 'hierarchical structure' whereby civil partners in addition to husbands are given "first shot" at parental status (McCandless and Sheldon 2010: 188). Those not in civil partnerships must seek licensed treatment if the non-carrying partner is to attain legal parentage, and are dealt with under separate provisions based on consent (section 44 of the 2008 Act). Legal parenthood is therefore conferred either as a result of status or by a contract-like arrangement; both of which are well-entrenched legal devices.

Civil partnership offers the incentive of being able to choose either licensed or unlicensed treatment, known or unknown donors, without the threat of challenge from that donor for parental status. As Glennon (2009) argues in a different context: 'These are ultimately questions of *accessibility* as prevailing norms are not disturbed but either simply extended, or modified to apply to alternative family structures' (177). Civil partnership is relevant to those same-sex parents who have experienced stigmatisation as it may be seen as an effective means of legitimating their relationships. It could also make legal recognition available for couples who wish to benefit from the protections of the 2008 Act but are unable to afford treatment at a licensed clinic (Luzia 2013; Nordqvist and Smart 2014: 41). Civil partnership operates here as marital status – with the non-carrying partner presumed to be the child's parent. In other words, the commitment read off from civil partnership also evidences intention to parent; an understanding deeply rooted in the historical traditions associated with marriage as the ideal institution for raising children. David Cameron's (2011) remark that he supports gay marriage not *in spite of* being a conservative, but *because* he is a Conservative – and believes in the power of commitment to strengthen society – reflects an assimilationist strategy to hetero-normalise relationships. Historically however, same-sex couples have developed their own norms, creating and negotiating their own ways of conducting relationships (Rolfe and Peel 2011: 317).

The equation of civil partnership with marriage means the dominance of the two-parent nuclear family is retained, reiterated and stabilised. Grigolo (2003) sees equality as demanding non-heterosexuals move from what has historically been seen as the negative side of the heterosexuality/homosexuality dichotomy to the positive side. In this context the positive side of heterosexuality would include, for example, stable, lasting, committed relationships as against those which are on the other hand constructed as unstable, transient and uncommitted (1041). The 2008 Act situates marriage and civil partnership at one end of the pole, and unlicensed and potentially unconventional PTP families sliding off the scale without a presence in the legal framework. Somewhere in between is the lesbian couple who chooses not to enter civil partnership but seeks licensed treatment rather than opting for self-insemination.

Some couples felt pressured into civil partnership even prior to the 2008 Act (Nordqvist 2012: 656), so it is at least questionable whether law should reify social norms – particularly where potentially transgressive and more radical possibilities are thereby forsaken and the social positioning at the margins of acceptability of those who fail to take up these incentives is further justified (Butler 2002). Jones (2010) argues that key possibilities arising from reproductive technologies are explicitly excluded from the legal provisions, such as the possibility of three or more parents being recognised as such concurrently. Her thesis is useful for flagging up how it is just as important to reflect on what the law does not do along with what it does. Jones (2010) considers these possibilities 'Beyond the Legal Imagination' (214). On the contrary, we argue that it is precisely *because of* the law makers' wild imaginings about the possibilities of multiple parents and the potential disorder that the assimilationist approach is adopted. During the reform process, the Department of Health actually considered the possibility of a child having three legal parents but concluded that the 2008 Act was not regarded as the correct forum for bringing about such 'wide-ranging reform of fundamental family law principles' (McCandless and Sheldon 2010: 191).

While assessment of which hetero-norm – genetic parentage or the dyadic nuclear family – is more dominant in wider society is generally moot, the 2008 Act is unambiguous. Offering protections for those who wish to oppose the former, it refuses to acknowledge challenges to the latter. At the top end of the hetero-normative continuum, then, there is the new legal framework that provides parental status and rights based upon the privileged legal relationship of civil partnership. Those not in civil partnerships must seek licensed treatment, and are conferred legal parenthood by a contract-like arrangement. These provisions confine reproductive relationships within the conventional two-parent paradigm, forestalling the possibility of a third legal parent. It is assumed that the *one* non-birth parent will care for the child together with the birth parent. Still further along that continuum, and perhaps not even on the line, are those at the forefront of reshaping family life since Weston (1991) coined the phrase 'families of choice' – defining their experiences of kinship by and for their specifically lesbian and gay subject positions, negotiating reproductive relationships to co-parent and form families that challenge the two-parent norm. Although opportunities have been limited due to an absence of legal support, empirical evidence suggests that there are various ways in which some lesbians and gay men negotiate prospective roles in order to support alternative models. Dunne's (2000) study revealed that some lesbian parents were keen to shun the traditional nuclear family in favour of 'extended family networks of friends and kin' (118). When, after more than two adults have agreed to conceive and raise a child and relationships break down, what has become clear is that intention is considered in the case law alongside other significant factors. However, the cases prove difficult to resolve when fathers have applied for court orders to strengthen their legal position in respect of the child(ren).

Protecting the lesbian nuclear family

Applying the logic of the 2008 Act, courts have expressed an explicit desire to protect the lesbian nuclear family. In *R v E and F* (2010), the application for parental responsibility and shared residence was dismissed, and contact not exceeding 50 days per year (which amounted to considerably less contact than enjoyed previously) was awarded. At the interim hearing in *Re P & L* (2012) the application for a residence order was struck out, and a defined contact order for contact between the men and the younger child was made at the full hearing. Because of the extent of the deterioration in the relationships, only indirect contact between the men and the older child was ordered, which was variable by agreement between the adults. On appeal in *A v B & C* (2012), the father was awarded defined contact for one meeting per fortnight, such that the child should know him but not so much as to 'fracture by frequent absence what is described as the nuclear family'.

As mentioned earlier, same-sex relationships have made ground in respect of achieving legal equality, gaining access to institutions which broadly mimic those already privileged in society. However, those further away from the preferential end of our continuum will face problems as family law courts struggle to deal with the range of issues that arise when relationships break down. When there is conflict between multiple parents an easy option is to contain the dispute, protecting the more familiar two-parent family by restricting paternal rights and responsibilities such as contact. This approach is apparent in the case law; the lesbian nuclear family is 'protected' by limiting relationships between children and gay fathers. It is not difficult to imagine how lesbian parents who have been historically disadvantaged in respect of their children come to feel vulnerable when rights claims are made by biological fathers. It is also unsurprising that family courts are concerned about the welfare interests of the child within the nuclear family. However, there was strong evidence in all three cases that there was a fairly high level of involvement from the fathers and in two, their male partners. Child welfare is context specific and courts look at cases on an individual basis. Our argument is that the court could also consider political motivations for embarking upon a PTP family project; where, for example, the parties involved attempt to break down traditional parenting paradigms, and where deliberate decisions have been made to incorporate gay fathers rather than heterosexual ones to co-parent children. There are a range of options available, and it is simply our concern that the courts are currently being too restrictive in their assessment of the nature and value of the relationship between gay fathers and the child.

Diduck (2007) identifies how the use of a known donor who takes up some kind of father role appears to challenge the nuclear family, while simultaneously reinforcing 'the heterosexual and patriarchal model of the family that requires a father or father figure and undermines the idea that women can parent alone' (citing Kelly 2004: 133). We are not sure that the case law to date suggests that gay fathers find themselves in such a strong position in respect of their children. It is unfortunate for them to be cast as agents of hetero-normative patriarchy when empirical evidence suggests that there is a sense amongst lesbian and gay prospective parents that the PTP family is a re-imagining and reshaping of family life with a shared aim of decentring the traditional two-parent family.

A significant factor in the research is that gay fathers were selected *not* because of the perceived importance of biological fathers to children but instead because of the belief that they represented a more 'appealing' (Ryan-Flood 2005: 200) or 'positive' (Dunne 2000: 117) form of masculinity. This research also revealed that lesbian couples believed that, should there be a dispute, a heterosexual father (especially a married one) would be in a stronger position than a gay one in respect of residence and contact disputes (Dunne 2000; Ryan-Flood 2005). This certainly seems to be borne out in the examination of the case law – for example the recent case of *Re SAB* (2014), which saw a heterosexual donor/father awarded contact on the basis that the court deemed it 'highly unlikely' that he would have agreed 'merely to be a sperm donor' (25). However, it is important, *especially* because PTP families are shaped by a political and personal desire to escape the hetero-normative framework and to parent in atypical ways, to reflect on how gay fathers are situated in respect of children when disputes arise.

A role for the gay father?

Kirkman (2004) describes the process of assessing the role of the donor/father as one imbued with both 'ambivalence and complexity' (328), to which the courts must be attentive. Nordqvist and Smart (2014), for example, identify parents 'trying to reshape parenthood away from the familiar twosome model' (17), even though no couples reported entering into a co-parenting agreement, or sharing parenthood equally with the donor/father, in their research project (117). Although there is evidence that lesbians see gay men as less of a threat to the stability of the family than heterosexual fathers, this might shift as more gay men express interest in involved parenthood (Almack 2006: 13). Empirical research into how these men construe their relationships with children suggests that their perspectives on this process may be equally complex (Riggs and Scholz 2011; Dempsey 2012). Nordqvist (2013) describes questions of kinship as 'multilayered' (14), emphasising the gendered power relationships at stake when men are included in lesbian parenting projects. Nevertheless, it remains important to avoid placing gay fathers in an overly prejudicial position in seeking to meet the needs of the dyadic lesbian family.

Each of the gay fathers in the decided cases sought to equate their position with that of heterosexual estranged fathers, though the courts, in all instances, rejected the view that the positions were comparable. In a crucial aspect of *A v B & C* (2012), Thorpe LJ made it clear that the case was 'not in any way analogous to a situation which has been referred to as the "divorce model"' because there had never been a cohabiting relationship between parent and child (12). Hedley J was equally clear in *MA v RS* (2011): 'It is all too easy in these cases for biological fathers to see themselves in the same position as in separated parent cases in heterosexual arrangements, whereas this arrangement is, and was always *intended* to be, quite different' (9). In *Re P & L* (2011) it was concluded that: 'the use of stereotypes from traditional family models was unreliable and the court should resist the temptation to squeeze a given set of facts to fit such a model' (1). Finally, in *R v E and F* (2010) it was held that the pre-conception agreement suggested that the 'mother and her partner were to be the child's parents, although the father was to have an important role […]. It would not be in the child's best interests to grant the father parental responsibility when the father was asserting that the four adults and the child comprised one family' (3). The court's response to the father's claim to be regarded in the same way as the heterosexual father is thus to hetero-normalise the female parental relationship while diminishing his significance.

It is hardly surprising that the fathers sought to put forward equality-based arguments when legislation has itself sought to achieve equality by adapting the mechanisms available for heterosexuals. Leckey (2011) calls this the 'liberal equality claim' (333). There has been an additional legislative drive throughout the years to equalise the position of women and men in relation to their children. The broader socio-legal landscape would suggest that such a strategy might have proven fruitful as fathers' rights groups garner support from the emphasis placed on the need of children for continuing relationships with their biological parents. The Children and Families Act 2014 has incorporated a presumption of parental involvement into the Children Act 1989 by getting rid of residence and contact orders in favour of the child arrangements order designed to eradicate the notion that there are winners and losers in family disputes and augment the position of the non-resident parent, most frequently the father (Ministry of Justice and Department for Education 2012: 23).[6]

It is difficult to ascertain the extent to which this presumption will feature in PTP family disputes and whether the courts will be compelled to incorporate the shared parenting presumption in the exercise of the welfare test. However, the current judicial approach has resisted the view that gay fathers are intended as having a central role in their children's lives and they have been portrayed as mere donors; even constituting a threatening presence to the lesbian family. Of course, this position could change – and may, should a future court go on to award substantive contact following the recent case of *Re G* (2013). This joint hearing saw both members of a gay couple denied leave to apply for parental responsibility and residence orders in respect of the children they had conceived with two separate lesbian couples, but gave leave to apply for contact. In contrast to the previous cases, both lesbian couples had registered civil partnerships; positioning their relationship at the preferential end of the hetero-normative continuum. The manner in which these men were characterised as 'fathers' whose rights had been deprived by the 2008 Act has been interpreted as constituting a shift in the judicial approach to lesbian families. Yeatman (2013) fears that, after *Re G* (2013), lesbian couples who allow a child to have any contact with their progenitor 'will open the door to an application for more contact if that is what the donor wants, because the courts will still regard him as a parent due to his genetic tie to the child' (1583). Yet substantively, Yeatman (2013) admits, the court could hardly refuse the men's application for leave to apply for contact 'as there is no such prohibition on others who are not legally connected to children' (1583). The disputes were resolved out of court, and the results from the parties' settlement will not be made public (Gamble 2013). Hence it remains to be seen whether such a shift will be borne out in subsequent case law; if a future court were to make a substantive order against the wishes of a lesbian couple who had taken active steps to normalise their relationship, then the legal position of gay fathers would be somewhat stronger than anticipated.

Courts are being forced to tread a difficult line between recognising the role that gay fathers have and want to play and the need to preserve and protect the relationships within the nuclear family. Although the PTP family is potentially transformative, the dominance of fathers' rights discourse in the broader social context and the undervaluing of women's caring role do raise issues in terms of rendering lesbian parents vulnerable (Kelly 2004). Court decisions are not made in a social vacuum, and the power of rhetoric promoting a paradigmatically hetero-normative conception of fatherhood (as either biologically or socially necessary) has been noted (Smith 2010: 56). This is particularly so where such arguments – from the likes of fathers' rights group Fathers 4 Justice – are made in conjunction with attacks on 'lesbo dads' (Land 2008). The judicial limits placed upon the father's rights can be seen *prima facie* as a sensitive response to the lesbian dyadic family but it is important to ensure that care is taken not to discriminate against gay fathers – who have yet to feature in these fathers' rights narratives. Whilst it is accepted that 'men have had systematically more material, institutional and discursive power to shape the process of social construction' this will vary depending on a range of factors including ethnicity, social class and sexuality (Boyd 2010: 140). The notion of third-party threat apparently draws upon an idea of dominant paternal authority historically associated with heterosexual fatherhood (Collier 1995). It is at least doubtful whether this notion of paternal authority is appropriate for gay fathers (Dempsey 2012). As empirical research has indicated, they have been viewed by lesbians as rather less of a threat in respect of family life and as offering a more acceptable form of masculinity. For heterosexual couples, social policy and law construct biological fathers as central to child welfare and the Children and Families Act 2014 with its presumption of parental involvement continues in this vein. The gay father's position is rather more ambiguous.

These cases raise questions about what level of involvement leads to a gay father becoming a parent and the political, social, legal and personal implications of being regarded as a father rather than a parent. It also requires some attention to the relative position of gay fathers in respect of family life. Intention to parent has some relevance for gay fathers and it is necessary to reflect critically upon what they have to do to have their input count as 'parenting' rather than as a mere father figure, and at what point one's intention to parent is evidenced. When lesbians and gay men actively seek to challenge the heterosexual and patriarchal model of family life, written agreements about future relationships are sometimes explicitly based on social solidarity, ongoing mutual support and flexibility rather than on fixed negotiated contract terms of future parenting (Dempsey 2010: 1153).

Although certain individual benefits may arise out of negotiations for sharing parenting (Dunne 2000; Ryan-Flood 2005), there remains an expectation of a 'social contract between the extended families of origin […] and goodwill and friendship between the adults parenting' (Dempsey 2010: 1153). One way to deal with the PTP family is to suggest that pre-conception agreements be legally enforceable (Zanghellini 2010; Callus 2012: 347). However, the difficulty with intention is all too readily apparent in these cases. Emotions can run high once a child is born and what was intended before conception can seem completely inappropriate afterwards. It is therefore important for courts to be able to draw upon the broader social context in which these disputes arise, including the political issues, while appreciating and initiating appropriate post-separation parenting arrangements that reflect actual caring relationships and responsibilities that existed before relationship breakdown.

The cases also raise important issues about how the role of fathers in the PTP family is perceived as compared with the heterosexual context. In that context biology is used to augment the links between men and children and it is assumed that parental responsibilities flow from that relationship when they may very well not. In contrast, PTP families' pre-conception agreements are frequently made as a result of a highly cognitive, negotiated process. It is clear from the cases that gay fathers are relegated to a subordinate role despite judicial disagreement over the terms 'primary' (or principal) and 'secondary' parents. This is so even when it is all too clear that children have been born of relationships based on intention, mutual respect, co-operation, flexibility and friendship. A gay father's role may be constrained from the start where disputes arise early on, as was the case in *A v B & C* (2012). The approach to the prospective roles for gay fathers needs to be sensitive to their wider social and political context as well as that of lesbian parents. It is understandable that the resident lesbian parents' position is protected when gay fathers seek additional involvement. Feminist and queer research has sought the legitimation of lesbian families and their protection by looking at wider society and discrimination suffered by lesbian families within it. This is also the approach in evidence in family courts. Yet there are welfare benefits for the child of the PTP family from having family law send out positive messages about their family arrangement. When parenting with multiple parents, it is frequently a political and social endeavour for lesbians and gay men to challenge the patriarchal nuclear family and it would be a shame to omit this from discussions about welfare considerations. Wider society also Stands to gain as a result of increased understanding and sensitivity towards diverse families and the eradication of discrimination based on sexuality. Similar arguments were made in the early battle to gain legal recognition and social acceptance of lesbian families. As Leckey (2008) has argued, family law now produces 'contextual subjects' who are 'rooted in their relationships and social settings' (3). It would be a pity if gay fathers were located on the margins of the hetero-normative nuclear family almost as if they typify the 'self-sufficient liberal individual who is autonomous' that the contextual approach seeks to avoid (Boyd 2010: 149–50).

Conclusion

The dyadic lesbian nuclear family can take solace from the protection offered by statutory reforms and the approach of the judiciary to date in England and Wales. Academic debates in Canada and the USA have been directed towards whether or not law reform should take this trajectory or rather focus upon extending the boundaries of family and parenthood to include multiple parents rather than just the two (Kelly 2004). In British Columbia, Canada, section 30 of the Family Law Act 2011 means it is now possible for a child to have multiple legal parents if such an arrangement has been made between the intending parents. It is arguable that, in the UK, motivations for entering into PTP arrangements may come to have more significance now that lesbian parents can protect their legal position vis à vis the donor by the formal means provided by the 2008 Act. In other words, will the choice of an informal arrangement – rather than civil partnership or licensed treatment – strengthen the gay father's (and his partner's) position in respect of the child, and is this desirable? Case law to date has protected the lesbian family from the 'threat' of the gay father by restricting his participation in the family; but that protection comes at the cost of marginalising children raised in diverse lesbian and gay extended families and omits the political dimension from consideration of child welfare.

It might be suggested that the protection of the dyadic lesbian family supports rather than challenges the two-parent only norm, reinforcing the 'dichotomy within which the "other" is defined' (Grigolo 2003: 1025). The 'other' here is the PTP family. As Grigolo (2003) has argued, 'the more a relationship or a family differentiates itself from the traditional sexual and biological requirements of "the" family based on marriage, the less likely recognition becomes' (1040). The dyadic lesbian family is approached sympathetically precisely because it can establish itself as belonging to the preferential end of the hetero-normative continuum. The gay father is located at the very end of that continuum when disputes arise and he can be constructed, and experienced, as an unwanted and disruptive source of conflict and intrusion. There is a need to consider whether or not to recognise more than two individuals as parents in order to convey the reality where there is clear evidence of multiple parent activity.

The provisions of the 2008 Act 'reinforce the traditional hetero familial ideal of two parents; the equality imposed upon lesbian partners […] imposes heterosexual norms upon them' (Diduck 2007: 466). Like the Human Fertilisation and Embryology Act 1990 before it, this is designed to provide a 'strong moral statement of the importance of the nuclear family' (Sheldon 2005: 527). When prospective parents choose to operate outside the formal framework and locate themselves at the very end (and constructed as the worst side) of the hetero-normative continuum, it may be that pre-conception discussions will figure more highly and courts may be swayed towards awarding parental responsibility where it looks like the decision to have a child is a PTP family project. Questions might be raised about whether this would be such a negative development.

The 2008 Act conceives of this question as a zero-sum game; whereas we reject the assumption that privilege must be redistributed by courts along a new (hetero-)normative continuum. Instead, we advocate dismantling such hierarchies so as enable different challenges to the hetero-normative family. What form that challenge takes – dyadic lesbian parents, PTP families, or neither – could be of little legal relevance as people care and support each other in families of choice without turning to law. However, while law privileges dyadic challenges – extending protections to lesbian couples beyond those who opt in to civil partnership or licensed treatment – it effectively denies the legitimacy of PTP families. In some cases these protections will be over-extended; were a court to find evidence that a PTP family may have been planned or functioning before the relationships broke down, it would seem highly unconscionable for it to ignore that evidence in order to exclude the gay father and 'protect' a dyadic lesbian family that may itself have formed only in reaction to that breakdown.

Although issues of gender, sexuality and power will form part of the contextual background (and may or may not be overtly dealt with), there is no doubt that they are important and relevant considerations which have been used to insulate the lesbian family but have not been fully developed in respect of gay fathers. Lesbian and gay communities have been at the vanguard of challenging hetero-normative models of the family, and parenting differently has been a shared and political enterprise. It is undeniable that there are risks, sometimes dangerous ones, involved in multiple-parenting projects.[7] However, issues of gender, sexuality and power shift, evolve and transmute according to prevailing socio-political contexts. Lesbian parents' families are gaining social and legal recognition, and, politically, it is important not to subject gay fathers to the same kind of marginalisation that lesbian mothers have suffered. Clearly, there are issues to confront. PTP families can present a greater set of challenges for law than those of the nuclear family. The difficulty in confronting these challenges will be for law to avoid hetero-normative assumptions about both fatherhood and the family form. There may nevertheless be great benefits to children from protecting all their meaningful relationships and sending out positive messages about diverse families to wider society.

Notes

1 We define a plus-two-parent (PTP) family as an intended parenting project, involving three or more adults assuming a 'parenting' role in varying degrees, depending on the agreement reached, in an earlier version of this article published

by Family Law (a publishing imprint of Jordan Publishing Ltd) in 2013 issue 4 of *Child and Family Law Quarterly*, at [2013] CFLQ 451.

2 See Thorpe LJ in *A v B & C* (2012), para [30].

3 'Family life' will exist between a birth father and his child where there has been cohabitation or other factors that show an actual or potential relationship of sufficient constancy and commitment to create *de facto* ties *Kroon v The Netherlands* (1994). Mere biological kinship is insufficient.

4 Though proof may be difficult, as *M v F and H* (2013) demonstrates.

5 Children Act 1989 s 4ZA.

6 This legislation is considered very much a response to the fathers' rights argument that family law privileges mothers. While heterosexual fathers have been very visible in these discussions, gay fathers have not.

7 An extreme example is *Re Patrick* (2002), which resulted in the biological mother killing herself and Patrick.

References

Almack, K., 'Seeking sperm: accounts of lesbian couple' reproductive decision-making and understandings of the needs of the child' (2006) 20(1) *International Journal of Law, Policy and the Family* 1–22.

Boyd, S., 'Autonomy for mothers? Relational theory and parenting apart' (2010) *Feminist Legal Studies* 137–158.

Butler, J., *Gender Trouble: Feminism and the subversion of identity* (Routledge, 1990).

——'Is kinship always already heterosexual?' (2002) 13(1) *Differences* 14–44.

Callus, T., 'A new parenthood paradigm for twenty-first century family law in England and Wales?' (2012) 32(3) *Legal Studies* 347–368.

Cameron, D., Conservative Party conference speech. Manchester, 5 October 2011 http://www.guardian.co.uk/politics/2011/oct/05/david-cameron-conservative-party-speech [accessed 4 September 2013].

Collier, R., *Masculinity, Law and the Family* (Routledge, 1995).

Dempsey, D., 'Conceiving and negotiating reproductive relationships: lesbian and gay men forming families with children' (2010) 44(6) *Sociology* 1145–1162.

——'More like a donor or more like a father? Gay men's concepts of relatedness to children' (2012) 15(2) *Sexualities* 156–74.

Diduck, A., '"If only we can find the appropriate terms to use the issue will be solved": Law, identity and parenthood' (2007) *Child and Family Law Quarterly* 458–480.

do Mar Castro Varela, M., Dhawan, N. and Engel, A., 'Introduction' in do Mar Castro Varela M, Dhawan, N. and Engel, A. (eds), *Hegemony and Heteronormativity: Revisiting 'The Political' in Queer Politics* (Ashgate, 2011a), 1–24.

——'Normative dilemmas and the hegemony of counter-hegemony' in do Mar Castro Varela, M., Dhawan, N. and Engel, A. (eds), *Hegemony and Heteronormativity: Revisiting 'The Political' in Queer Politics* (Ashgate, 2011b), 91–120.

Duggan, L., *The Twilight of Equality: Neoliberalism, Cultural Politics, and the Attack on Democracy* (Beacon Press, 2003).

Dunne, G., 'Balancing acts: on the salience of sexuality and sexual identity for understanding the gendering of work and family-life opportunities' in Spearling L. and Owen, M. (eds), *Women and Work: The age of post-feminism?* (Ashgate, 2000), 109–132.

Gamble, N., 'Lesbian parents and sperm donors: re G and re Z' (2013) *Family Law* 1426–1429.

Glennon, L., 'The limitations of equality discourses on the contours of intimate obligations' in Wallbank, J., Choudhry, S. and Herring, J. (eds), *Rights, Gender and Family Law* (Routledge, 2009), 169–198.

Grigolo, M., 'Sexualities and the ECHR: introducing the universal sexual legal subject' (2003) 14(5) *European Journal of International Law* 1023–1044.

Jackson, S., 'Gender, sexuality and heterosexuality: the complexity (and limits) of heteronormativity' (2006) 7(1) *Feminist Theory* 105–121.

Jones, C., 'The (im)possible parents in law' in Lind, C., Keating, H. and Bridgeman, J. (eds), *Taking Responsibility, Law and the Changing Family* (Ashgate, 2010), 201–220.

Kelly, F., 'Nuclear norms or fluid families? Incorporating lesbian and gay parents into Canadian family law' (2004) 21 *Canadian Journal of Family Law* 133–178.

Kirkman, M., 'Saviours and satyrs: ambivalence in narrative meanings of sperm provision' (2004) 6(4) *Culture, Health & Sexuality* 319–348.

Land, J., 'Fathers 4 Justice protestors confronted over "homophobic" banner' (24dash.com, 2008) http://www.24dash.com/news/communities/2008-09-19-fathers-4-justice-protestors-confronted-over-homophobic-banner [accessed 30 July 2013].

Leckey, R., *Contextual Subjects: Family, State, and Relational theory* (University of Toronto Press, 2008).

——'Law reform, lesbian parenting, and the reflective claim' (2011) 3 *Social and Legal Studies* 331–348.

Lind, C. and Hewitt, T., 'Law and the complexities of parenting: parental status and parental function' (2009) 31(4) *Journal of Social, Welfare and Family Law* 391–406.

Ludwig, G., 'From the "heterosexual matrix" to a "Heteronormative hegemony": initiating a dialogue between Judith Butler and Antonio Gramsci about queer theory and politics' in do Mar Castro Varela, M., Dhawan, N. and Engel, A. (eds), *Hegemony and Heteronormativity: Revisiting 'The Political' in Queer Politics* (Ashgate, 2011), 43–62.

Luzia, K., 'Present absences: hidden geographies of lesbian parenting' in Taylor, Y. and Addison, M. (eds), *Queer Presences and Absences* (Palgrave Macmillan, 2013), 203–221.

McCandless, J. and Sheldon, S., 'The Human Fertilisation and Embryology Act (2008) and the tenacity of the sexual family form' (2010) 73(2) *Modern Law Review* 175–207.

Ministry of Justice and Department for Education, *The Government Response to the Family Justice Review: A system with children and families at its heart*, Cm 8273 (The Stationery Office, 2012).

Nordqvist, P., '"I don't want us to stand out more than we already do": Lesbian couples negotiating family conceptions in donor conception' (2012) 15(5/6) *Sexualities* 644–661.

——'Bringing kinship into being: connectedness, donor conception and lesbian parenthood' (2013) 48(2) *Sociology*, 268–283.

——and Smart, C., *Relative Strangers: Family Life, Genes and Donor Conception* (Palgrave Macmillan, 2014).

Riggs, D.W. and Scholz, B., 'The value and meaning attached to genetic relatedness among Australian sperm donors' (2011) 30(1) *New Genetics and Society* 41–58.

Rolfe, A. and Peel, E., '"It's a double-edged thing": The paradox of civil partnership and why some couples are choosing not to have one' (2011) 21(3) *Feminism & Psychology* 317–35.

Ryan-Flood, R., 'Contested heteronormativities: discourses of fatherhood among lesbian parents in Sweden and Ireland' (2005) 8(2) *Sexualities* 189–204.

Sheldon, S., 'Fragmenting fatherhood: the regulation of reproductive technologies' (2005) 68 *Modern Law Review* 523–553.

Smith, L., 'Clashing symbols? Reconciling support for fathers and fatherless families after the Human Fertilisation and Embryology Act 2008' (2010) 22(1) *Child and Family Law Quarterly* 46–70.

——'Tangling the web of legal parenthood: legal responses to the use of known donors in lesbian parenting arrangements' (2013) 33(3) *Legal Studies* 355–381.

Wallbank, J., 'Channelling the messiness of diverse family lives: resisting the calls to order and de-centring the hetero-normative family' (2010) 32(4) *Journal of Social Welfare and Family Law* 353–368.

Warner, M., 'Introduction' in Warner, M. (ed.), *Fear of a Queer Planet: Queer Politics and Social Theory* (University of Minnesota Press, 1993), vii–xxxi.

Weston, K., *Families We Choose: Lesbians, Gays, Kinship* (Columbia University Press, 1991).

Yeatman, L., 'Lesbian co-parents: still not real mothers' (2013) *Family Law* 1581–1587.

Zanghellini, A., 'Lesbian and gay parents and reproductive technologies: the 2008 Australian and UK reforms' (2010) 18 *Feminist Legal Studies* 227–251.

Cases

Kroon v The Netherlands (1994) 19 EHRR 263

Re Patrick (2002) 28 Fam LR 579 (Australia)

Re D (contact and parental responsibility: lesbian mothers and known father) [2006] EWHC 2 (Fam), [2006] 1 FCR 556

Re B (Role of Biological Father) [2007] EWHC 1952 (Fam), [2008] 1 FLR 1015

R v E and F (Female Parents: Known Father) [2010] EWHC 417 (Fam), [2010] 2 FLR 383

T v T [2010] EWCA Civ 1366, [2011] Fam Law 240

ML, AR v RW, SW [2011] EWHC 2455 (Fam), [2012] 1 FLR 1056

A v B & C [2012] EWCA Civ 285, [2012] 2 FLR 607

MA v RS (Contact: Parenting Roles) [2011] EWHC 2455 (Fam), [2012] 1 FLR 1056.

Re P & L (Contact) [2011] EWHC 3431, [2012] 1 FLR 1068.

Re G (A Child) [2013] EWHC 134 (Fam), [2013] 1 FLR 1334

M v F and H (Legal Paternity) [2013] EWHC 1901 (Fam)

Re SAB [2014] EWHC 384 (Fam)

Chapter 11

Judging the Act

Civil partnership disputes in the courtroom and the media

Daniel Monk

Introduction

Judges make law. And in the decade prior to the enactment of the Civil Partnership Act 2004 (the CPA), the judiciary expressed their views about same-sex relations on a number of occasions (Harper et al. 2014: 9–23). By 2004 the case law not only reflected an explicit judicial commitment to liberal values (in marked contrast to earlier case law) but also, in some areas, effectively established formal legal equality. Arguably the highpoint of judicial action was *Ghaidan v Godin-Mendoza* [2004] UKHL 30; for here the House of Lords held that the statutory expression 'living together as husband and wife' could refer to a same-sex couple. In other words, in recognising same-sex relationships the judiciary beat Parliament to it.[1]

Creative judicial interpretations are not new. The Human Rights Act 1998 may have provided an additional legitimacy, but judicial creativity is at the heart of the common law tradition, and what makes it such a rich historical source. And of course it is not always progressive. For example a statutory reform introduced in 2009 to prevent 'sexual infidelity' being an acceptable ground to reduce a murder charge to one of manslaughter has only recently been restrictively reframed by judicial creativity.[2] So what have the judges made of the CPA? This chapter explores this question by a close reading of three cases where provisions under the CPA have been open to interpretation. The cases all received varying degrees of media attention and examining this coverage alongside the formal case reports provides a contrasting space for exploring public representations and understandings of same-sex relationships.

Arguments both for and against the CPA, and gay marriage more generally, frequently make broad claims about their effects. For example, within 'progressive' circles, supporters claim that the legislation will 'modernise' the institution of marriage (for the better), while detractors claim that the institution will 'normalise' gays and lesbians (for the worse). These causal arguments are often crude. On both sides ideological aspirations are too often expressed as empirical predictions. A key argument here is that the case law where judges are called on to apply or adjudicate on provisions within the CPA provides a space for assessing some of the claims about its real and potential impact.

Case law is, of course, a weak empirical source. It does provide a window into and an account of the lives of real people. But against this it is important to acknowledge two things. First, very few people resort to law to resolve their conflicts (in other words they are atypical from the start), and even fewer reach the appellate courts. This renders reported decisions, in some ways, simply anecdotal. And the transformation of a dispute into a legal dispute is a complex process involving an array of gatekeepers and extraneous factors (in particularly economics) (Felstiner et al. 1980–81). Second, and perhaps more significant, is the fact that legal narratives are never neutral. Law requires that a real life story is framed and described in a very particular way. So law's stories are just that: stories. But they are powerful stories, which is to say that they are more productive than descriptive; as Gewirtz notes, legal narratives are 'artifacts that reveal a culture, not just policies that shape that culture' (1996: 3). Legal subjects consequently may be mythical but it is precisely this fact – and particularly in a juridical age – that renders law's stories their significance beyond law.

Living 'as civil partners'?

Baynes v Hedger and others [2008] EWHC 1587 (Ch) was an inheritance dispute. Mary Watson and Margot Baynes were lovers, but not in a civil partnership. On Watson's death, Baynes argued that she had not been adequately provided for and made an application to contest Watson's will. Under the Inheritance (Provision for Family and Dependants) Act 1975 an unmarried partner can bring such a case, as long as the claimant can first satisfy the court that he or she was 'living as the husband or wife of the deceased' (s1(1A)(b)); Kerridge 2009: 163–65, 189). The CPA extended these provisions to include those living 'as civil partners'.[3] This statutory legal test is used in housing and other areas of law and, consequently, the case has significance beyond inheritance disputes. Previous case law – prior to the enactment of the CPA – had established that a same-sex couple could be considered to be living 'as husband and wife';[4] and so it could be argued that in this context legal equality was in place prior to the CPA. However, in this case the judge – Lewison J – held that the couple had not lived 'as civil partners' and, consequently, Baynes's claim failed. Whether Baynes ought to have received more from Watson's estate is debatable but not the focus here. For what is interesting in this context is the approach adopted to interpreting the new statutory expression 'living as civil partners'.[5]

Lewison J, applying previous case law, held that one of the tests to be applied to determine whether or not they were living 'as civil partners' was:

'Is the relationship one which has been presented to the outside world openly and unequivocally so that society considers it to be of permanent intent – the words "til death us do part" being apposite?' (para [120]). He also held that this was an 'essential qualification'; that 'it is not possible to establish that two persons have lived together as civil partners unless their relationship as a couple is an acknowledged one' (para [150]), as 'both a marriage and a civil partnership are publically acknowledged relationships' (para [125]).

While Lewison J considered himself bound by earlier decisions, he noted that these tests (established by previous case law and not statute) were 'statements of general principles' and, as such, 'must of course be read in the light of facts of the case' as 'human relationships are many and various' (para [121]).

Moreover, and perhaps surprisingly considering the conclusion he subsequently reached, Lewison J demonstrated a sensitive understanding of why, in this particular case, the relationship was not 'presented to the outside world openly and unequivocally'. In summarising the facts of the case he noted that:

> Many of the witnesses who saw them together described them as a couple. They were seen as a couple by Margot's children. But they were of a generation for whom a same-sex relationship was not an acceptable lifestyle, and their relationship was not openly acknowledged ... They were of that age when that sort of thing was unacceptable and it would have upset them ... I conclude that Mary and Margot had a loving relationship which spanned 50 continuous years ... There was no falling out between them, and their relationship carried on until Mary's death. But their relationship was a private relationship. ... Had any sexual element in the relationship been suggested, they would have denied it.
>
> (Paras [34] [35])

Despite the discretion that he acknowledged the law enabled him, he treated 'living as civil partners' in an identical way as 'husband and wife' and in doing so chose not to take into account the need, both real and sensed, for same-sex couples (especially older couples) to be less open about their relationship.[6]

Requiring a same-sex couple that have not opted for a civil partnership to produce evidence of openness is little more than a form of legal 'outing'.[7] And the potential violence of law here is significant. No comparable danger faces opposite-sex partners; there may be reasons why they might wish to keep a relationship from public view but the dangers of exposure of their sexual orientation are non-existent.

In the CPA debate in the House of Lords, Baroness Rendall argued for the availability of private registrations for civil partnerships on the basis that, 'In many areas of society and of the workplace, openly declaring one's sexual orientation is a risky business'.[8] That Parliament rejected this proposal partly legitimises Lewison's finding. Consequently, the case is a classic example of discrimination and substantive inequality resulting from 'blind' equal treatment.

The inappropriateness of failing to acknowledge difference here is clearer still if one examines the gendered basis of the 'openness' rule. For the requirement that marital status be public and visible has traditionally been, and still is, imposed by cultural norms far more on women than men. Wedding rings, change of surname, the title 'Mrs' and, in many cultures, dress codes are all examples of gendered rules and conventions that render the marital status of women visible. Premised, often explicitly, on the double standards of sexual fidelity, they indicate to men that a woman is 'taken' and 'unavailable'. Concerns about the legitimacy of children have traditionally been crucial here, and partly explain why sexual fidelity plays a far less central role in same-sex relations (Barker and Langdridge 2010; Hoff and Beougher 2010).

Lewison J, as quoted above, appears to imply that openness about a sexual relationship between the women, was, at the very least, a factor in determining the public nature of the relationship. Yet had he wished to he could have distinguished 'civil partners' from 'husband and wife' by reference to the CPA, for none of the marriage laws relating to sexual acts (adultery, non-consummation) apply to civil partnerships, and this distinction remains between same- and opposite-sex marriage (Barker 2006). It is therefore at least valid to question not only whether Watson and Baynes were living 'as civil partners', but why openness is a requirement that should apply to same-sex couples at all.

The case received considerable media attention. Baynes's daughter, who also contested Watson's will, had previously been married to the film director Ken Russell and, no doubt because of this, the story appeared in the 'showbiz' sections of the *Daily Mail* and the *Daily Telegraph* under the following respective headlines: 'Ken Russell's wife in court battle over her mother's lesbian lover's £2.3million estate' (Camber 2008) and 'Ken Russell's ex-wife sues over lesbian's estate' (Singh 2008; see also *Evening Standard* 2008 and *Metro* 2008). Perhaps surprisingly the liberal broadsheet newspapers reported the case in a similar fashion. The headline in the *Independent* was 'Ken Russell's former wife contests will of mother's lesbian lover' (26 June 2008), while in the *Guardian*, this time in the 'Law' section, the headline was 'Actor loses court battle over £2.3m estate of mother's lesbian lover' (Lewis 2008).

A tenuous link to celebrity and a story that can combine death, sex and money offer an obvious explanation for the coverage; and there is a long history of the reporting and avid public interest in wills and inheritance disputes (Monk 2013a). But the reporting here also demonstrates the extent to which non-conventional sexualities are still represented as in some ways salacious.[9] The publicity that a case can attract can also be used as a strategic device against gay and lesbian beneficiaries fearful about being open about their sexuality.[10] Moreover, in *Baynes* there is a certain cruel irony to the resulting publicity as the openness of the relationship between the women was a critical factor in Baynes losing her case. Significantly, neither news story mentioned this legal point or the possible consequences for other same-sex couples. Indeed, while the creation of civil partnerships and gay marriage have attracted considerable attention the failure of the media to address the implications of judicial interpretations of the CPA on real people is a recurring theme.

Revoked wills and 'legitimate' couples

Court and others v Despallieres [2009] EWHC 3340 (Ch) also concerned an inheritance dispute, but of a very different kind and raising distinct legal issues. The facts were simple. Peter Ikin – a rich music business executive – made a will in 2002 leaving his estate to a mixture of friends and relatives. In August 2008, he made a new will leaving everything to his lover, Alexandre Despalliers. In October 2008, Ikin and Despallieres entered into a civil partnership and in November 2008 Ikin died. Allegations of foul play were raised but not established and were not relevant to the questions raised by the case.

The case was brought by the executors and beneficiaries under the first will from 2002. Their argument was that the 2008 will was invalid as a result of a long-standing statutory rule whereby wills are revoked by subsequent marriages; a rule that was extended to include civil partnerships on identical terms.[11] The motive underlying the claim was simple: if the 2008 will was held to be invalid, Ikin would be deemed to have died intestate and under the intestacy rules Despallieres would have only been entitled to the surviving spouse/civil partner's 'statutory legacy' (then £450,000) and half the residue.[12] And as Ikin's estate was approximately £7 million, in this case the result would have been that instead of Despallieres getting everything, half of the residue would have passed to Ikin's surviving relatives.[13]

Despallieres argued that the 2008 will was valid on the basis of the following statutory exemption to the revocation rule:

> if it appears from a will (a) that at the time it was made the testator was expecting to form a civil partnership with a particular person, and (b) that he intended that the will should not be revoked by the formation of the civil partnership …
>
> (Section 18B(3) of the Wills Act 1837)

That the 2008 will was made only two months before the civil partnership was a fact relied on. But the key question for the court was the interpretation of clauses 2 and 4 of the will, which read as follows:

> ... this, my last Will and Testament shall not be revoked by neither subsequent marriage, Civil Union Partnership. ... (cl 2)
>
> I give AND BEQUEATH to Alexandre Renaud Marcel Despallieres the entirety of my estate as a sole beneficiary (cl 4).

The judge hearing the case – Arnold J – held against Despalliers on the basis that the will 'did not show that the deceased person expected to form a civil partnership, let alone with a particular person', and that there was 'nothing in the will to indicate that there is any connection between clause 2 and clause 4 (para 12).

The law relating to the interpretation of wills is complex; there is a long-standing debate between 'literal' and (less orthodox) 'intentionalist' approaches, which have a particular relevance in the context of 'home-made' wills such as the one in this case (Kerridge and Rivers 2000). The point here is not that Arnold J was in any way wrong in reaching the decision he did, but, simply, that legitimate judicial discretion could have supported a different conclusion and that there was more at stake here than will-drafting skills (Monk 2011).

It is often hard to predict the outcome of inheritance cases. This is particularly the case with claims under the 1975 Act where the courts are explicitly required to make a 'value judgment' (Douglas 2014: 241). But even in cases, such as the one here, where the focus is on identifying the intent of a testator, judicial sympathies are often thinly veiled. While the case was eventually settled out of court, Arnold J's ruling would have resulted in Despalliers receiving a very considerable sum – after a very short relationship, and a civil partnership lasting just over one month – with the remainder of the estate being distributed amongst Ikin's relatives, which the 2002 will indicated he had good long-term connections with. Many might consider this outcome fair and indeed it coheres with public opinion about the circumstances in which a 'surviving spouse' should not inherit the whole estate (Williams et al. 2008; Humphreys et al. 2010: para 2). The only individuals in the case that receive nothing are Ikin's friends and god-children named in the 2002 will. Their absence from this legal resolution reflects the exclusive focus on couples and biological relatives in the law of intestacy. While this approach, again, coheres with public opinion (Douglas et al. 2011), research that has focused on gays and lesbians indicates the important place of non-biological relatives and friends within constructions of their inheritance family (Monk 2014). This case consequently is a reminder that will-making is particularly important for people living outside conventional families and a stark warning to the many same-sex couples who made wills prior to entering a civil partnership of the need to make new wills (Monk 2013b).

Advocates for the CPA, both in parliamentary debates and more widely, placed considerable emphasis on the plight of surviving partners. There is consequently a degree of irony that in one of the first post-CPA cases the surviving partner 'loses out' as a *result* of having entered a civil partnership. The argument here is not that this outcome is necessarily unfair; rather, it indicates the significance of constructions of deserving claimants – that all couples are not viewed as equal – and in this context media coverage of the case is particularly revealing.

The case attracted considerable media attention, particularly in the Australian press – where Ikin originated from and was a well-known figure. As in the *Baynes* case, tenuous links to celebrity explain the coverage, and the salaciousness here was abundant with the added Ingredient of a possible murder (albeit unproven). In the media stories Despallieres was portrayed as a money-grabbing opportunist – little more than a high-class male prostitute. And conversely Ikin was portrayed as a man deeply committed to his family who had fallen prey to the seductiveness of a handsome and much younger man. Ethnicity also played a part here: with the earthy wholesomeness of a family-loving Australian pitted against an untrustworthy but charming Frenchman. The following headlines in various newspapers give a sense of these representations: 'Peter Ikin married French boyfriend weeks before death' (*Daily Telegraph* 2008); 'Gay lover of the late Peter Ikin quizzed over secret will' (*Daily Telegraph* 2009); 'Gay Frenchman accused of killing friend of Elton John freed on bail' (*Daily Mirror* 2011); 'The Talented M. Despalliéres' (Stone 2012); 'A dead man, a forged will, a £10m inheritance, and a ruined reputation' (Hutchins 2012); 'Ikin's lover admits forging will, denies kill plot' (Connolly 2012); 'Young gay husband Alexandre Despallieres gets Peter Ikin millions in will' (Fife-Yeomans and Miranda 2009).

Whatever the truth of the stories, they demonstrate the contingency of the idealised nature of 'the couple'. Unlike Baynes and Watson, who despite a 50-year loving relationship were not considered to be living 'as civil partners', Ikin and Despallieres *were* civil partners, but legal recognition here was qualified by other values; what was contested explicitly in the media (and arguably implicitly by the judge) was the authenticity of the relationship as one deserving the full privilege of the law. Despallieres was most certainly not the 'poster boy' grieving partner – a figure that played a critical role in the parliamentary debates in support of the CPA (Monk 2011). Cases such as this consequently provide narratives through which it is possible to trace shifting cultural and social investments in marriage. One way of teasing out these values is to question responses to the case had Despallieres been a similar age as Ikin, or if the relationship had been of much longer duration, or if Despallieres had performed a more conventional caring role.[14] Official statistics, as well as anecdotal evidence, indicate that the age gaps between male civil partners are proportionately significantly greater than that between both opposite-sex married couples and female civil partners (Ross et al. 2011: 6–8). This case suggests that these relationships may be viewed with suspicion when judged against prevailing norms of equality between partners. Another critical variation would be to imagine the same facts but opposite genders: would a woman marrying an older rich man be viewed in the same way as a man doing the same thing? Introducing gender as a framework for thinking about the case moreover serves to question the applicability of the revocation rule.

Prior to 1837 the rule only applied to women, reflecting their loss of legal identity on marriage. Men's wills were only revoked by marriage *after* the birth of a child of the marriage. Gender neutrality was introduced by late amendments to the Wills Act 1837, against the recommendation of the Real Property Commissioners (Law Reform Committee 1979: para 21) and its purpose was to protect not only a wife but also her property. However, with the subsequent Married Women's Property Acts enabling women to own property after marriage and the introduction of provisions enabling spouses to challenge wills, the original justifications for the revocation rule have far less weight. Consequently it could be compared to the Scots reset rule – which with the introduction of same-sex marriage was removed from the law of marriage for everyone (see Norrie in this collection).

It is important to emphasise that questioning the revocation rule is not necessarily to valorise financial independence, nor indeed to overlook the protection it provides. Rather, the point here is to simply challenge the reification of inequality through *assumptions* based on marital status as opposed to an *explicit* focus on the realities of need and dependency. As the final case indicates these questions are as acute on dissolution (and divorce) as they are on death.

Divorcing equally

Lawrence v Gallagher [2012] EWCA Civ 398 is the first reported case about a financial dispute arising on a dissolution of a civil partnership. As such, it was long awaited by legal scholars (Allen and Williams 2009; George 2012; Herring 2012; Bendall 2013). The basic facts of the case were simple. Lawrence and Gallagher had lived together – or cohabited – since February 1997. They entered into a civil partnership in December 2007, separated in September 2008 and the civil partnership was dissolved in 2009. Both men were successful in their careers; but Lawrence, an equity analyst in the City, was considerably richer than Gallagher, who was an actor. Gallagher's claim was that – as a civil partner – he was entitled to a larger share of their combined wealth than Lawrence was willing to agree to. In the High Court Parker J held that Gallagher was entitled to 42 per cent of their combined wealth. But in the Court of Appeal, Thorpe and Moses LJJ and Ryder J reduced Gallagher's entitlement to 37 per cent.

Thorpe LJ opened the lead judgment in the Court of Appeal with an unequivocal statement about equality between opposite and same-sex couples:

> the fact that the claim arises from the dissolution of a Civil Partnership rather than a marriage is of little moment since it is common ground

> that the language of schedule 5 of the Civil Partnership Act 2004 is identical to the language of s 25 of the Matrimonial Causes Act 1973
>
> (Paras 1, 2)

As George has commented: 'The Court of Appeal thinks it so obvious that there can be no difference between analogously placed married couples and civil partners that it is *not even worth discussing the issue*' (2012: 358, emphasis added). Formal equality here consequently results in a judicial silence, one that renders gender invisible. Whether this results in a fair or appropriate decision is a matter of debate. But it is also questionable whether this commitment to equality is adhered to. In other words it is possible to argue that had the case, with identical facts, concerned a man and woman, the court would have reached a different decision. In reading the case in this way it is necessary to read between the lines, as Bendall notes, 'what the court does not say might be considered more interesting than what it does' (2013: 306). Challenging the judgment in this way is far from straightforward because the outcome of financial claims on divorce are always notoriously complex to predict. A lack of clarity exists because the law enables wide judicial discretion and because at the highest level judges have endlessly worked and reworked the meaning of the guiding principle of 'fairness' (Herring 2013: 227–51).

Legal commentators have noted that the initial decision by the High Court was not in any way unreasonable. This is important because it is questionable then whether there was any legitimate reason for the Court of Appeal to substitute its own assessment of a fair outcome (Bailey-Harris 2012; George 2012).

One explanation for the approach adopted by the Court of Appeal is to view it as part of a general shift away from the principle of 'equal sharing', itself a relatively recent development, towards a more individualistic approach that emphasises financial autonomy and a norm of independence between partners (at least or especially where no children are involved). This latter approach emphasises gender equality as an ideal. But, as George notes, it could at the same time result in 'a return to the days of valuing financial earnings above other forms of contributions to family life' (2012: 361), an approach that overlooks deeper structural gendered economic inequalities.

This concern is arguably justified. For what enabled the Court of Appeal to move away from equal sharing was the fact that in their judgment, and in contrast to the High Court, as Bendall has noted, 'No mention is made as to how household labour was conducted within the relationship. Such discussion is consistently present in the context of heterosexual couples (normally with reference to the wife)' (2013: 307). In other words, economic vulnerability resulting from care is seen as a particularly 'feminine affliction' (Bendall 2013: 307; Chan 2013) and as Harper et al. argue, 'the pressure to correct systemic imbalance does not arrive in civil partnerships ... because there is no disparity of gender' (2014: 139). The inclination to take care more seriously when it is a women providing the care was evident in the Supreme Court's high-profile judgment about pre-nuptial agreements in *Radmacher v Granatino* [2010] UKSC 42. Here eight male judges were unsympathetic to a man who argued for a larger payout from his much richer wife (and the only woman judge in that case dissented, emphasising the implications of the ruling on women) (Miles 2011; Herring 2013: 260–65).

At stake here is the ongoing complex paradox that results from aspiring to be 'post-gender' in what remains a highly gendered world. 'Equality' as a guiding principle points in two different directions: *assuming* equality between the genders or *imposing* equal sharing to correct gendered imbalances. The former approach of course benefits men more than women. And in this same-sex case it benefited the man who was the higher wage earner – the banker as opposed to the actor. While the Court of Appeal did not go as far as to argue that this was a case of independent dual careers, at the same time the possibility of male economic dependency and male homemaking does not appear to have received the degree of judicial recognition that is, more often, accorded to women. It is perhaps noteworthy that in *Lawrence*, as in *Radmacher*, a woman judge – emphasising 'homemaking' – was overruled by the views of the male judges. 'Perhaps', because while it is simplistic to reduce an analysis of judicial thinking to the gender of a judge, the burgeoning scholarship on diversity in the judiciary and feminist law-making highlights the value and nuanced ways of exploring this dimension (Hunter et al. 2010).

The case attracted considerable media attention and what is striking is the extent to which in this context gender roles were centre stage, in marked contrast to the Court of Appeal's judgment. This was communicated – implicitly but very effectively – by the images used to illustrate the story. In a number of newspaper articles the photograph of Lawrence was that of a typical City man in a suit and tie. The photographs used for Gallagher captured him in his starring West End role as the drag queen Bernadette in the musical (based on the film) *Priscilla Queen of the Desert* (Gibb 2012; Long 2012; Wrenn 2012). Another image of him – in a suit and tie leaving the court – was available, but the picture of him in drag was the preferred image. Accompanying these visual representations were quotations from his lawyers that emphasised that he 'had played the major domestic and home making role' and that he 'helped create and maintain a lovely home in the flat in various ways – soft furnishings, planting on balconies, improvement of layout and fixtures, redecoration' (Gibb 2012: 5).

The headlines also served to subtly emphasise the very different gendered roles. Lawrence was described as 'the millionaire banker' (Allen and Parveen 2012; Wrenn 2012) and as a 'City high-flier' (*Daily Telegraph* 2012); whereas Gallagher was described as the 'actor lover' (Allen and Pareveen 2012; Wrenn 2012) and a 'Gay actor' (*Daily Telegraph* 2012) and 'Gay "homemaker"'

(Gibb 2012). There were no references to 'gay banker' or 'high flying actor'; and the media in these various ways consequently constructed a narrative in which the differences between the men – both economic and in terms of male roles – were constantly emphasised, rendering them more 'husband and wife' than 'husband and husband'.

It would be overly optimistic to suggest that the media in these accounts is subtly making an argument premised on a feminist ethics of care and the inevitability and importance of inter-dependence and challenging gender roles. More likely what these stories do is implicitly tease the reader with the idea that in same-sex relationships one party is 'the man' and the other 'the women'. Consequently, while superficially very distinct, what is at stake in both the judicial and the media readings of the case is the contingency of masculinity – what it means to be a man.

Concluding thoughts

One could dismiss *Baynes*, *Despalliers* and *Lawrence* as simply three stories about a few rich people fighting over money. There is some truth to this (and the same could be said about most civil litigation). And despite the fact that the cases all relate to the CPA, it could be argued that the sexuality of the parties was irrelevant, or in the words of Thorpe LJ in *Lawrence*, 'of little moment' (para 2).

In both these respects they appear very distinct from the non-discrimination cases that were heard at around the same time; those concerning access to B&Bs and the employment rights of 'homophobic' employees (a local authority registrar, marriage guidance counsellors and prospective foster parents).[15] None of these cases required the courts to interpret provisions under the CPA (and consequently are not the focus here). Significantly, these public law cases all received far greater and a very different type of media (and academic) attention. Unlike the three discussed here, these were perceived as clear-cut human rights claims, they fitted neatly into a 'victim of homophobia' claim paradigm, and this was reinforced by the vocal and lead role played by Stonewall. In other words they were explicitly political and most 'progressive' people, although not all, found it easy to take sides.

While the aim here is not to assert a hierarchy of victimhood, it is, however, worth noting that the actual harm that those cases provided redress for was either minimal (the right to stay in a particular B&B) or non-existent (no one in Islington was prevented from entering a civil partnership by the refusal of one registrar). By contrast the real and potential vulnerability of people at the end of relationships (on death or dissolution) – as in the cases here – is if not more at least as significant. Yet they are in effect depoliticised, categorised in law and by the media as simply 'private' disputes. When gays and lesbians are pitted against each other (as they are in *Baynes* and *Lawrence*) as opposed to against 'homophobes', they are more complex, they do not lend themselves to campaigns and taking sides is harder. Stonewall is silent about them, yet 'equality' as a principle is no less significant here, just messier.

In *Baynes*, formal legal equality results arguably in a form of indirect discrimination, exposing gays and lesbians who have opted not to enter a civil partnership to the dangers of having to be publically open about relationship as a prerequisite for claims in the context of not just inheritance but housing and social welfare. Taking a long view of the 'openness' rule reveals the underlying significance of gender and assumptions of dependency. Gender is also central to a critical reading of the revocation rule in *Despalliers* and financial obligations or fairness on dissolution in *Lawrence*. In thinking about what they tell us about the institutions of civil partnership and marriage it is worth returning to the crux of Lady Hale's judgment in *Ghaidan v Godin-Mendoza* for treating a gay couple as 'husband and wife':

> Once upon a time it might have been difficult to apply those words to a same-sex relationship because both in law and in reality the roles of the husband and wife were so different and those differences were defined by their genders. That is no longer the case. The law now differentiates between husband and wife in only a very few and unimportant respects. Husbands and wives decide for themselves who will go out to work and who will do the homework and childcare. Mostly each does some of each. *The roles are inter-changeable. There is thus no difficulty in applying the term 'marriage-like' to same-sex relationships.*
>
> (Para [144], emphasis added)

For Hale, consequently, same-sex partnership rights are simply a logical extension of women's rights. While few would disagree with the outcome of that case, the subsequent cases discussed here while demonstrating the same commitment to formal equality all reveal the deep ongoing significance of gender; through the application of rules premised on gendered roles to same-sex couples and by reading between the lines of judges in cases where discretion enables flexibility but also the masking of gendered value judgments. Whether the outcome of the cases here are fair or not is less important than evaluating the impact of the CPA more widely on the malleability of the institution. In *Baynes*, the distinctiveness of same-sex relations was marginalised, but in *Lawrence*, arguably, it did have an impact (for better or worse).

These disputes will inevitably increase and taking them seriously, by looking beyond the individual merits of the parties' claims in order to identify their historical and cultural importance, provides new challenges. The decisions in these cases impact not just on other people who go to court in the future but on people who seek advice from lawyers (Diduck 2000) and more subtly on understandings of law. In particular, they shift the focus away from debates about the right to legal recognition and address instead the implications of being recognised. In other words, they tell us what exactly it is that gay men and lesbians are signing up to when they enter civil partnerships or get married. They flesh out the terms and conditions of the marriage contract.

Notes

1 See Cretney (2006: 43) for an analysis of the relationship between Parliament and the judges.
2 Coroners and Justice Act 2009, s 55(6)(b). *R v Clinton* [2012] EWCA Crim 2.
3 Inheritance (Provision for Family and Dependants) Act 1975, s 1(1B) (as inserted by CPA 2004, s 71, Sch 4). See Harper et al. (2014: para 4.6).
4 *Ghaidan v Godin-Mendoza* [2004] UKHL 30. See Harper et al. (2014: 20, 56).
5 The case also raised questions about the meaning of separate households and domestic economies which are important for the increasing number of people 'living apart together' (Duncan et al. 2013). Baynes' daughter, who was a god-daughter of Watson, also challenged the will and her case questioned the legal definition of a 'child of the family': *Baynes v Hedger* [2009] EWCA Civ 374. On the significance of the god–child relationship to gay men and lesbians, see Monk (2014).
6 See Heaphy in this volume about generational differences and also Monk (2014).
7 For a discussion of the concept and practices of 'outing', see Gross (1993).
8 *Hansard*, HL Deb, 22 April 2004, vol 660, col 414.
9 For other recent examples, see: 'Muriel Spark leaves millions to woman friend rather than son': *Evening Standard*, 14 April 2007; 'Why did this decadent peer leave his millions to his manservant?': *Daily Mail*, 20 June 2011; 'Gay-lover-of-dead-flamboyant-TV-presenter-loses-legal-battle-over-property-portfolio': *Daily Telegraph*, 10 August 2011.
10 In the US case *In re Anonymous* 75 Misc 2d 133, 347 NYS 2d 263 (Sur Ct 1973) a gay beneficiary under his partner's will had the following dilemma: risk self-incrimination for crimes of homosexuality (then in existence) or lose his entitlement; see Sherman 1981: 233.
11 Wills Act 1837, s 18B (as inserted by CPA, s 71).
12 Administration of Estates Act 1925, s 46(1) (as amended by CPA, s 71, Sch 4, Pt 2, para 7).
13 The law has subsequently been changed and, as Ikin had no children, under the current law Despalliers would have been entitled to the whole estate: Inheritance and Trustee's Powers Act 2014, s 1. For background to this reform, see Cooke (2009); Law Commission (2009).
14 See, for example, the claimant in *Ghaidan v Godin-Mendoza* [2004] UKHL 30 and conrast this with the the gay claimant in *Nutting v Southern Housing Group Limited* [2004] EWHC 2989, who failed to satisfy the court that his relationship was one of 'mutual lifetime commitment' as opposed simply to 'the living together of lovers'.
15 *Ladele v London Borough of Islington* [2009] EWCA Civ 1357; *McFarlane v Relate Avon Ltd* [2010] IRLR 872, CA (these were both subsequently heard in the European Court of Human Rights: *Eweida and others v United Kingdom* (Application Nos 48420/10, 36516/10, 51671/10, 59842/10) [2013] IRLR 231); *Bull and another v Hall and another* [2013] UKSC 73; *R (Eunice Johns and Owen Johns) v Derby City Council and EHRC* [2011] EWHC 375 (Fam).

References

Adams, S. (2009) 'Music executive's "husband" cut out of £7 million will', *Daily Telegraph*, 17 December 2009. Available at: http://www.telegraph.co.uk/news/6833917/Music-executives-husband-cut-out-of-7-million-will.html. [Last accessed 3rd March 2015]

Allen, N. and Williams, H. 2009. 'The law and financial provision on the dissolution of a civil partnership', *Family Law*, 39: 836–841.

Allen, V. and Parveen, N. (2012) 'The millionaire banker, his actor lover and their landmark £1.7m "divorce" settlement', *Daily Mail*, 8 March. Available at: http://www.dailymail.co.uk/news/article-2112280/Banker-Peter-Lawrence-actor-lover-Don-Gallaghers-1-7m-divorce-settlement.html [Last accessed 3rd March 2015].

Bailey-Harris, R. (2012) 'Financial orders: civil partnership', *Family Law*, 42: 646–47.

Barker, M. and Langdridge, D. (2010) 'Whatever happened to non-monogamies? Critical reflections on recent research and theory', *Sexualities*, 13(6): 748–72.

Barker, N.J. (2006) 'Sex and the civil partnership act: the future of (non) conjugality?', *Feminist Legal Studies*, 14(2): 241–259.

Bendall, C. (2013) 'A break away from the (hetero)norm?: *Lawrence v Gallagher* [2012] EWCA Civ 394', *Feminist Legal Studies* 21(3): 303–10.

Camber, R. (2008) 'Ken Russell's wife in court battle over her mother's lesbian lover's £2.3million estate', *Daily Mail*, 26 June 2008. Available at: http://www.dailymail.co.uk/tvshowbiz/article-1029346/Ken-Russells-wife-court-battle-mothers-lesbian-lovers-2-3million-estate.html [Last accessed 3rd March 2015].

Campbell, E. (2009) 'Baynes v Hedger & Anor: a lesson for charities?', *New Law Journal*, 16 October 2009.

Chan, W. (2013) 'Cohabitation, civil partnership, marriage and the equal sharing principle', *Legal Studies*, 33(1): 46–65.

Connolly, E. (2012) 'Ikin's lover admits forging will, denies kill plot', *Sydney Morning Herald*, 2 July. Available at: http://www.smh.com.au/national/ikins-lover-admits-forging-will-denies-kill-plot-20120701-21b1f.html#ixzz37ov1jivG. [Last accessed 3rd March 2015].

Cooke, E. (2009) 'Wives, widows and wicked step-mothers: a brief examination of spousal entitlement on intestacy', *Child and Family Law Quarterly*, 21(4): 423–42.

Cretney, S.M. (2006). *Same Sex Relationships, From 'Odious Crime' to 'Gay Marriage'.* Oxford: Oxford University Press.

Daily Mirror (2011) 'Gay Frenchman accused of killing friend of Elton John freed on bail', 31 March. Available at: http://www.mirror.co.uk/news/uk-news/gay-frenchman-accused-of-killing-friend-119495 [Last accessed 3rd March 2015].

Daily Telegraph (2008) 'Peter Ikin married French boyfriend weeks before death', 11 December.

——(2009) 'Gay lover of the late Peter Ikin quizzed over secret will', 18 December.

——(2012) 'Gay actor and City high-flier fight over separation payout', 9 March.

Diduck, A. (2000) 'Solicitors and legal subjects', in J. Bridgeman and D. Monk (eds) *Feminist Perspectives on Child Law.* London: Cavendish Press.

Douglas, G. (2014) 'Disappointed "heirs" as a socio-legal phenomenon', *Oñati Socio-legal Series*, 4(2): 243–63.

Douglas, G. et al. (2011) 'Enduring love? Attitudes to family and inheritance law in England and Wales', *Journal of Law and Society*, 38(2): 245–71.

Evening Standard (2008) 'Ken Russell's wife in court battle over her mother's lesbian lover's £2.3million estate', 25 June. Available at: http://www.standard.co.uk/showbiz/ken-russells-wife-in-court-battle-over-her-mothers-lesbian-lovers-23million-estate-6839461.html [Last accessed 3rd March 2015].

Felstiner, W., Abel, W.R. and Sarat, A. (1980–81) 'The emergence and transformation: naming, blaming, claiming', *Law and Society Review*, 15: 631–54.

Fife-Yeomans, J. and Miranda, C. (2009) 'Young gay husband Alexandre Despallieres gets Peter Ikin millions in will', *Daily Telegraph*, 4 July. Available at: http://www.couriermail.com.au/news/young-gay-husband-alexandre-despallieres-gets-peter-ikin-millions-in-will/story-e6freon6–1225745870694?nk=88ab1e391637ade4da127c94af12bfd8 [Last accessed 3rd March 2015].

George, R. (2012) '*Lawrence v Gallagher* [2012] EWCA Civ 394 – playing a straight bat in civil partnership appeals?', *Journal of Social Welfare and Family Law*, 34(3): 357–362.

Gewirtz, P. (1996) 'Narrative and rhetoric in the law', in P. Brooks and P. Gewirts (eds) *Law's Stories*. New Haven, CT: Yale University Press.

Gibb, F. (2012) 'Gay "homemaker" and banker fight over £5m divorce', *The Times*, 9 March, p. 5.

Gross, L. (1993) *Contested Closets: The Politics and Ethics of Outing*. Minneapolis: University of Minnesota Press.

Harper, M., Chelvan, S., Downs, M., Landless, K. and Wilson, G. (2014) *Same Sex Marriage and Civil Partnerships*. Bristol: Family Law/Jordan.

Herring, J. (2012) 'Breaking bonds', *New Law Journal*, 25 May.

——(2013) *Family Law* (6th edn). Harlow: Longman/Pearson.

Hoff, C.C. and Beougher, S.C. (2010) 'Sexual agreements among gay male couples', *Archives of Sexual Behavior*, 39(3): 774–787.

Hunter, R., McGlynn, C. and Rackley, E. (2010) *Feminist Judgments: From Theory to Practice*. Oxford: Hart.

Humphreys, Alun, Mill, Lisa, Morrell, Gareth, Douglas, Gillian and Woodward, Hilary. (2010). *Inheritance and family: Attitudes to will-making and intestacy*. London: National Centre for Social Research.

Hutchins, C. (2012) 'A dead man, a forged will, a £10m inheritance, and a ruined reputation', *London Evening Standard*, 10 August. Available at: http://www.standard.co.uk/lifestyle/esmagazine/a-dead-man-a-forged-will-a-10m-inheritance-and-a-ruined-reputation-8026886.html [Last accessed 3rd March 2015].

Kerridge, R. (2009) *Parry and Kerridge: The Law of Succession* (12th edn). London: Sweet & Maxwell.

Kerridge, R. and Rivers, J. (2000) 'The construction of wills', *Law Quarterly Review*, 116: 287–317.

Law Commission (2009) *Intestacy and Family Provisions Claim on Death*. Law Commission Consultation Paper No 191. London: HMSO.

Law Reform Committee (1979) *The Making and Revocation of Wills*. Consultative Document.

Lewis, P. (2008) 'Actor loses court battle over £2.3m estate of mother's lesbian lover', *Guardian*, 14 July. Available at: http://www.theguardian.com/uk/2008/jul/14/law.theatre [Last accessed 3rd March 2015].

Duncan, S., Carter, J. and Phillips, M. (2013) 'Why do people live apart together?', *Families, Relationships and Society*, 2(3): 323–338.

Long, B. (2012) 'Analysis: the multi-million pounds "gay divorce"', *Pink News*, 13 April. Available at: http://www.pinknews.co.uk/2012/04/13/analysis-the-multi-million-pound-gay-divorce/ [Last accessed 3rd March 2015].

Metro (2008) 'Actress loses £800,000 case over mother's lesbian lover', 14 July. Available at: http://metro.co.uk/2008/07/14/actress-loses-800-000-case-over-mother-s-lesbian-lover-271580/ [Last accessed 3rd March 2015].

Miles, J. (2011) 'Marriage and divorce in the Supreme Court and the Law Commission: for love or money?', *Modern Law Review*, 74: 430.

Monk, D. (2011) 'Sexuality and succession law: beyond formal equality', *Feminist Legal Studies*, 19(3): 231–250.

——(2013a) 'E. M. Forster's will: an overlooked posthumous publication', *Legal Studies*, 33(4): 572–597.

——(2013b) 'Those in civil partnerships need to be aware of what happens to wills', *Pink News*, 3 April. Available at: http://www.pinknews.co.uk/2013/03/04/comment-those-in-civil-partnerships-need-to-be-aware-of-what-happens-to-wills/ [Last accessed 3rd March 2015].

——(2014) 'Reading (gay and lesbian) wills', *Oñati Socio-legal Series* [online], 4 (2), 306–322. Available from: http://ssrn.com/abstract=2431093 [Last accessed 3rd March 2015].

Ross, H., Gask K. and Berrington, A. (2011) *Civil Partnerships 5 Years On*. Population Trends nr 145. London: Office for National Statistics.

Singh, Anita (2008) 'Ken Russell's ex-wife sues over lesbian's estate', *Daily Telegraph*, 25 June 2008. Available at: http://www.telegraph.co.uk/news/celebritynews/2193978/Ken-Russells-ex-wife-sues-over-lesbian-lovers-estate.html [Last accessed 3rd March 2015]

Stone, B. (2012) 'The talented M. Despallières', *Bloomsbury Business Week*, 28 June. Available at: http://www.businessweek.com/articles/2012-06-28/the-talented-m-dot-despalli-res [Last accessed 3rd March 2015].

Independent (2008) 'Ken Russell's former wife contests will of mother's lesbian lover'.

Williams, Catherine, Potter, Gary and Douglas, Gillian. 2008. Cohabitation and intestacy: Public opinion and law reform. *Child and Family Law Quarterly* 20(4): 499–521.

Wrenn, E. (2012) 'Millionaire banker wins battle with his actor lover over £1.7million landmark "divorce" settlement after their civil partnership ends', *Daily Mail*, 29 March. Available at: http://www.dailymail.co.uk/news/article-2122048/Banker-Peter-Lawrence-actor-lover-Don-Gallaghers-civil-partnership-goes-appeal-1-7m-divorce-settlement.html [Last accessed 3rd March 2015].

Chapter 12

Dissolution or disillusion

The unravelling of civil partnerships

Rosemary Auchmuty

No one had any idea, when civil partnerships were first introduced, how many same-sex couples would take up the opportunity to formalise their relationships under the law. No one knew whether civil partnerships would appeal primarily to men or to women, to older or to younger people. But, then, no one really knew the demographic characteristics of gays and lesbians in the UK generally, let alone those in couples. In a few short years, we had come from near-invisibility to full legal recognition. It was with some interest, then, that the earliest statistics were greeted and analysed, and it was found that that men were much more eager to embrace the new institution than women (Shoffman 2006). In the first month of the Civil Partnership Act 2004's operation, December 2005, men registered almost twice the number of civil partnerships as women; in the following year, with over 16,000 registrations (the high point; numbers started to decline thereafter), the proportions were 60 per cent men to 40 per cent women. As the years went by, men continued to register more civil partnerships, but the gap was narrowing, and in 2010 it disappeared; in 2012, the latest year for which figures are available, women registered 51 per cent (ONS 2013a).

In 2007, the first dissolutions became available. Here again the statistics were interesting: in the first year, 13 male couples dissolved their civil partnership, compared with 28 female. In other words, women were more than twice as likely to dissolve, even though there were many fewer female civil partnerships. From then on, women continued to dissolve more civil partnerships than men; in 2011 almost twice as many, and in 2012 57 per cent. By the end of 2012, out of a total of more than 5,000 dissolutions, 3.2 per cent of male civil partnerships and 6.1 per cent of female civil partnerships had been dissolved (ONS 2013a). 'Lesbians, it seems, are cutting their losses more quickly than gay men', noted the *Independent* on the day the statistics were released (Dent 2013).

In 2011, I embarked on an empirical study of the dissolution process,[1] the full results of which will be published separately. I interviewed people who had entered into, and then dissolved, their civil partnerships in the first six years of the Act's operation, with a view to finding out what this new experience was like and, in particular, whether those who underwent it had been surprised by the legal effects of civil partnership registration and dissolution. To these ends, I asked participants (14 women and five men, with an age range of 29–69) why they had entered into a civil partnership, as well as why they had dissolved it. I found quite profound differences in expectations and experiences of the law. These differences appeared to be determined largely by sex and age (and also by class, where it intersected with gender), and it occurred to me that my findings could be helpful, in conjunction with other work on sexuality, in explaining the interesting demographic trends revealed by the Office for National Statistics.

This chapter therefore considers the following three questions:

- Why did more men register a civil partnership initially than women?
- Why has the gender ratio equalised?
- Why have women dissolved their civil partnership at a consistently higher rate than men?

I also looked at comparisons between divorce and dissolution. After four years of the Act's operation, civil partnerships were less than half as likely to end in dissolution as marriages of the same length in divorce: 2.5 per cent, as compared with 5.5 per cent (Ross et al. 2011: 15–16). By 2012, however, the gap was beginning to close. 'Now gay marriages are hit by seven-year itch', proclaimed the *Daily Mail* (incidentally demonstrating the appropriation of the term 'marriage' for civil partnerships). 'Civil partnership break ups approach same rate as heterosexual couples' (Doughty 2013). This shift in turn led me to think about another issue that was aired in the same-sex marriage debates of the 2000s, given these statistics:

- What has happened to the argument that same-sex unions will be different from, or better than (with its assumption of longer-lasting), heterosexual unions?

In exploring answers to these four questions, the chapter aims to demonstrate the limitations of the modern tendency to assume an identity of interests among lesbians and gay men,[2] a feature of much writing on sexuality and law that focuses on the attainment of 'equality' and 'rights' without any critique of the comparator group or concern about the content of those rights.

Why did more men register civil partnerships initially?

Introducing the Civil Partnership Bill, the Labour government predicted that between 11,000 and 22,000 gays and lesbians might register a civil partnership in the first five years. In fact, four times as many did (ONS 2013a: pdf

Bulletin, 2). This can be explained in three ways: first, that there were many more gays and lesbians in the UK than the government imagined (or were prepared to admit) when promoting the legislation; second, that there were many more gay and lesbian *couples* than it thought there were (and in these days of equality and respectability it is worth remembering that throughout most of the twentieth century, the dominant images of homosexuality were of unchecked promiscuity and/or the lonely closet); and third, that there was greater appetite for legal recognition and the privileges of quasi-marriage than anyone expected. All these factors seem to have been true.

It is clear that none of the Bill's proponents, still less its enemies, had any idea how many gays and lesbians there were. Often the best that anyone could come up with was the clichéd 'one in ten'. This statistical black hole was compounded by the fact that not everyone who embarked on a same-sex relationship identified as gay or lesbian, as well as the fact that people moved (and still do) between gay and heterosexual identities and relationships. It is very likely that many people living a heterosexual lifestyle might have decided to come out as gay once this became not only acceptable but legally protected. One of the clearest findings of my dissolution research was that many of my interviewees had been in heterosexual relationships – several had been married – prior to entering into a same-sex one. One woman, indeed, went on to marry a man after the dissolution of her civil partnership (while still, interestingly, identifying as 'gay'). If my research shows anything, it is that sexuality and identity are not fixed or inborn, but fluid and changing. So, for many people, the advent of civil partnerships may have offered an opportunity to come out publicly and officially; and I suggest that this opportunity was especially attractive to men, for the following reasons.

First, the early 'backlog' group of gay men – those who had been in relationships for a long time and were getting on in years – were more likely to have practical reasons for registering a civil partnership than women. Fifty per cent of civil partners who registered in December 2005 were aged 50 or more (National Statistics 2006: 2). They were more likely to have property that might be subject to inheritance tax, because only about 5 per cent of the population is wealthy enough to be liable (Toynbee 2014) and men (especially older, childless men with good jobs or pensions) are on average richer than women. In London, unlike anywhere else in the country, male civil partnerships have consistently outnumbered female by around 3:1; this distinction could well be associated with the high property values in the capital (ONS 2013a: Table 3) and, if wealth bears any relation to class, as may be assumed, it also suggests that civil partnerships are more of a middle-class phenomenon.

Large age differences between partners are much more common in male partnerships than female (Ross et al. 2011: 6) – in 2012, 87 men aged 55–64 entered into civil partnerships with partners more than 20 years younger, while only 11 women did this (ONS 2013a: Table 5) – making 'protection' of the younger person a priority in the event of the older one's death. In addition, as my dissolution study revealed, many men (though also some women) had partners from overseas and wanted to make it possible for them to stay in the country.

The flipside of gendered inequalities in wealth is that women tend to be disproportionately represented among the poorest social groups. The Civil Partnership Act 2004, in equalising the position of gays and heterosexuals, actually removed an advantage enjoyed up to that point by same-sex couples, which was that they were not viewed as a 'household' (as unmarried heterosexual couples had been since 1966) for the purposes of benefits assessment. Drawing attention to your relationship could well mean a reduction in benefits if you were assessed as a couple rather than two individuals (Scott 2005). Yvette Taylor's study of working-class lesbians, undertaken before the Civil Partnership Act 2004, shows that many older lesbians were resistant to the possibility of legal regulation because they knew they would be worse off if their benefits were assessed on a household basis (Taylor 2007); this was confirmed by Rosie Harding's post-Act research (Harding 2008: 747). Here again, class plays a role in making some women disinclined to engage with civil partnerships for financial reasons.

A second impetus for gay men to register a civil partnership was their long and bitter history of being subject to the criminal law, which provided a powerful symbolic reason to have their relationships legally acknowledged and protected. Homosexual acts between men were illegal between 1885 and 1967, and prosecutions for private sexual behaviour could, and did, destroy lives. When I attended the civil partnership ceremony of two gay friends, this history was explicitly recalled, as it was in *Our Gay Wedding – the Musical*, shown on Channel 4 in early 2014. For lesbians, however, invisibility has long been our accustomed position (Auchmuty 2007: 116) so, for women, there was less incentive to go public.

A third explanation is that men, unlike women, have no history of oppression in marriage and no suspicion of it as the site of patriarchal power. I have argued elsewhere that the massive decline in the marriage rate over the past 40 years has been due to a much more conscious rejection of the institution by women than has previously been acknowledged (Auchmuty 2012). This rejection was spearheaded by second-wave feminism which simultaneously exposed the way that marriage operated to keep women in dependence on men and fought to create the conditions within which equality-based models of relating could flourish. For women who had been part of this movement or influenced by it, marriage and marriage-like institutions held no attraction and might even be viewed with abhorrence.

That this analysis has passed most gay men by was brought home to me in my interviews. Some of the men seemed to have absolutely no awareness of power within relationships, naively assuming (for example) that a union with a much younger man from a third-world country whom the older man was supporting financially, along with members of his family, could not be based on anything but love. 'My plan was that we'd buy a house there and we'd live happily ever after', S told me. The mercenary aspect, so familiar to women who for generations have *had* to marry for financial support, had simply not occurred to him.

Why has the gender ratio equalised?

The main reason for the gender convergence in civil partnership formation is that, now all the older long-term couples who wished to register a civil partnership have done so, the age of entry into a civil partnership has fallen, and the younger generation of gays and lesbians have a very different world-view and different practical concerns from those who lived through the great social and attitudinal shifts of the last 40 years. In the first month after the Civil Partnership Act 2004 came into force, the mean age of registrants was 54 for men and 46 for women. It has been dropping ever since, to 40 for men and 37.6 for women in 2012 (ONS 2013a: pdf Bulletin, 4–5). Younger lesbians, like gay men, have no shared memory of the oppressiveness of marriage: marriage for them is simply a lifestyle choice. Similarly, younger gay men have no shared memory of outlaw status. Both sexes act upon the confident, if sometimes misplaced, assumption that their relationships will be 'equal' with those of heterosexuals.

A recent study of 50 younger civil partner couples aged 35 and below by Heaphy et al. (2013) offers stark testimony to how the relationship terrain has changed since the introduction of civil partnerships. The great majority of participants in that study espoused conventional notions of marriage, seeing the couple as the ideal relational form and monogamy as the most 'mature' way to relate. This conventionality derived, the authors deduce, from these young people's strong sense of 'ordinariness' and equality with heterosexuals (82) – the result, no doubt, of successful gay rights campaigns over the past 50 years which have made social and family acceptance of gays and lesbians the norm.

Conceptions of civil partnership

That younger and older civil partners had very different attitudes to legal regulation of their relationships became apparent when I asked participants why they had entered into a civil partnership. For the older women, the reasons were largely *practical* ('it was primarily an economic decision', said E. 'We wanted to be absolutely sure that we would get each other's pension contributions') and *political*: they were keen to celebrate the achievement of 'equality with heterosexuals', as A put it. They wanted to step away from the invisibility that has cloaked lesbians for centuries and 'stand up and be counted' (H). These women did not consider a civil partnership to be the same thing as marriage ('we were not a husband and wife', F declared) and they did not imagine that registration of their (usually longstanding) relationship would have any substantive impact on it. Only on its breakdown did they discover the difference that legal regulation makes.

The younger people I interviewed shared the attraction to legal rights and 'protection' but rarely spoke of making a public statement. Instead, they saw the civil partnership as 'the next step' after falling in love and moving in together, perhaps as a prelude to thinking about a family, or creating a new family for children already present. This was as true of the men as of the women. My findings here were similar to those of Heaphy et al. (2013). About half of their interviewees viewed civil partnerships as a 'natural progression' in their relationship (93), with many being encouraged to marry by family and friends (94). None of the 100 claimed marriage as a political act (104) and 'feminist concerns about the need to keep a degree of financial independence hardly surfaced at all' (114). Only four of the 25 female couples did not want children, and eight of the 25 male couples mentioned fostering and adoption in the future (162). For these younger people, as Rosie Harding has observed:

> The creation of a legal framework for same-sex relationships becomes a mapping out of how things are supposed to go – two people meet, fall in love, enter into a civil partnership, become more emotionally mature, become financially dependent on each other, and so on – mirroring heteronormative discourse around societal expectations of marriage and life
>
> (2008: 748)

In modelling their civil partnership on heterosexual marriage, these young couples adopted its symbols and ceremonies, not to speak of its language (Heaphy et al. 2013: 3–4): the book is titled *Same-Sex Marriages* for this reason. This I too found with the younger participants in my study. B, for example, used the language of marriage throughout the interview: 'she was my wife, I was married to my wife'. K, another woman, told me unprompted, 'We still call it married, we don't say civil partnered'. L, a young man, agreed that he and his partner spoke of their 'marriage' and when I asked if he referred to him as his husband or wife he laughingly admitted that he spoke of his wife ('but that was just a joke'). For younger participants, civil partnership *was* marriage.

The older women in my study were much less likely to use the language of marriage, and some explicitly repudiated it. 'No. […] We hated that', said E. P never used the words 'marriage' or 'wife' herself, but said her partner did: '[She] viewed it as a sort of "roses round the door" thing, which I never did […] I've never wanted to be married'.

I found that those who embraced the language of marriage were also more likely to embrace the customs and traditions associated with the institution.

One interviewee had hyphenated her surname with her partner's when they registered the civil partnership (and was now in the process of changing it back) while another spoke of choosing an entirely new name for himself and his current partner in anticipation of future children, so that the family could all have the same name. Whether and how the event was celebrated was also testimony to the different views. Those who were registering primarily for practical reasons – that is, the older people – usually had very simple ceremonies with only a handful of people present: 'we didn't want to make a big song and dance about it', said E, a woman. F had a small registration and the two large parties that followed were celebrations of equality for gays and lesbians more than her own union.

It was generally the younger women who had the 'big white wedding'. K described hers with enthusiasm:

> I was in white, a long flowing train and everything, and she wore like a nice dress from Monsoon, […] a pink one, and then we had […] four bridesmaids, and two pageboys, and they were in like cerise pink, and the boys were in like suits, with the cerise pink ties and cerise pink cummerbunds, and with my dad as well. So yes, I did the full works [*laughing*].

But gay men love a party too, as described by S:

> We had a quickie civil partnership, with five friends […] and then we had my fairy tale marriage ceremony that I had in mind […] It was a beautiful wedding. We had a hundred guests … we each had three best men […] two of them wore suits, standard lounge suits, and one wore Pakistani dress, and his three wore traditional Balinese costumes, so it was all quite colourful and eh … and lots of love on the day.

In spite of the fact that these relationships ended unhappily, the wedding day was often recalled with pleasure. J's colourful account was tempered by the rueful comment that when friends spoke of it now, they said, 'Oh well, we had a lovely day'. Q recalled that, 'Even when I told some work colleagues that I was splitting up, they went, "oh well, still the best wedding do we've ever been to!"'.

Social and family acceptance

There can be no doubt that the advent of civil partnerships has transformed social attitudes to homosexuality in England. The most telling change is that the tabloid press now writes approvingly of celebrity gay weddings such as that of Elton John and David Furnish. One of my interviewees, O, a teacher, told me that she had had to leave her first school because of the homophobic bullying. At the second, however, 'I was completely out to all of the students and all of the teachers, and it was very positive'. That's not to say that homophobia has disappeared, but it does mean that civil partnerships have provided a forum for families to 'come out' in support of a gay son or lesbian daughter in a socially acceptable and traditional way.

Marriage was historically about family alliances and even today, when the love-match is the dominant form, family involvement in their children's marriages tends to be located along a continuum from actually choosing the spouse to paying for the wedding, giving the bride away, or at the very least approving the child's partner. In the past, however, the unpopularity of a gay or lesbian child's sexual choices frequently led to estrangement from their families of origin, which were replaced by 'families of choice' – that is friends and former lovers. When I asked participants in my research if their families had been supportive of their civil partnerships, responses from some of the older lesbians reflected this estrangement. 'I', for example, hoped that her civil partnership would change negative attitudes among her family members (it did not). A, however, was able to overcome her father's religious reservations: he 'actually enjoyed the whole day' because 'he had completely taken on board that it was about the world paying me some respect and credibility for my relationships'.

The position was strikingly different for the younger participants. Families were uniformly accepting of their child's sexuality and generally welcoming to the partner. 'I always got on fine with his parents', M assured me. 'Never an issue'. Where there was family opposition, it was usually not to the same-sex relationship but to the individual partner. 'I don't think [my mother] liked my ex very much', O confided; but her mother felt quite differently about her new partner, telling her, 'You're part of the family – we love you to bits'. Not only parents, but colleagues, too, were openly supportive, as K found when she told her headmaster about her relationship breakdown.

These generational differences help, I think, to explain why younger women and gay men did not have the reservations about civil partnership that many older people did. This in turn explains why the civil partnership rate, after steady decline, started to rise again in 2010, and why the gender balance has equalised.

The same shift has occurred in the rate of traditional (heterosexual) marriage which, long in decline, reached a low of 8.4 persons marrying per 1,000 population in 2009 before starting to rise again. In 2012 it stood at 9.3 (ONS 2014b). This suggests that age is more important than sexuality in determining attitudes to marriage/civil partnership. Young gays and lesbians believe they have as much 'right' to access to marriage and marriage-like institutions as heterosexuals. But my findings also suggest that marriage itself has become less significant. The younger generation grew up with families where the parents lived together and apart, moved on to other partners and other children, where family forms were mixed and varied. They see marriage as an institution which can be chosen or not, undone and re-done, and this has led them not so much to a more positive as to a more *neutral* view of the institution. Second-wave feminist critiques (e.g. Smart 1984) were made at a time when divorce was much less common and much more stigmatised. As M (a man of 29, the youngest person I interviewed) put it: 'I don't think anyone who enters into marriage or civil partnership actually, in this day and age, necessarily expects it's always going to be for ever',

Why do more women than men dissolve their civil partnerships?

It has long been recognised that more women initiate divorce proceedings than men. I have always found this perfectly explicable in terms of men's bad behaviour; *of course* men are more likely to be the cause of the problem and *of course* that will lead women to have to divorce them. But the fact that women are more likely to dissolve a civil partnership – and this statistic has remained fairly constant since dissolution became possible in 2007 – suggests that the explanation lies not only in men's bad behaviour but also in something about women.

Here my research into civil partnership dissolution threw up some interesting findings. Of all the reasons given by the 14 women I interviewed for the dissolution of their partnership, two stood out: unacceptable infidelity or disputes over monogamy, and a partner's substance abuse or mental health issues. Though men sometimes mentioned these, they experienced and dealt with them quite differently.

Infidelity

Unlike the corresponding provisions governing divorce in the Matrimonial Causes Act 1973, the Civil Partnership Act 2004 does not allow for 'adultery' as a ground for dissolution – a fact that amazed some of my interviewees and amused others (mainly the men). It was clear, however, that monogamy had been assumed in many of the women's relationships, whether or not the question had ever been discussed. An affair by one partner, in a relationship premised on fidelity, was an event that precipitated dissolution for no fewer than seven of my 14 female interviewees. Five of the women who had been unfaithful (including two of the women I interviewed) ended up in a new relationship with the person they had had an affair with (four with another woman and one with a man) – in other words, they went from one monogamous relationship (via adultery) to another. Most of their former partners had also moved on to new relationships, one having married a man.

That is not to say that non-monogamy is never an accepted feature of lesbian relationships. Indeed, non-monogamy has often been a principled feature of both feminist and gay rejections of heteronormativity (Barker and Langdridge 2010). Three participants in my study chose to dissolve their civil partnership because their partner wanted to open up the relationship to other lovers: C's partner to resume the polyamorous lifestyle they had both enjoyed before the marriage, D's to explore polyamory and E's to explore her heterosexuality. But C's account is instructive in its detail on the challenges involved and the reasons why she was no longer prepared to go down that route:

> I was non-monogamous until I met [my ex]. We tried having a non-monogamous relationship for about three months, and [my ex] said, 'No, I'm too old-fashioned, I can't do this – this is going to make me go nuts,' and I thought, well, she gave it a go, I'll see if I can give it a go, and I found I didn't miss it, not even slightly.

Her partner then changed her mind and suggested they return to non-monogamy:

> And I went, 'No, absolutely not, I'm not going back there – it's too difficult.' There's too many discussions that have to take place. There's too many other people involved. […] the amount of work that I would have to put into it, and the amount of communication, and the amount of trust that has to happen […] and the likelihood for drama is exponentially increased, so […] I just don't have the energy for it [*laughing*]!

More than one participant pointed out that a decision to open up a relationship was often symptomatic of existing problems. B said:

> We'd been having sexual problems for quite a while before the – in fact, we'd opened our relationship up […] which wasn't unusual at the time, like we knew lots of poly-people. […] [N]ow, looking back, I think it kind of allowed me to ignore the fact that she was kind of losing interest in me.

Fidelity was not an issue for any of the men, who did not expect monogamy. Four of the five had had an open relationship, and L expressed the view that the civil partnership reflected this norm: '[the legislature] are trying to say that gay men are generally much more promiscuous so they're going to sleep around and we're not going to let you get divorced for being unfaithful'. My conclusion is that, while fidelity matters more to many (clearly not all) women than to most men, what is more significant is that lesbians are less likely to accept disagreement about the role of monogamy within their relationships, and gay men are more likely to see non-monogamy as unproblematic. Moreover, if they do have sex outside the relationship, women are more likely to replace one monogamous relationship with another, leading them to want to dissolve the first.

Gender is, of course, socially constructed, and I am not saying for a minute that women are naturally more monogamous and men more promiscuous (though there is an extensive literature saying precisely this, e.g. Katz 2014). Instead, what my interviews suggest is that, if one partner finds it impossible to forgive infidelity or tolerate non-monogamy, then dissolution (perforce under the 'unreasonable behaviour' ground if the parties are not prepared to wait two years) is likely to follow; and that women are much more likely than men to adopt this position.

Men's attitudes may, however, be changing. As civil partnerships become more popular, as memories of the outlaw status fade and with it the need to seek sex in public spaces, more men may start rejecting the promiscuous lifestyle in favour of normative monogamy. When the Civil Partnership Act 2004 was under discussion, advocates hoped and opponents feared that one of its effects would be to 'domesticate' gay men, and I found evidence that this might be happening. L, although he had been in an open relationship with his ex, said he expected his current partner to be faithful. R, on the other hand, had agreed with his new partner to have an open relationship – but neither acted on it. The agreement simply represented his refusal to be told how to behave. He told me: 'I really liked the sex, and in the old days, I was having sex everywhere. [But] I love [my current partner] so much that I just don't feel the need to'. Most people, of course, feel like this in the early days of a relationship; attitudes may shift once familiarity sets in, and we may well see a return to agreed promiscuity within a relationship or even the rise of prostitution for married gay men, parallelling heterosexual male norms.

Mental health problems and substance abuse

These were also mentioned by seven of the women I interviewed. A former partner's depression, self-harm, and suicide threats and attempts featured in many accounts. P's partner, for example, was pathologically jealous: 'I couldn't go out for a pint of milk, for example, without being either timed or accompanied'. J's partner's alcoholism created havoc at home. 'I like a drink, but X turned it into an Olympic sport'. Only one of the five men I interviewed, however, linked the dissolution of his civil partnership to mental health issues.

One factor stood out in the relationships of the women I interviewed. Several confessed, unprompted, to being drawn to a caring role, or identified this quality in their ex-partner:

C: I tend to be a massive caretaker, and I burnt myself out doing that.

H: [My ex] liked to look after people she thought were vulnerable. When I met her, I was a single mum, a trainee solicitor [with] two young children. […] I was never really needy, but she liked to be the mother figure, and [her ex's new partner] has got mental health issues and alcohol issues, and I think [my ex] likes looking after her, and I didn't need looking after [*laughing*].

P: [My ex was] very controlling and possessive. [She] wanted to run the relationship very much like a sort of parent/child thing – she's 15 years older than me.

In P's case, that very age difference meant that the caring would eventually become reciprocal, and she gave as a reason for entering into the civil partnership that it would give her partner 'some surety. It put us on a sort of … a sort of caring level, I felt'.

Whether women are drawn to a caring role or not, it is certainly expected of us, and to a far greater degree than it is of men. None of the men mentioned caring in the same way and, indeed, the sight of a male carer tends to evoke admiration and surprise, not to speak of pity and assistance. I was struck by the very different responses given to one of my female participants from the one given to the one man who sought help from an advice agency. O, the woman, went to Citizens Advice to find out what she could do about her partner's escalating expenditure because 'financially it was crippling us that she wasn't working'. She was told that the best thing she could do was to leave her job and become a full-time carer, because she would be paid for this. R, the man, had a partner whom he described as alternately loving and abusive, both emotionally and physically: 'two different people'. *He* was advised to leave the relationship immediately. Clearly, the symptoms O and R presented were different but exploitation and mental abuse were present in both situations (as indeed they were in P's and J's). Yet no one suggested that O should leave her partner if she wanted to end the exploitation and abuse. Instead, the assumption was that she should immerse herself still further in the caring role.

Equally significantly, the women themselves interpreted their situations in terms of the partner's mental health or drink problems rather than her abusive behaviour, leading one to wonder whether what might in a heterosexual or gay male couple be recognised as domestic violence could only be conceptualised as illness when the perpetrator is a woman in a lesbian relationship. This should not surprise us, of course, since feminist criminologists long ago revealed that male criminals tend to be seen as 'bad' and female as 'mad', and lesbianism has an equally long heritage as a mental illness.

The law in our relationships

One of the proudest boasts of lesbians and gays in the 1990s was that they could teach heterosexuals a thing or two about relationships. Gillian Dunne, for example, asked: 'What is it about lesbian relationships that appear to turn upside down many of the assumptions which shape heterosexual practice and maintain the status quo?' Her empirical findings about how lesbians conduct their lives underpinned a view of lesbian relationships as more egalitarian and less role-bound; as one of her interviewees put it: 'We've got no role models in terms of how we divide our duties, so we've got to work it out afresh as to what suits us. … We try very hard to be just to each other and … not exploit the other person' (Dunne 1999: 211; see also Dunne 1997).

Likewise, Weeks, Heaphy and Donovan in their ground-breaking study *Same-Sex Intimacies* (2001) documented 'the emergence of the new relationship ethic in the non-heterosexual world' which they called 'families of choice', premised on a range of 'new relational possibilities' (vii–viii). Among couples, they too perceived a 'negotiated egalitarian' style as the 'dominant one today' (the research took place in 1995–96) (106). Many of the (mostly youthful) gays and lesbians they interviewed rejected the role-playing models (for instance, butch and femme) of many older gays and lesbians (115). One 28-year-old woman explained how she felt heterosexual relationships imposed, or at least facilitated, destructive *emotional* roles, 'I don't mean roles as in housework or breadwinner – I mean roles as in game playing, manipulation, being passive, being victim-like', Lesbian relationships, she asserted, were free of these and based on 'freedom … on not owning a person and not dictating to the person what they can and can't do' (Weeks et al. 2001: 113).

My research, however, found plenty of evidence of game-playing and manipulation in the relationships (and especially their breakdown) of the women I interviewed, many of whom must have been of the same generation as the Weeks team's interviewees, 15 years later. Among the reasons given to me for dissolution were:

- *Disagreements over whether to have children.* This was only raised by women in my study, presumably because up until recently women have occupied the childrearing role, but I suspect it will follow for men as it becomes more common for gay men to want to parent. K's partner, who had three children, married on the understanding that they would have children of their own. She later taunted K, saying, 'I never wanted to have children with you anyway'.
- *Money problems.* With the women, these tended to take the form of excessive spending by one woman of her partner's hard-earned cash, but with the men it was more usually about the belittling and control felt by the poorer partner because of the couple's disparity of income. (An exception was the man with a younger dependent partner who had a gambling habit.) Spending is of course the archetypal female role, whereas men have traditionally exercised power in domestic relationships through being the breadwinner.

- *Disputes over the housework.* While these doubtless go on in heterosexual households, in lesbian relationships they can be exacerbated by the fact that men have traditionally not been expected to contribute much in this department – so expectations are higher for women, and disappointment correspondingly more common.
- *Communication problems.* Women have been socialised to be sensitive to others' needs in ways that are not expected of men. They are supposed to do the listening and caring in relationships and so, in the stories I heard, 'little' failings like neglecting or misreading partners' needs or not apologising for bad behaviour quickly mounted up in the women's relationships to become a 'big' issue that contributed to the break.

All this led to me to wonder whether the legal regulation of the relationship made a difference in how these issues were handled. In other words, were these just problems for lesbian couples, or were they problems of civil partnerships? Only one of my interviewees expressed the view that registration had played any role in the ending of her relationship. J observed that her partner, who had an alcohol problem, changed her behaviour after the ceremony and began to act as her father acted towards her mother: 'drunk, she reminds me of her dad […] she'd become a bully with the civil partnership certificate […] I think it's just a control thing'.

Although this observation was not made by anyone else, other interviews suggested to me that the mutual obligations of marriage and civil partnership do *facilitate* abuse. K, O, P and Q all had partners who exploited them emotionally, practically and financially. When you are in a relationship of care and dependence, the law's promise of security (pensions, next-of-kin rights) offers an attractive form of protection. As O said, for her partner 'the legal situation was a big thing, first of all, obviously, with the Jehovah's Witness thing, and also with her work, because she was off sick for four or five years'. Some of my participants felt, if not quite pressured, unable to resist the dependent partner's eagerness to formalise the relationship. Once formally linked, these people could more easily maintain the pattern of dependence and abuse, while it became correspondingly harder for their partners to resist the legal as well as the moral responsibility for caring and support.

My conclusion is that women have higher expectations of relationships than men. This may be partly due to the failure of marriage to live up to its romantic ideal and, for women in opposite-sex relationships, the realisation that the promise of gender equality is, as yet, unrealised. But with same-sex relationships, the fact that women are brought up to do the caring work in society means that we expect more of our women partners. We expect women to fulfil our trust in them, to listen and share, to treat us well and not to abuse us. When men behave badly, however disappointing, it is only what society assumes and takes for granted. When women do, there is a real sense of betrayal – a sense that they have let our sex down. And that is why more women dissolve their civil partnership than men.

What has happened to the argument that same-sex unions will be different from, or better than, heterosexual unions?

In an article in the *Observer* (3 February 2008), the editor of the gay site http://www.pinknews.co.uk, Tony Grew, opined that gays and lesbians took civil partnerships:

> more seriously than many people who get married. The people who go for it are older, have been together longer and have more committed relationships. That's why we won't see the 40 per cent or 50 per cent divorce rates we see in heterosexual relationships.
>
> (Campbell 2008)

By 2012, everything about this statement seemed wide of the mark.

The 2012 figures for *divorce* in England and Wales showed a small increase of 0.5 per cent on the previous year's. Of the almost 120,000 divorces, almost half occurred in the first ten years of marriage, and 65 per cent were as a result of petitions by women. The most common ground was 'unreasonable behaviour', for which women were almost three times as likely to petition as men (ONS 2014a). The Office for National Statistics estimates that 42 per cent of marriages will end in divorce (ONS 2013b).

The 2012 figures for *dissolution of civil partnerships* in England and Wales show a much greater increase on the previous year's – a full 20 per cent. Of the 794 dissolutions, all of which have taken place within the first five years of registration, 57 per cent were of women's partnerships (ONS 2013a: 7–8). The Office for National Statistics does not publish figures for grounds for dissolution, though almost certainly the most common ground is 'unreasonable behaviour', nor does it make predictions about how many civil partnerships will end in dissolution. In 2010, marriages were more than twice as likely to end in divorce after four years than civil partnerships in dissolution. Ross et al. (2011) noted that 'it is too early to say whether this trend will continue beyond the fourth anniversary' (15). But that 20 per cent increase in dissolutions in 2012 suggests that dissolutions are catching up. It follows that not only are same-sex couples not immune to the problems suffered by opposite-sex couples but also that destructive (or at least short-term) dynamics might actually be built into our legal model of marriage.

When Weeks, Heaphy and Donovan undertook their research into *Same-Sex Intimacies* in the mid-1990s, they found little enthusiasm for the legal regulation of gay and lesbian relationships. 'The very idea is really quite abhorrent', said one woman (107). And another: 'marriage has never been in women's interests – ever' (Weeks et al. 1999: 48). Among women this finding can be explained by the (by then well-recognised) feminist concerns about marriage as a site of women's oppression, while some gay men still harboured a well-founded suspicion of law's interventions in their private lives. In the USA, however, in a debate largely dominated by conservative men, a few feminist voices were raised in support of same-sex marriage: Cheshire Calhoun (2000), for example, argued the necessity of inhabiting the heterosexual space of family in order to transform it, while Nan Hunter (1995) saw lesbian spouses modelling what egalitarian marriage might look like. In arguing that same-sex marriage would be 'different' (and better) than opposite-sex marriage, pro-marriage feminists were actually drawing on some of the same behavioural ideals as those revealed by Weeks, Heaphy, Donovan and Dunne, and argued by some anti-marriage feminists such as myself (Auchmuty 2003). But where *we* identified marriage as a tool of social conformity to traditional roles and power structures, and argued against the privileging of the couple, *they* believed that the egalitarian model could survive and, indeed, flourish within an institution which in other respects had so much to offer gays and lesbians – inclusion, status, and family and community support.

The question is whether those claims about difference and the superiority of gay and lesbian modes of relating were ever fulfilled in practice, or remained in the realms of unrealised ideals. Brian Heaphy has cautioned against our tendency as gays and lesbians to 'confuse analysis with prescription and actualities with potentialities', and to generalise from 'small and exclusive groups of lesbians and gay men … *as if* it illuminated general experience' (2008: 1, 6). Did we in fact arrange our domestic lives differently from heterosexuals? Did we live in 'families of choice'? Or does the popularity of civil partnerships reveal these claims to be purely rhetorical?

Certainly, the large numbers of gay and lesbian couples who have entered into civil partnerships once the institution was introduced suggest that the romantically or domestically linked couple relationship has retained its normative power. But it must be remembered that no other relationship is capable of legal regulation: who knows what would have happened had the government offered the possibility of registering any other family form? Having a partner does not preclude living differently from the conventional married couple. Let us analyse the claimed areas of difference.

In their mid-1990s study of both gay men and lesbians, Weeks, Heaphy and Donovan identified 'families of choice' as the distinctive feature of gay and lesbian relationships. Both male and female respondents claimed that 'the friendships I have are family' (2001: 10), so much so that the book devoted a whole chapter to friendship. Interviewees with children spoke of different family structures with up to four parents – all 'family' (34) – and, while many interviewees lived alone or in couples, there were some genuinely alternative families. Roy, for instance, a gay man, lived with his female ex-lover, their biological and non-biological children, his ex-partner's male lover and the last-named's mother (98). Gillian Dunne's study of urban lesbians of the same period made a similar point about the importance of ex-lovers as 'family', another recognised feature of gay and lesbian relationships (1997: 203). Her findings, however, focused more on the egalitarian nature of couple relationships, clearly very much influenced by lesbian feminism. Of her 60 respondents 53 said that the main way their relationship differed from heterosexual ones was that it was 'more equal'. Dunne comments: 'This was manifested through their adherence to an egalitarian perspective as an ideal or a political principle, which appeared to be constructed around notions of individual autonomy' (181). This certainly resonates with the ways the older participants in my own research saw their relationships, with close attention being paid to financial independence and autonomy (dual careers, minimising inequalities of income, separate bank accounts).

But lesbians also embraced the notion of families of choice. It seems to me, however, that the words meant different things to lesbians and gay men. Among gay men it was likely to refer to the replacement by friends and gay community of a birth family from which they were estranged. Among lesbians, while it might also have that meaning, there was often superimposed a feminist critique of the 'nuclear' family with its patriarchal structure and gendered roles (e.g. Barrett and McIntosh 1982) which led them consciously to reject prioritisation of the couple and, while still often having a recognised partner with whom they might or might not live, to construct alternative family arrangements where friends, ex-partners and kin all played a central part. Take my friend, for example, an older single lesbian who once lived communally with other lesbians (including my partner, which is how I know her), and who now shares her home with a lesbian lodger whose partner lives in another city. My friend's ex-partner lives nearby with her current partner and child, whom my friend helps to mind. My friend sometimes goes on holiday by herself, sometimes with friends, and sometimes with her ex-partner while *her* partner stays at home with the child. That was the arrangement the couple made when the child was adopted. So here we have couples and a child, but in domestic arrangements a far cry from the families we all grew up in.

It may be argued that these alternative family structures can also be seen in opposite-sex families – in part because of the rise in divorce and the large numbers of families with multiple sets of parents and carers. In the 1980s, however, when Smart (1984) and Barrett and McIntosh (1982) were writing their critiques of contemporary marriage and the family, it was gays and lesbians who were actively pioneering different ways of living that challenged the nuclear structures, from which they were excluded, and in self-conscious and deliberate rather than simply pragmatic ways. It is arguable that the more egalitarian forms of opposite-sex marriage and relationships we see today are in fact indebted to the models provided by same-sex couples, just as Hunter (1995) predicted.

From my interviews and the 2013 study by Smart, Heaphy and Einarsdottir, however, it is clear that the dominant view of same-sex relationships today bears little relation to the ideals of the 1980s and 1990s. This, I would argue, is because most of the 'different' and 'egalitarian' qualities of same-sex relationships disappeared with the advent of civil partnerships, to be replaced by a rhetoric of sameness – 'We are just like you' – and of normative legal assumptions premised on traditional marriage and divorce. This had two consequences. First, it caused shock and heartache among the older participants in my study when their long-term relationship broke down and their ex-partner, encouraged by her lawyer, moved swiftly into 'divorcee' mode. As A put it, the law 'doesn't understand homosexual relations, so it sees everything from a heterosexual lens'. In her case, on dissolution her ex-partner was able to present herself as dependent and vulnerable, whereas their 19-year relationship had been based on a very different model of autonomy and independence. Second, for the younger generation who had grown up in legal 'equality' with heterosexuals, the arrival of civil partnerships suppressed not simply the conscious negotiation of roles and repudiation of heterosexual models by same-sex couples, but the very *knowledge* that such ideals and critiques had ever existed.

One of the young women in my study, for example, planned to give up her teaching job when she and her new partner started a family; in spite of her previous bad experience in a civil partnership, she seemed to have given little thought to the financial consequences. Gendered roles, albeit modified as a result of feminist successes, often seem to be the only roles younger gays and lesbians recognise. Resistance is made difficult, of course, by institutional structures that force a breadwinner/dependent role on less affluent couples with children. While the greatest publicity is given to millionaire gay male parents such as Elton John and David Furnish, we never see the much more usual lesbian couples struggling on benefits. The *Observer* ran a column in 2012 called 'Two dads, one mum – one family' in which actor Charlie Condou recounted his experiences as a gay father of two children and his shared parenting arrangements. But civil partnerships do not recognise a relationship of three, so the 1990s 'families of choice' with their 'new relational possibilities' appear to have been snuffed out with the legislation.

In light of all this, the reasons for the rise in dissolution become clear. Civil partnerships increasingly appeal to young people; civil partnerships increasingly resemble traditional marriage; a high proportion of shorter (less than ten years) marriages end in divorce; so too will shorter civil partnerships end in dissolution, and for the same reasons. In spite of all the optimistic predictions, civil partnerships will, in fact, prove to be no more egalitarian or enduring than marriages.

Conclusion

Several conclusions may be drawn from this brief examination of the statistics of civil partnership formation and dissolution. First, given the rocketing dissolution rate, it is obvious that civil partnerships have not been an unqualified success. Second, insofar as they suit anyone, they suit older gay men with property (though the most high-profile dissolution cases have also come from this group), rather than older lesbians or young people generally. This had been predicted (Auchmuty 2007: 111) and chimes with Jessie Bernard's revelation 40 years ago that marriage works for men but makes women ill (Bernard 1972). Third, these two facts demonstrate the shortcomings of a simplistic equal-rights approach to sexuality and law, since this formal equality measure has brought neither substantive equality nor, it seems, lasting happiness to many people.

A fourth conclusion to be drawn from the evidence is that, in accepting the heterosexual model of couple recognition and regulation, we have lost a great deal of what was distinctive about same-sex, especially lesbian, relationships. I put this down to the drowning-out of feminist perspectives by the dominant equal-rights discourse around same-sex marriage. Mainstream knowledge has always been strikingly resistant to feminism but, on this subject, the first- and second-wave feminist analyses of power within marriage and the family simply disappeared under the weight of formal equality discourses, leaving younger lesbians as well as gay men of all ages vulnerable to the *structural* inequalities.

Notes

1 I am grateful for the assistance of a British Academy Small Grant which enabled me to undertake this project. I also wish to thank all those who helped me in carrying it out, particularly the 19 participants who agreed to be interviewed, my research assistant Anisa de Jong, and Alison McPherson, who transcribed the interviews.

2 Or, worse still, that catch-all phrase 'LGBT' (lesbians, gay men, bisexuals and transgender people) – or even 'LGBTIQ' (the above, plus intersex and queer people). Such communities simply do not exist, so very different are the respective interests of the different groups.

References

Auchmuty, R. (2003) 'When equality is not equity: Homosexual inclusion in undue influence law', 11 *Feminist Legal Studies* 163–90.

——(2007) 'Out of the shadows: Feminist silence and liberal law' in C. Stychin and V. Munro (eds) *Sexuality and the Law: Feminist Engagements* (Routledge).

——(2012) 'Law and the power of feminism: How marriage lost its power to oppress women', 20 *Feminist Legal Studies* 71–87.

Barker, M. and Langdridge, D. (2010) 'Whatever happened to non-monogamies? Critical reflections on recent research and theory', 13 *Sexualities* 748–72.

Barrett, M. and McIntosh, M. (1982) *The Anti-Social Family* (Verso).

Bernard, J. (1972) *The Future of Marriage* (World Publishing).

Calhoun, C. (2000) *Feminism, the Family, and the Politics of the Closet* (Oxford University Press).

Campbell, D. (2008) 'Honeymoon is over for gay weddings', *Observer* 3 February.

Condou, C. (2012) 'The three of us', *Guardian* 14 July.

Dent, G. (2013) 'How come it's lesbians rather than gay men that are giving up on civil partnerships?' *Independent* 10 October.

Doughty, S. (2013) 'Now gay marriages are hit by seven-year itch', *Daily Mail* 9 October.

Dunne, G. (1997) *Lesbian Lifestyles: Women's Work and the Politics of* Sexuality (Macmillan).

——(1999) 'What difference does "difference" make? Lesbian experience of work and family life' in J. Seymour and P. Bagguley (eds) *Relating Intimacies: Power and Resistance* (Macmillan).

Harding, R. (2008) 'Recognizing (and resisting) regulation: Attitudes to the introduction of civil partnership', 11 *Sexualities* 740–60.

Heaphy, B. (2008) 'The sociology of lesbian and gay reflexivity or reflexive sociology?' *Sociological Research Online*, 21 March: http://www.socresonline.org.uk/13/1/9.html [Last accessed 4 March 2015].

Heaphy, B., Smart, C. and Einarsdottir, A. (2013) *Same-Sex Marriages: New Generations, New Relationships* (Palgrave Macmillan).

Hunter, N. D. (1995) 'Marriage, law and gender: A feminist inquiry' in L. Duggan and N. D. Hunter (eds) *Sex Wars: Sexual Dissent and Political Culture* (Routledge).

Katz, E. M. (2014) 'Is monogamy harder for men or for women?': http://www.evanmarckatz.com/blog/sex/is-monogamy-harder-for-men-or-women/ [accessed 24 June].

National Statistics (2006) 'More than 15,500 civil partnerships formed', 4 December.

ONS (Office for National Statistics) (2013a) 'Civil partnerships in the UK 2012', published 8 October: http://www.ons.gov.uk/ons/rel/vsob2/civil-partnership-statistics – united-kingdom/2012/stb-civil-partnerships-2012.html [accessed 6 June 2014].

ONS (2013b) 'What percentage of marriages ends in divorce?', 9 February: http://www.ons.gov.uk/ons/rel/vsob1/divorces-in-england-and-wales/2011/sty-what-percentage-of-marriages-end-in-divorce.html [accessed 6 June 2014].

——(2014a) 'Divorces in England and Wales, 2012', 6 February: http://www.ons.gov.uk/ons/rel/vsob1/divorces-in-england-and-wales/2012/stb-divorces-2012.html [accessed 6 June 2014].

——(2014b) 'Marriages in England and Wales, 2012 (provisional)': http://www.ons.gov.uk/ons/rel/vsob1/marriages-in-england-and-wales–provisional-/2012/stb-marriages-in-england-and-wales – provisional – 2011.html [accessed 24 June 2014].

Ross, H., Gask, K. and Berrington, A. (2011) 'Civil partnerships five years on', 145 *Population Trends* (Office for National Statistics, Autumn) 1–31.

Scott, M. (2005) 'Gay wedding bells a wake-up call for all partners' *Observer* 4 December.

Shoffman, M. (2006) 'Over 15,500 gays and lesbians are civil partners': http://www.pinknews.co.uk/2006/12/04/over-15000-gays-and-lesbians-are-civil-partners/ [accessed 6 June 2014].

Smart, C. (1984) *The Ties That Bind* (Routledge & Kegan Paul).

Taylor, Y. (2007) *Working Class Lesbian Life: Classed Outsiders* (Palgrave Macmillan).

Toynbee, P. (2014) 'Scrap inheritance tax and leave the dead to rest in peace', *Guardian* 2 May.

Weeks, J., Heaphy, B. and Donovan, C. (1999) 'Partnership rites: Commitment and ritual in non-heterosexual relationships' in J. Seymour and P. Bagguley (eds) *Relating Intimacies: Power and Resistance* (Macmillan).

Weeks, J., Heaphy, B. and Donovan, C. (2001) *Same-Sex Intimacies: Families of Choice and Other Life Experiments* (Routledge).

Chapter 13

After the wedding, what next?

Conservatism and conjugality

Nicola Barker

Introduction

Same-sex marriage in England and Wales was introduced with an announcement from a Conservative prime minister that he supports gay marriage not in spite of but *because* he is a Conservative (Cameron 2011). It was presented as the most Conservative of endeavours, a way to recognise long-term relationships and reward 'responsible' families. Loving, committed, married same-sex couples fit comfortably within a broader conservative policy package of state austerity and privatised family responsibility.[1] However, this is not the end of the story. Some (mostly but not exclusively Conservatives) did not share Cameron's sentiment and instead expressed fears that same-sex marriage would mark a radical transformation in the institution of marriage itself. The 'slippery slope' arguments, that same-sex marriage will inevitably lead to polygamy and incest, were much less prominent in the UK than in the USA, though they were still present here. For example, during the debates on the same-sex marriage legislation in the Scottish Parliament, the Labour MSP Elaine Smith expressed concerns that largely echoed those of the Coalition for Marriage that 'redefining marriage' would, amongst other things, lead to unions of three or more people (Smith 2013).[2]

What is striking about the UK debates though is that in 2004 it was opponents of civil partnerships who were trying to initiate descent down the slippery slope, arguing that the marriage-like institution *should* be extended to siblings and other close family members (see further Chapter 1 in this collection). In an interview with the *Big Issue* during the same-sex marriage debates in 2013, Lord Tebbit returned to this theme, facetiously declaring a sexual attraction towards his brother whilst making a more fiscally concerned point about the unfairness of not allowing siblings to marry and thus inherit each other's property tax-free once same-sex marriage was introduced (Delaney 2013). These interventions were designed to undermine both the recognition of same-sex relationships and the unpopular (amongst conservatives) inheritance tax provision. However, Conservatives opposing same-sex relationship recognition without wanting to appear homophobic are not the only ones questioning why inheritance tax breaks and other legal consequences of marriage should be reserved for those in conjugal relationships. Some legal academics have also been calling for a shift away from conjugality and towards care as the basis for legal recognition of (interdependent) relationships. I explore these suggestions and consider whether this may lead to a more radical legal family form, whether the next step after same-sex marriage might be to focus legal attention on caretaking relationships and what that might mean for those in such relationships. Is this the beginning of a new expansion of relationship recognition, and does that mean the beginning of the end for conjugality as the principal way in which the law constitutes a family, through marriage?

The Conservative proposal for same-sex marriage and the future of the welfare state

The recent history of the Conservative Party in general and David Cameron in particular, including their opposition to repealing Section 28 of the Local Government Act 1988 in 2003, does not (despite the subsequent apology: see Watt 2009) suggest that within a decade they would have introduced same-sex marriage. The Conservatives began to court the so-called 'gay vote' in 2004 as part of their attempt to cast off their image as 'the nasty party' (McLean 2004). However, same-sex marriage is not simply an attempt to appeal to socially liberal and gay voters. It fits comfortably within Conservative ideology for all those except the most homophobic, and it also fits well within the politics of state austerity. Examining the reasons advanced by Conservatives for introducing same-sex marriage alongside other Conservative policies, particularly those relating to 'family values' and to the cuts to the welfare state (a primary target of austerity measures), highlights the ways in which same-sex marriage contributes to a broader Conservative policy package.

Examining the (mainstream Conservative) discourse in favour of same-sex marriage tells us about more than simply rhetorical and/or political strategy, though this was undoubtedly also a factor. Peter Tatchell, taking credit for '[winning] the government's commitment to marriage equality', explains how the Equal Love campaign 'pitched our arguments to appeal to their Conservative values' and notes how closely the language of David Cameron's speech echoes their briefings (Tatchell 2011):

> Conservatives rightly encourage and approve loving, stable relationships because enduring care and commitment are good for individuals, families and for the well-being of society as a whole. If marriage is a Conservative value, then same-sex marriage is consistent with this value. Far from undermining marriage, gay marriage strengthens it. Conservatives

> believe in marriage. They should therefore support same-sex marriage precisely because they are Conservatives
>
> (Tatchell 2011)

> And to anyone who has reservations, I say: Yes, it's about equality, but it's also about something else: commitment. Conservatives believe in the ties that bind us; that society is stronger when we make vows to each other and support each other. So I don't support gay marriage despite being a Conservative. I support gay marriage because I'm a Conservative
>
> (Cameron 2011)

The language of commitment and mutual support are strikingly similar to the language of 'encouraging responsibility' used by New Labour in introducing the Civil Partnership Act 2004. These terms are not particularly surprising in that they are frequently used when politicians discuss marriage in general, but they are not empty rhetoric. Behind them is a troubling economic policy: the privatisation of care and dependency. This refers to the burdens and costs of social reproduction (for example raising a child) being borne almost exclusively by the family unit as the state retracts welfare provision and support services. For example, as Susan Boyd (1997: 14) has argued, an expectation that childcare will be done in the home for free by mothers is linked to both childcare work being underpaid and the absence of publicly funded daycare. It can also refer to an expectation of mutual support between partners, which results in the reduction or withdrawal of state support such as unemployment benefits based on a partner's income.

This privatisation was particularly evident in the advocacy for civil partnerships, which focused on access to spousal inheritance tax breaks and pensions (see, for example, Stonewall 2004). In order to make those arguments, Stonewall had to concede that same-sex couples should also be disadvantaged in exactly the same ways as similarly situated heterosexual couples:

> The taxpayer would actually save money in the area of benefit and tax credit payments. Same-sex partners currently claim benefits as two individuals, meaning that they will receive more money than if their needs had been assessed as a couple. This Bill will treat same-sex couples in the same way as heterosexual couples.
>
> (Stonewall 2004)

The consequences of civil partnerships for the poorest same-sex couples was a reduction in income for same-sex couples who were claiming as two individuals and now must claim as a couple. While same-sex couples who want to take advantage of the inheritance tax breaks[3] need to marry or get a civil partnership to be able to do so, it is impossible for the poorest couples to avoid the loss of income because cohabitants are treated the same as spouses for the purposes of assessing benefit entitlements, even though there is no legal obligation on a cohabitant to financially support their partner. However, this effect of the Civil Partnership Act 2004 was hidden within a discourse of accepting responsibilities alongside rights, obscuring the fact that some of the economic consequences of spousal status are different depending on the income-level of the individuals within the couple, and also obscuring the economic vulnerability of a low-income partner or couple who have part of their income withdrawn in the process of the lesbian and gay community more broadly achieving formal equality.

In this sense, marriage and civil partnership play a key role in supporting the politics of state austerity and the rolling back of the welfare state. This is motivated not only by immediate financial concerns but also by an ideology that reifies a small state. The state recognises same-sex relationships in order to encourage lesbians and gay men to take on these care burdens and financial (inter)dependencies as part of the process of welfare retrenchment (Conaghan and Grabham 2007). In other words, the £18 billion of cuts to the welfare state that is to take effect this fiscal year (2014–15) and further £10 billion by 2016–17 (Browne et al. 2012) needs to be absorbed by families. It is not necessary for a homophobic government to recognise same-sex families through civil partnership and now marriage but, by doing so, they are able to both demonstrate that they are 'not homophobic' and encourage more families to take on responsibility for privatised care and dependency.

The creation of civil partnerships in 2004 already enabled this privatisation, so what does the language of marriage add for the Conservatives in government? Arguing that marriage is 'conservatising' and drawing heavily on the work of American conservative gay commentator Andrew Sullivan, Tim Montgomerie (editor of *Conservative Home*) provides the clearest example of why the language of marriage matters to the agenda of privatisation:

> [The] social trinity of a good family, a good education and a commitment to work represent the superior conservative alternative to the socialist emphasis on a large welfare state. … If marriage is embraced as an institution of relevance to all people I hope we will begin to see the kind of pro-marriage public policy that exists in nearly all other developed countries. By making social conservatism if not fashionable again, but certainly acceptable, I think, for example, it will be easier to see the kind of pro-marriage tax policies that exist in almost every other European state.
>
> (Montgomerie 2012)

Montgomerie highlights how same-sex marriage not only would support but also is *necessary* to justify explicitly 'pro-marriage' public policy. He also hints at the link between 'pro-marriage' policies and a smaller welfare state. Civil partners are already treated the same as married couples for these purposes so there would be nothing to prevent such policies being created to apply to both spouses and civil partners, but the existence of civil partnership as a separate institution that also receives these tax breaks undermines the pro-*marriage* rhetoric. Conservative commentators in the USA have, for example, lamented the same-sex marriage prohibition for bringing about a 'proliferation of alternatives' to marriage, such as civil union and domestic partnership (Rauch 2004).

The idea that a 'good family' in the form of marriage will enable reduction of the welfare state was adopted by the Bush administration in the USA, though in this case it did not extend to same-sex marriage. In that context, Priya Kandaswamy (2008) has demonstrated a link between work requirements (also one of the most controversial aspects of the UK coalition government's welfare reform) and sexual regulation in the form of 'marriage promotion'. She argues that 'the language of marriage has effectively been used to undermine welfare rights and to depoliticize economic inequality altogether' (2008: 707). In other words, Kandaswamy argues that the so-called 'welfare queen' – sexually promiscuous women, racialised as Black or Latina, who supposedly use welfare to both avoid the labour market and fund life outside the normative family – is in poverty not because of broader racial and class inequality, the difficulty of combining paid work, particularly precarious low-paid work, with raising children, or the difficulty of finding employment, but because of her own 'deviant' lifestyle.

Same-sex marriage advocates in the UK who made arguments to appeal to conservatives implicitly, and sometimes explicitly, accept the premise of such policies by highlighting how same-sex marriage would both 'civilise'[4] gay men by discouraging promiscuity and encouraging responsibility and also contribute to the core Conservative message that the married state is morally superior (see, for example, Tatchell, above). In the *Daily Telegraph*, Matthew d'Ancona explains this, also mentioning David Cameron's desire to introduce a tax allowance for married couples:

> The extension of marriage to include gay couples will entrench the idea of the married estate as a social good as well as a private condition. Marriage encourages reliance upon a spouse rather than the state: a wedding is the ritual in which the individual recognizes publicly that he or she is not alone, and that, choosing a spouse, promises love to, and accepts lifelong responsibility for, that person.
>
> (d'Ancona 2012)

The blame rhetoric that was behind the recent UK government reforms to welfare (see DWP 2010a) is not as explicitly tied to (racialised) sexuality as the 'welfare queen' discourse in the USA, but, as this quote suggests, it does bear some of its hallmarks. In response to the welfare reforms, the Child Poverty Action Group has noted the government's 'disproportionate focus' on the claimant without sufficient focus on the 'ability of the labour market to create flexible, well remunerated jobs' (DWP 2010b). The Social Security Advisory Committee also warned that an increase in 'labour market flexibility' has led to an increase in part-time and temporary jobs, many of which are 'also very low-paid and insecure', leading to 'a cycle of low-paid work, to out of work benefits, and back to low-paid work' (SSAC 2010). However, the government dismissed these concerns and instead proceeds under the assumption that people are unemployed or underemployed either because they are insufficiently committed to finding work or they insufficiently skilled in the art of finding work.[5]

While this appears to lack the *sexual* regulation that Kandaswamy identified in the USA, marriage promotion is not absent from Conservative policy and sits comfortably alongside this individualism and privatisation of responsibility for poverty. Although it is yet to be implemented, the Centre for Social Justice, directed by Iain Duncan Smith, who also oversaw the welfare reforms as Secretary of State for Work and Pensions, recommended that a transferrable tax allowance should be introduced for married couples that would provide an additional £20 per week, designed to encourage low-income couples to transition from cohabitation to marriage, and 'thereby increase the stability of their relationship' (Centre for Social Justice 2010). This was in the Conservative Manifesto in order to 'send an important signal that we value couples and the commitment that people make when they get married', as opposed to the existing tax and benefits system, which 'rewards people when they split up' (Conservatives 2010). David Cameron highlighted 'commitment' as a key Conservative value that was to be encouraged in order to strengthen society, while Douglas Murray noted that those who object to the 'perceived promiscuity' of gay men ought to 'welcome gay acceptance into the marital fold' (Murray 2012). In other words, the increasing acceptance of gay marriage 'represents not the making gay of marriage but the making conservative of gays' (ibid.). Both Murray and other commentators also note the need for 'renewal and restoration' of the institution of marriage itself, particularly at a time when heterosexuals are increasingly rejecting marriage. For example, Matthew d'Ancona (2012) notes the 'stabilising force' of gay couples being 'recruited to, and reinforcing, an ancient institution'. This renewal of marriage would also be accompanied by the renewal of the Conservative Party. According to Tim Montgomerie:

> What David Cameron has embarked upon is an incredibly important project – to make social conservatism fashionable again. Marriage is civilizing, stabilizing, a hugely important institution for bringing people

> together. But if marriage is fossilized and exclusive, that has only limited reach. His attempt to enlarge and modernize the institution should not be seen as a threat to marriage but as its saviour.
>
> (Interviewed in Grice 2012)

In other words, the Conservative proposal of same-sex marriage is also a proposal to the lesbian and gay communities to renew both the institution of marriage and the reputation of the Conservative Party. Behind that proposal lies an intention of sexual regulation of both low-income couples more generally and 'sexually promiscuous' gay men through financial incentives to marry and remain married.

This is not inevitably the future but it will take the continuing engagement of those who have fought for social justice in the form of same-sex marriage to prevent same-sex marriage from reinforcing the existing inequalities and injustices within the institution of marriage, including the economic vulnerability of carers and those reliant on state benefits, and the stigmatisation of non-normative sexualities, whether these are homosexual or heterosexual. The next step after same-sex marriage should be one of resistance to this conservative agenda.

Despite this deeply conservative rhetoric in favour of same-sex marriage, there was not a consensus amongst conservatives or the Conservative Party, with the government relying on the votes of Liberal Democrat and Labour MPs to pass the Marriage (Same Sex Couples) Bill 2013. Those who are more traditional social and/or religious conservatives (or just homophobic) focus not on the links between same-sex marriage and these broader Conservative policy objectives but on the supposed 'redefinition' of marriage. For them, same-sex marriage represents a threat to the institution rather than its saviour and signals, perhaps, the end of conjugality.

The end of conjugality?

During the parliamentary debates on the Marriage (Same Sex Couples) Bill 2013, Sir Roger Gale MP (Conservative) referred to same-sex marriage as 'Alice in Wonderland territory – Orwellian almost' before suggesting that 'a way forward' was that marriage ought to be abolished as a legal institution and replaced with civil unions that can be entered into by anyone including brothers and sisters (*Hansard*, HC Deb, 5 February 2013, col 152). The slightly facetious call to abolish marriage (from a thrice married man) aside, the expansion of some spousal rights to non-conjugal caretaking relationships is a possibility that has been called for not only by Conservatives but also by legal academics from the other end of the political spectrum.

The absence of conjugality in both civil partnerships and same-sex marriage, in that there is no consummation requirement and adultery is not listed as a factor demonstrating irretrievable breakdown of the relationship for the purposes of divorce/dissolution (see further Chapter 1 in this volume), provides the opportunity to question why these provisions should be limited to sexual partners. Each time there has been a major development in same-sex relationship recognition, those who want to oppose the measure have taken advantage of this absence by calling for it to be expanded to siblings and other family relationships. These calls are largely disingenuous and are a strategy to undermine same-sex relationship recognition as much as anything else, as evidenced by the fact that they tend to disappear the minute the legislation recognising same-sex relationships is passed.[6] The most prominent example of this was the Christian Institute full-page newspaper advert[7] and the amendments proposed by Baroness O'Caithain, Lord Tebbit and others during the Civil Partnership Bill debates in 2004. They were ostensibly concerned about the so-called 'spinster sisters' who lived together all their lives yet the surviving sister would have to pay inheritance tax after the death of her sister. This was presented as deeply unfair in contrast to a same-sex partner who may have been in a short civil partnership prior to the death of their spouse yet would have a tax-free inheritance. Baroness Deech (2010) subsequently described this as English law displaying a preference for the 'idle sexual partner' over the 'deserving family member'.[8]

Although these amendments failed the issue surfaced again during the debates on the Marriage (Same Sex Couples) Bill 2013, though with much less prominence and fewer proponents than the first time around. Instead the focus of opposition this time was largely on whether religious bodies or individuals would be forced to perform, teach or accept the equal validity of same-sex marriages (see Chapter 1 in this volume). Lord Tebbit, though, returned to the issue of spousal tax breaks for family members in his interview with the *Big Issue*, saying:

> It's like one of my colleagues said – we've got to make these same-sex marriages available to all. It would lift my worries about inheritance tax because maybe I'd be allowed to marry my son. Why not? Why shouldn't a mother marry her daughter? Why shouldn't two elderly sisters living together marry each other? I quite fancy my brother!
>
> (Delaney 2013)

The fact that once the provision has passed these proponents of spousal rights for siblings seem to drop the issue suggests that this is a strategy of opposition rather than a serious attempt to have caretaking relationships recognised, though these people did seem to sincerely hold the belief that there ought to be wider inheritance-tax exemptions.

The argument that civil partnerships should be available to siblings was tested in the European Court of Human Rights by the Burden sisters, who claimed that they were discriminated against in their right to enjoy their property because sisters were unable to become civil partners and thus would be liable for inheritance tax. Picking up the theme of deserving versus undeserving, Joyce Burden was quoted as saying:

> This government is always going out of its way to give rights to people who have done nothing to deserve them. If we were lesbians we would have all the rights in the world. But we are sisters and it seems we have no rights at all.
>
> (Slack et al. 2006; Gibb 2008)

The Civil Partnership Act 2004 played a prominent role in the sisters' submission to the court for two reasons: first, because the absence of a sexual relationship does not preclude them from the analogy to civil partnership as it might to marriage;[9] and, second, because of the unsuccessful amendments tabled during the parliamentary debates that would have included them. Their submission quotes at length from the speech of Baroness O'Cathain,[10] who emphasises the caretaking that takes place between sisters, or a daughter looking after an elderly mother, for example, to argue that the hardship caused to same-sex couples through exclusion from the legal protections of marriage also applies to these cases.

The judgments in both the Chamber (*Burden v United Kingdom* (2007) 44 EHRR 51) and the Grand Chamber (*Burden v United Kingdom* (2008) 47 EHRR 38) went against the sisters, and there may be little sympathy for wealthy applicants who are trying to avoid paying tax.[11] However, the case does illustrate the potential injustices in giving extra privileges to a marriage/civil partnership that has lasted a short time whilst refusing to recognise a long-term caring, non-sexual relationship, whether this is a sibling relationship or a caretaking relationship between those who are not (legally recognised) family members. However, the conservative approach is to expand recognition only as far as those in conventional close family relationships, such as siblings, and only for the purposes of tax avoidance (see further Barker 2014).

In contrast to the conservative approach, a number of academics have proposed ways of recognising relationships through care and other means that move away from conjugality. These proposals share some commonalities with the conservative arguments that sexual partners should not be legally privileged over other 'deserving' family members, but they do not restrict this to those already in (legally recognised) family relationships and they do not restrict it only to tax-related issues. Many relationships are both sexual and caring but it is for those for whom sex and care exist in separate relationships that this distinction becomes crucial (such as a single parent who has a casual sexual partner or partners), as well as for those for whom a non-sexual caring relationship is the most important in their life (such as close friends who have been cohabiting for many years). However, there is also a broader argument to be made. Those who advocate for care, rather than sex, to be the signifier of a legally privileged relationship point to the important societal benefits of care as well as to the economic vulnerability of the carer. Martha Fineman's work is seminal in this regard. She notes that dependency is both inevitable (everyone is dependent at some point in our life) and creates derivate dependency (the caretaker is, in turn, dependent on resources necessary to carry out care work, whether state aid or private resources within the family). As such, Fineman argues that:

> The universal nature of inevitable dependency is central to the argument for the imposition of societal or collective responsibility. The realization that this form of dependency is inherent in the human condition is the conceptual foundation upon which can be built a claim to societal resources on the part of the caretakers of inevitable dependents, in order to facilitate their care. Justice demands that society recognize that caretaking labor produces a good for the larger society. Equality demands that this labor must not only be counted, but also valued, compensated, and accommodated by society and its institutions
>
> (2004: 38)

The sexual family structure means that derivative dependency is hidden within the family, 'its public and inevitable nature concealed' (ibid.). It is not merely, as for example is assumed in provisions relating to the division of marital assets on divorce, that the individual receiving or benefiting from care work ought to provide compensation to the carer. Society as a whole owes a *collective* debt to carers, who produce and reproduce society (2004: 48). Fineman argues that one way to recognise this 'dependency deficit' is to redraw the boundaries of familial relationships from the sexual unit to caretaking or dependency units, such as parent and child (2004: 293; see also Fineman 1995).

In the UK context, Jonathan Herring also argues that caring and interdependent relationships are 'of greater importance to society and need promotion' as well as being the type of relationship that is 'most likely to cause the greatest disadvantage, especially in economic terms and, therefore need the protective and adjustive work of family law'. He adds that:

> Family law should seek to protect those abused within relationships; structure decision-making on relationship breakdown; promote and protect those relationships which are important to the state. The relationships where these are needed are not those marked by sex, but rather by care and commitment.
>
> (2009: 3)

Unlike the conservative proposals and the *Burden* case, discussed above, which would have merely expanded the protections afforded to those within the legally recognised family who cohabit (providing certain conditions were met), Fineman and Herring seek to abolish the marriage model and move away from the sexual family entirely.[12] This is a goal that I support but I am less convinced that care is a suitable alternative framework, particularly if our concern is with the economic vulnerability of the carer (and cared for). The recognition of non-sexual caring relationships would fit neatly into the neoliberal agenda of increasing privatisation of care in the same way as same-sex marriage has. If caring relationships were to be recognised for the purposes of tax-free inheritance for the wealthy, it is inevitable that they would also be recognised for the purposes of benefit reductions for the poor in just the same way as civil partnerships were used to extend financial disadvantages to same-sex couples on benefits. I would suggest that in this circumstance, recognition and support for care and dependency would be likely to operate as another form of welfare retrenchment by encouraging broader categories of people to take on these roles privately in return for rewards in the form of tax-free inheritance from the family estate, or tenancy succession, and allowing the welfare state to retract further, without consideration of whether private wealth or other benefits such as a statutory tenancy are actually available to support the individual carer.

Structuring legal recognition around care is more justifiable than structuring it around conjugality: as Fineman points out, state subsidies for marriage do not make sense when we consider that some married couples are dual-income with no caring responsibilities, whereas some parents are single and so the support or state subsidy should be more effectively targeted.[13] However, shifting the focus from conjugality to care is likely to also result in the deepening of that privatisation, the retraction of subsidies for the poor while the wealthy gain access to tax breaks. Nevertheless, it is an interesting proposition to think about care as an alternative framework or, more likely, an additional framework to conjugality (see further Herring 2014). It could allow families of choice[14] to be recognised and end the dominance of the conjugal model. But when we are looking for a more radical family form we have to be keenly aware of the possible economic consequences of alternative models, and that is something that was overlooked or conceded too quickly in the civil partnership debates. The idea that the poorest same-sex couples, those who were claiming benefits, would have to 'accept the responsibilities alongside the rights' and take the reduction in their income that came along with the introduction of civil partnership, regardless of whether the couple themselves actually became civil partners (Section 137(A) of the Social Security Contributions and Benefits Act 1992), is deeply problematic and we should be wary of extending this to caretaking relationships. The facts of a recent case highlights the difficulties for both those claimants who are now assumed to be a same-sex couple and carers:

> The appellant had been married to a man and was now widowed. She was incapable of work, and lived with Ms R in the house they jointly

> owned as tenants in common. Ms R was her friend, companion and carer, she said; there was no intimate relationship. … The Secretary of State had accepted that were not civil partners but contended they lived together as if they were civil partners. … This was material because Ms R was in full-time remunerative work, which disqualified Ms P from IS if they were members of a couple.
>
> (Case Comment 2014: 90)

It is worth noting, though, that in this case the women's appeal against the finding that they were living as civil partners succeeded because of the precedent set by the case of *Baynes v Hedger* [2008] EWHC 1587 (Ch), that a relationship must be publicly acknowledged in order to meet this definition (see further Monk in this volume). Therefore, although same-sex couples who remain closeted will avoid being treated as civil partners for the purposes of benefits claims, those who are out will be unable to avoid the financial penalty.

The Law Commission of Canada made an alternative proposal that could potentially avoid this. It rejected an approach based on relationships, whether sexual, caring or otherwise. Instead, its focus was to take each individual legal provision (such as inheritance tax exemption, intestacy, spousal pension rights, etc.) and ask what the objective of this particular provision is, creating an objective-based criterion rather than asking how 'deserving' a particular relationship is of legal recognition. This approach was based on a number of principles, central to which were values of equality and autonomy (Law Commission of Canada 2001: xi). The Law Commission of Canada proposed a methodology for determining whether a law or proposed law meets these principles. This involves asking four questions:

> First, are the objectives of the law still legitimate? If the objectives of a law are no longer appropriate, the response may be to repeal or fundamentally revise a law rather than to adjust its use of relational terms. Second, if a law is pursuing a legitimate objective, are relationships relevant to the objective at hand? If relationships are not important, then the legislation should be redesigned to allocate the rights and responsibilities on an individual basis. Third, assuming that relationships are relevant, could the law allow individuals to decide which of their close personal relationships should be subject to the law? Fourth, if relationships do matter, and self-definition of relevant relationships is not a feasible option, is there a better way for the government to include relationships?.
>
> (2001: 29–30)

This is a radical set of proposals because it involves dismantling and fundamentally redistributing the 'package' of rights and responsibilities that are associated with marriage. This proposal also rejects any other 'one size fits all' framework, including those based on care rather than sex. For example, the Burden sisters might be eligible for a provision such as a tax exemption not by virtue of either being sisters or having a caring relationship but according to the same principled criteria as anyone else. Determining these criteria would involve looking at the purpose of the inheritance tax exemption and considering whether it should be revised to attach to the individual rather than a relationship status or to apply to a broader range of relationships. This would be an advantage in considering cases such as the Burden sisters, who have a reasonable claim that there is not really a good justification for treating them differently than if they were a lesbian couple, but at the same time avoid addressing this issue by introducing another method of tax avoidance for the wealthy. This methodology avoids a conclusion either where sisters are excluded based on circular and unprincipled reasoning (such as the Grand Chamber's judgment that sisters are unlike spouses because they are forbidden from marrying because they are sisters) or where rich sisters (and others) gain a method of tax avoidance.

This methodology provides a principled way in which it is possible to begin to think about family differently, to move away from the sexual family. The extension of a legal consequence to any relationship is not on a wholesale 'one size fits all' basis, but rather in situations where there is a good reason why relationships should be central to a legal provision. That provision can then be either designated by the relevant individual, or expanded to include a range of relationships that have some familial function or other relevant significance to the legal provision concerned. The absence of a single comprehensive provision along the lines of either marriage or a caring relationship model means that there is less certainty but there is also more scope for nuanced recognition of the realities and complexities of people's intimate (whether sexual or not) associations and parenting arrangements. It would not be possible under this type of reform to assume that maternity leave, for example, can be self-funded from within the family resources because 'the family' would have little legal meaning or recognition by virtue of status alone. Instead, there would be a series of 'relational definitions' that vary according to the objective and nature of the particular policy. Without the family unit to shoulder the burden of privatised care the relationship between providing care and derivative dependency would be impossible to ignore.

Conclusion

Same-sex marriage is, despite homophobic opposition to it from some within the Conservative Party, compatible with broader conservative policy goals, particularly in relation to promoting marriage and encouraging privatised responsibility for care and dependency. Amongst others, conservative commentators have highlighted this by explaining that conservatives should welcome gay marriage as a counter to the 'promiscuity' of gay men and as representing the 'making conservative' of the gay community, as well as restoring both the institution of marriage and the reputation of the Conservative Party. Whether these aims will be achieved will depend partly on the extent to which gays and lesbians can resist becoming complicit with the anti-benefits and privatisation discourse and the stigmatisation of non-normative relationships and sexualities when marriage is the norm for same-sex couples.

In 1991, Kath Weston wrote about families of choice within the lesbian and gay communities in the USA. These were networks of close friends, ex-lovers and other significant people in one's life who became family, often in the absence of good relationships with biological kin. The defining feature of chosen families was love: 'they quite consciously incorporated symbolic demonstrations of love, shared history, material or emotional assistance, and other signs of enduring solidarity' (1991: 109). These families were significant throughout the AIDS crisis and beyond, with Weeks et al. (2001) and Roseneil and Budgeon (2004) also finding chosen families taking on increasing significance in the UK. This was not limited to the LGBT communities, but it may be that same-sex marriage marks the beginning of a decline in the significance of these relationships, as lesbians and gay men retreat into the normative coupledom of marriage.[15] However, the conservative discourse embraced to gain same-sex marriage does not need to inevitably become the dominant narrative. Another possibility is that same-sex marriage might mean the beginning of the end for conjugality, ironically partly due to the efforts of conservatives who were trying to 'protect' the institution of marriage from same-sex couples. The debates around civil partnership and then same-sex marriage began a discussion about the fairness of rewarding conjugal relationships but not relationships of care and dependency that are not sexual. This discussion may fade away amongst conservatives now there is no same-sex provision to try to derail with a wrecking amendment. However, there are good reasons to take this issue seriously, albeit in a way that is careful not to further contribute to the privatisation of care. An approach similar to that of the Law Commission of Canada may be a way to do this.

Notes

1 I am not using conservative in a party political sense here. These policies are very similar to those of New Labour when they introduced civil partnerships and the language used by them, as I discuss later, demonstrates these same goals.

2 Perhaps predictably, the reference for this concern is to the Netherlands having 'conducted its first ceremony to unite three people in a relationship' after same-sex marriage was introduced there in 2001. Smith's comment was then reported in the media as referring to the Netherlands having 'civil union arrangements for three or more people which has been dubbed "polygamy in all but name"' (Macnab 2013). However, this is not accurate. The Netherlands does not have a civil union but rather a provision called registered partnership, which is in fact restricted to two partners. The ceremony referred to by Smith and numerous other opponents of same-sex marriage (mostly from the Christian right) is presumably a ceremony commemorating a cohabitation agreement. Dutch law does not permit

polygamous marriage or registered partnership, and in 2010 the Minister of Justice sought to 'restrict the recognition of polygamous marriages concluded abroad by foreign nationals' who subsequently relocate to the Netherlands (Government of the Netherlands 2010). This would be more restrictive than the UK, which only refuses recognition to polygamous marriages conducted abroad if any party was at the time of the marriage domiciled in the UK (Matrimonial Causes Act 1973, s11(d)).

3 This would be a very small number of same-sex couples as only the wealthiest are liable for this tax: in 2011–12, only 20,000 estates paid inheritance tax, equivalent to 3.5% of all deaths that year (Browne and Roantree 2012: 25).

4 The homophobic language of marriage 'civilising' gay men comes from a US (gay) law professor: Eskridge (1996).

5 In response, they have increased the level of conditionality and introduced a 'claimant commitment' to ensure that claimants understand their obligations and introduced a more punitive 'Work Programme' to provide training and 'instill the habits and disciplines of regular employment' (DWP 2010b).

6 For example, during the Civil Partnership Bill 2004 debates, the government gave assurances that the Law Commission would consult on the question of those excluded from civil partnerships. Instead of addressing the issue of 'spinster sisters', the Law Commission's consultation focused on the financial consequences of the termination of sexual cohabiting relationships (Law Commission 2006 and 2007). There was no public complaint about this focus from those who had advocated for sisters to be included in civil partnerships.

7 This appeared in *The Times* on 30 November 2004.

8 See also in the Australian context: Graycar and Millbank (2007).

9 See further Barker (2006). As Rosemary Auchmuty notes, it would have been inconceivable for the sisters to argue for inclusion within marriage (2009: 211).

10 Sam Grodzinski (Counsel for the Applicants) 'Observations of the Applicants on the Merits and Admissability of Application No. 13378/05 made by (1) Miss Joyce Mary Burden and (2) Miss Sybil Dorothy Burden; Responding to the Observations of the United Kingdom Government' (on file with the author). I would like to thank Nancy Polikoff for providing me with this document.

11 In addition to their house, they jointly owned adjoining land, two further properties and other assets worth up to £475,000 (*Burden v United Kingdom* (2008) 47 EHRR 38, para 11). Their tax liability was estimated to be £191,000 (Auchmuty, 2009: 212), meaning that the sisters could comfortably pay the tax bill without having to sell their home, contrary to media reports at the time.

12 There are also other proposals that would occupy a middle ground between these propositions. For example, Maxine Eichner and Nancy Polikoff have argued in favour of more subtly decentring the marriage model by expanding the range of forms of relationship recognition available in addition to marriage or civil partnership. See Polikoff (2008); Eichner (2007).

13 This is arguably one reason why the majority of Liberal Democrat and Labour MPs who voted for same-sex marriage have so far resisted the Conservative proposals of tax breaks for married people.

14 See Weston (1991); Weeks et al. (2001); Roseneil and Budgeon (2004), discussed below.

15 This is unlikely to be the sole factor. There is also arguably a generational difference here, as families of origin become more accepting of LGB relationships, perhaps helped on this journey through civil partnership and marriage ceremonies (Shipman and Smart 2007), yet friendship and chosen family remain central for older lesbian, gay and bisexual people (Westwood 2013). See also Heaphy, and Auchmuty, in this volume, on generational differences.

References

Auchmuty, R., 2009. 'Beyond couples: Burden v United Kingdom', *Feminist Legal Studies*, 17(2), pp. 205–18.

Barker, N., 2006. 'Sex and the Civil Partnership Act: the future of (non)conjugality?', *Feminist Legal Studies*, 14(2), pp. 241–59.

——2014. 'Why care? "Deserving family members" and the conservative movement for broader family recognition', in Wallbank, J. and Herring, J. (eds) *Vulnerabilities, Care and Family Law*. Abingdon and New York: Routledge.

Boyd, Susan B. (ed.) (1997) Challenging the Public/Private Divide: Feminism, Law and Public Policy (Toronto: University of Toronto Press).

Browne, J., Hood, A. and Joyce, R., 2012. 'The £10 billion question: where could the Chancellor find welfare cuts?', Institute for Fiscal Studies (8 October): http://www.ifs.org.uk/publications/6362 [accessed 14 June 2014].

Browne, J. and Roantree, B., 2012. *A Survey of the UK Tax System: IFS Briefing Note BN09*: http://www.ifs.org.uk/bns/bn09.pdf [accessed 12 August 2014].

Cameron, D., 2011. 'David Cameron's Conservative Party conference speech in full', *Guardian* (5 October): http://www.guardian.co.uk/politics/2011/oct/05/david-cameron-conservative-party-speech [Acccssed 5th October 2011].

Case Comment, 2014. 'Living together as if civil partners (income support): Civil Partnership Act 2004', *Journal of Social Security Law*, 21(2), pp. 89–91.

Centre for Social Justice, 2010. *Green Paper on the Family*, www.centreforsocialjustice.org.uk, pp. 19–20.

Conaghan, J. and Grabham, E., 2007. 'Sexuality and the citizen carer', *Northern Ireland Legal Quarterly*, 58(3), pp. 325–41.

Conservatives, 2010. *Invitation to Join the Government of Britain: The Conservative Manifesto, 2010:* http://www.conservatives.com/~/media/Files/Activist%20Centre/Press%20and%20Policy/Manifestos/Manifesto2010 [3rd December 2014].

d'Ancona, M., 2012. 'The case for gay marriage is fundamentally conservative – it will strengthen Britain's social fabric', *Telegraph*, 10 March: http://www.telegraph.co.uk/news/politics/david-cameron/9135181/The-case-for-gay-marriage-is-fundamentally-conservative-it-will-strengthen-Britains-social-fabric.html [Accessed 19th April 2012].

Deech, R., 2010. 'Sisters sisters – and other family members', *Family Law*, 40(April), pp. 375–80.

Delaney, S., 2013. 'Lord Tebbit: gay marriage, a lesbian queen – full interview', *The Big Issue* (30 May): http://www.bigissue.com/features/interviews/2438/lord-tebbit-gay-marriage-lesbian-queen-full-interview [accessed 1 July 2013].

Department for Work and Pensions (DWP), 2010a. *21st Century Welfare*, Cm7913.

——2010b. *Consultation Responses to 21st Century Welfare*, Cm7971, p. 20.

Eichner, M., 2007. 'Principles of the law of relationships among adults', *Family Law Quarterly*, 41(3), pp. 433–53.

Eskridge, W. N. Jr., 1996. *The Case for Same-Sex Marriage: From Sexual Liberty to Civilized Commitment*. New York and London: The Free Press.

Fineman, M. A., 1995. *The Neutered Mother, the Sexual Family and other Twentieth Century Tragedies*. New York: Routledge.

——2004. *The Autonomy Myth: Lies We Tell Ourselves About Dependency and Self-Sufficiency*. New York: The New Press.

Gibb, F., 2008. 'Sisters Joyce and Sybil Burden lose legal appeal over death duties', *The Times* (London, 30 April): http://www.thetimes.co.uk/tto/news/uk/article 1918370.ece [accessed 7 August 2014].

Government of the Netherlands, 2010. 'Hirsch Ballin restricts recognition of foreign polygamous marriages', *Press Release* (27 January): http://www.government.nl/issues/family-law/documents-and-publications/press-releases/2010/01/27/hirsch-ballin-restricts-recognition-of-foreign-polygamous-marriages.html [accessed 21 May 2014].

Graycar, R. and Millbank, J., 2007. 'From functional family to spinster sisters: Australia's distinctive path to relationship recognition', *Wash U J L & Pol'y*, 24, pp. 121–64.

Grice, A., 2012. 'Prominent Tory disowns "religious right" and supports gay marriage', *Independent* (6 February): http://www.independent.co.uk/news/uk/politics/prominent-tory-disowns-religious-right-and-supports-gay-marriage-6579531.html# [accessed 4 June 2013].

Herring, J., 2009. 'Sexless family law', *Lex Familiae, Revista Portuguesa de Direito da Familia*, 11, pp. 3–20.

——2014. 'Making family law more careful', in Wallbank, J. and Herring, J. (eds) *Vulnerabilities, Care and Family Law*. Abingdon and New York: Routledge.

Kandaswamy, P., 2008. 'State austerity and the racial politics of same-sex marriage in the US', *Sexualities*, 11(6), pp. 706–25.

Law Commission, 2006. *Cohabitation: The Financial Consequences of Relationship Breakdown: A Consultation Paper* (Law Com No 179).

——2007. *Cohabitation: The Financial Consequences of Relationship Breakdown* (Law Com No 307, Cm7182.

Law Commission of Canada, 2001. *Beyond Conjugality: Recognizing and Supporting Close Personal Adult Relationships.*

Macnab, S., 2013. 'Polygamy could follow gay marriage, warns MSP', *The Scotsman* (28 September).

McLean, G. 2004. 'Can you be pink and true blue?', *Guardian* (26 March): http://www.guardian.co.uk/politics/2004/mar/26/gayrights.conservatives [accessed 8 August 2014].

Montgomerie, T., 2012. 'A Conservative Case for Gay Marriage', *A Tory Diary: Conservative Home* (6 February): http://conservativehome.blogs.com/thetorydiary/2012/02/a-conservative-case-for-gay-marriage.html [accessed 4 June 2013].

Murray, D., 2012. 'Why Conservatives should welcome gay marriage', *The Spectator*, 5 October: http://blogs.spectator.co.uk/coffeehouse/2011/10/why-conservatives-should-welcome-gay-marriage/ [accessed 8 August 2014].

Polikoff, N. 2008. *Beyond (Straight and Gay) Marriage: Valuing All Families Under the Law.* Boston: Beacon Press.

Rauch, J., 2004. 'Bush's Case for Same-Sex Marriage', in Baird, R. M. and Rosenbaum, S. E. (eds) *Same-Sex Marriage: The Moral and Legal Debate*, 2nd edn. New York: Prometheus Books.

Roseneil, S. and Budgeon, S. 2004. 'Cultures of intimacy and care beyond "the family": personal life and social change in the early 21st century', *Current Sociology*, 52, p. 135.

Shipman, B. and Smart, C. 2007. '"It's made a huge difference": recognition, rights and the personal significance of civil partnership', *Sociological Research Online*, 12 (1): http://www.socresonline.org.uk/12/1/shipman.html [accessed 12 August 2014].

Slack, J., Salkeld, L. and McDermott, N., 2006. 'Euro-court denies sisters the same tax breaks as gay couples', *Mail Online* (12 December): http://www.dailymail.co.uk/news/article-422225/Euro-court-denies-sisters-tax-breaks-gay-couples.html [accessed 7 August 2014].

Smith, E., 2013. 'Marriage and Civil Partnership (Scotland) Bill, Further Submission from Elaine Smith MSP Scotland' (30 August) *5th Report, 2013 (Session 4): Stage 1 report on the Marriage and Civil Partnership (Scotland) Bill*, SP Paper 415, EO/S4/13/R5.

Social Security Advisory Committee (SSAC), 2010. *21st Century Welfare: A Response by the Social Security Advisory Committee*: http://ssac.independent.gov.uk/pdf/response-by-ssac.pdf.

Stonewall, 2004. *Parliamentary Briefing: Civil Partnership Bill, House of Commons Second Reading* (12 October): http://www.stonewall.org.uk/documents/oahq_Commons_Second_Reading_Sep_2004.doc [accessed 1 August 2014].

Tatchell, P., 2011. 'How the Tories were won to marriage equality' (13 October): http://www.petertatchell.net/lgbt_rights/partnerships/how-the-tories-were-won-to-marriage-equality.htm [accessed 14 June 2014].

——2014. 'It was a long fight for equal marriage – finally, it's here', *New Statesman* (28 March): http://www.newstatesman.com/politics/2014/03/it-was-long-fight-equal-marriage-finally-it-s-here [accessed 21 May 2014].

Watt, N., 2009. 'David Cameron apologises to gay people for section 28', *Guardian* (2 July): http://www.guardian.co.uk/politics/2009/jul/02/david-cameron-gay-pride-apology [accessed 8 August 2014].

Weeks, J. Heaphy, B. and Donovan, C., 2001. *Same-Sex Intimacies: Families of Choice and Other Life Experiments*. London and New York: Routledge.

Weston, K., 1991. *Families We Choose: Lesbians, Gays, Kinship*, rev. edn. 1997. New York: Columbia University Press.

Westwood, S., 2013. '"My friends are my family": an argument about the limitations of contemporary law's recognition of relationships in later life', *Journal of Social Welfare and Family Law*, 35(3), pp. 347–63.

Index